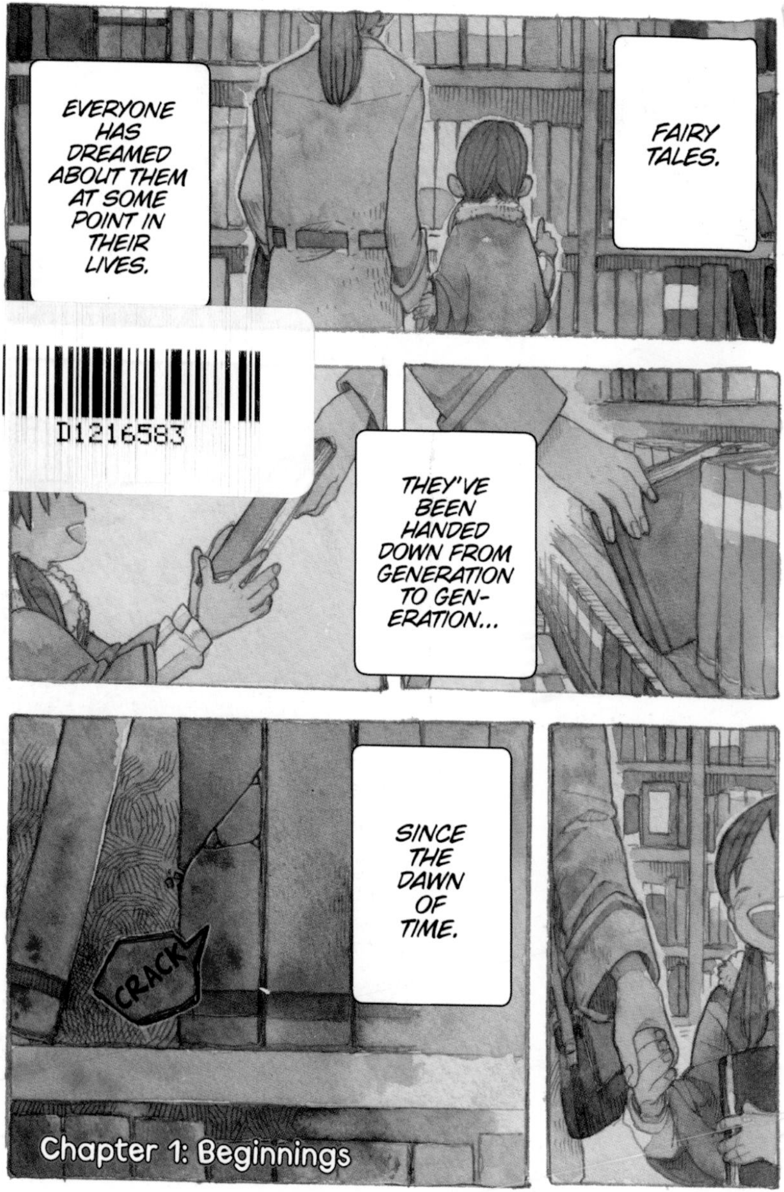
FAIRY TALES.
EVERYONE HAS DREAMED ABOUT THEM AT SOME POINT IN THEIR LIVES.
THEY'VE BEEN HANDED DOWN FROM GENERATION TO GEN-ERATION...
SINCE THE DAWN OF TIME.
CRACK
Chapter 1: Beginnings

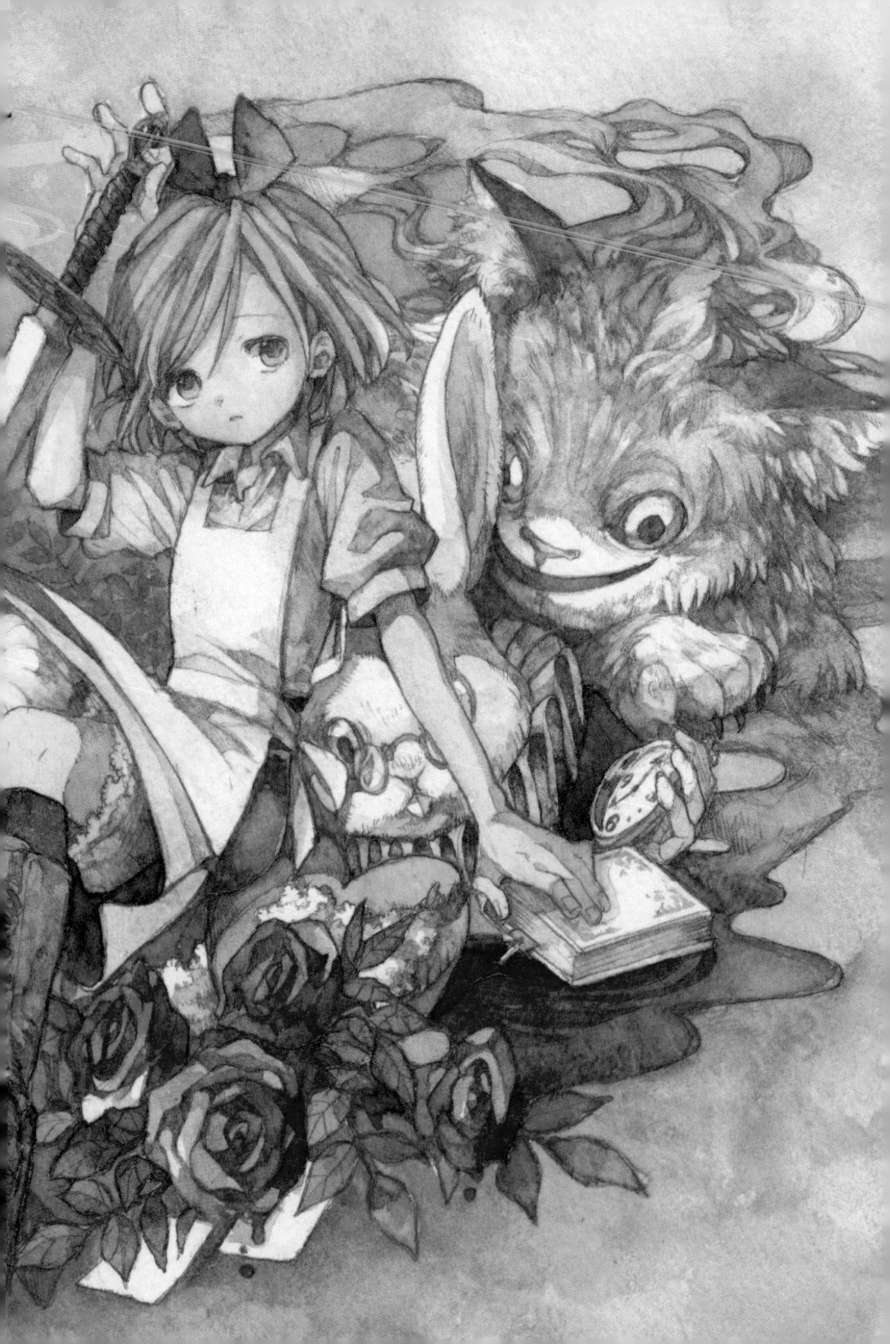

FAIRY TALE BATTLE ROYALE

1

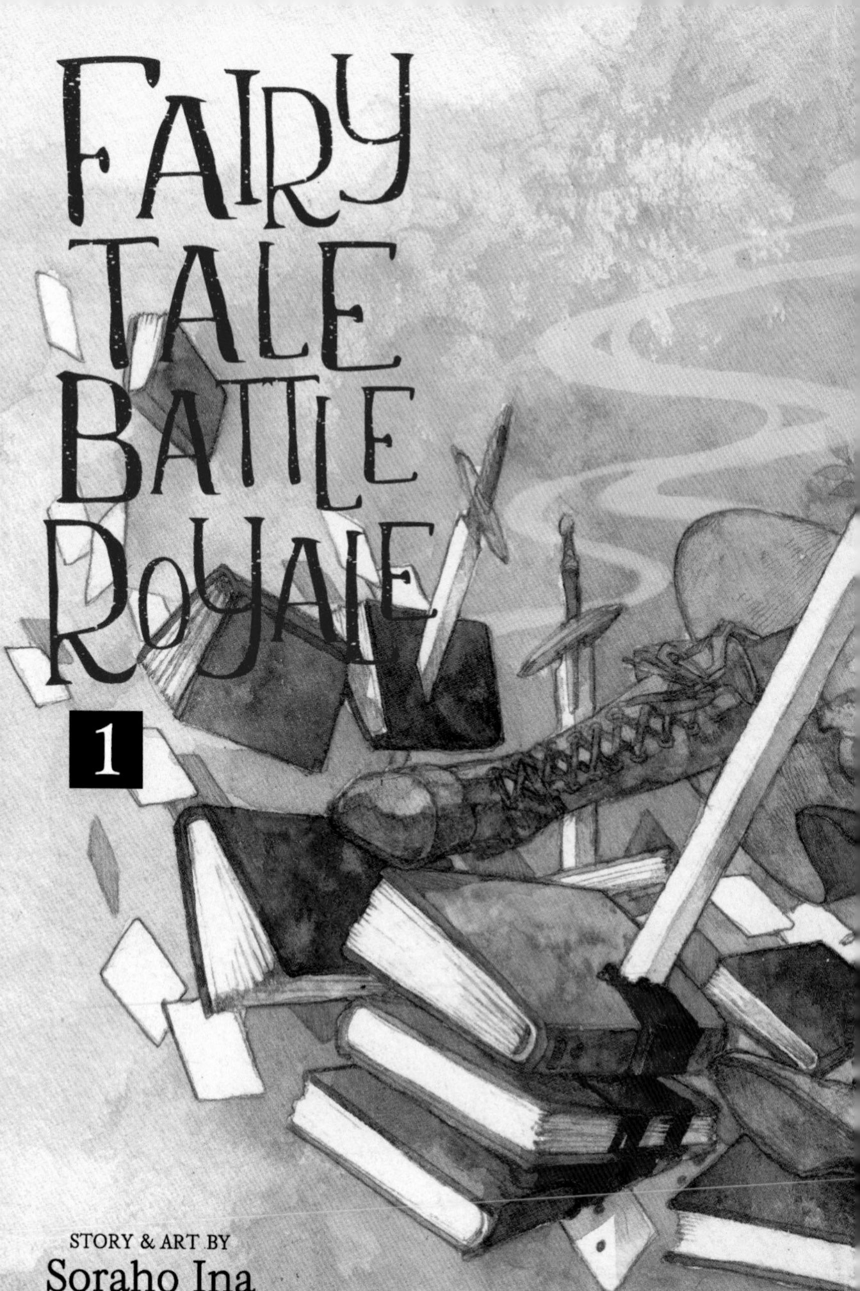

STORY & ART BY

Soraho Ina

Contents

Chapter 1: Beginnings

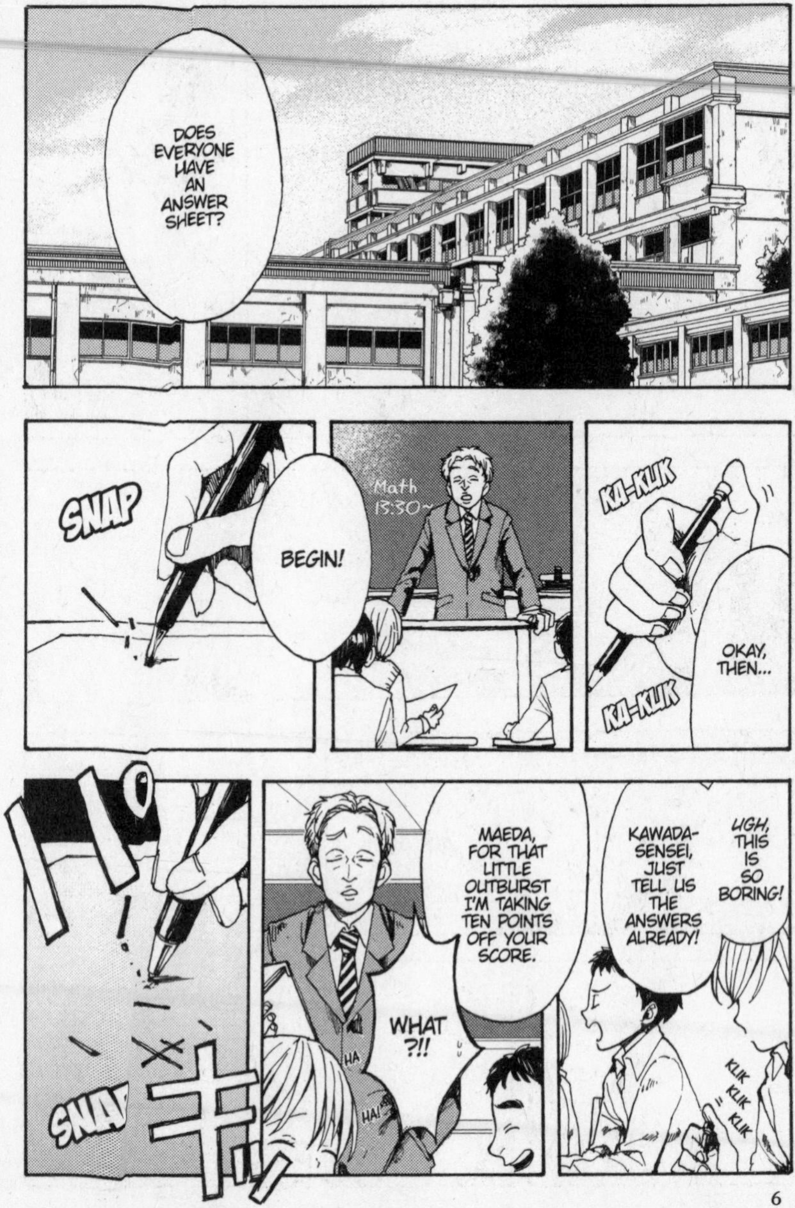
DOES EVERYONE HAVE AN ANSWER SHEET?
KA-KLIK
OKAY, THEN...
KA-KLIK
Math 13:30~
BEGIN!
SNAP
UGH, THIS IS SO BORING!
KAWADA-SENSEI, JUST TELL US THE ANSWERS ALREADY!
KLIK KLIK KLIK
MAEDA, FOR THAT LITTLE OUTBURST I'M TAKING TEN POINTS OFF YOUR SCORE.
WHAT?!!
HA
HA!
SNAP

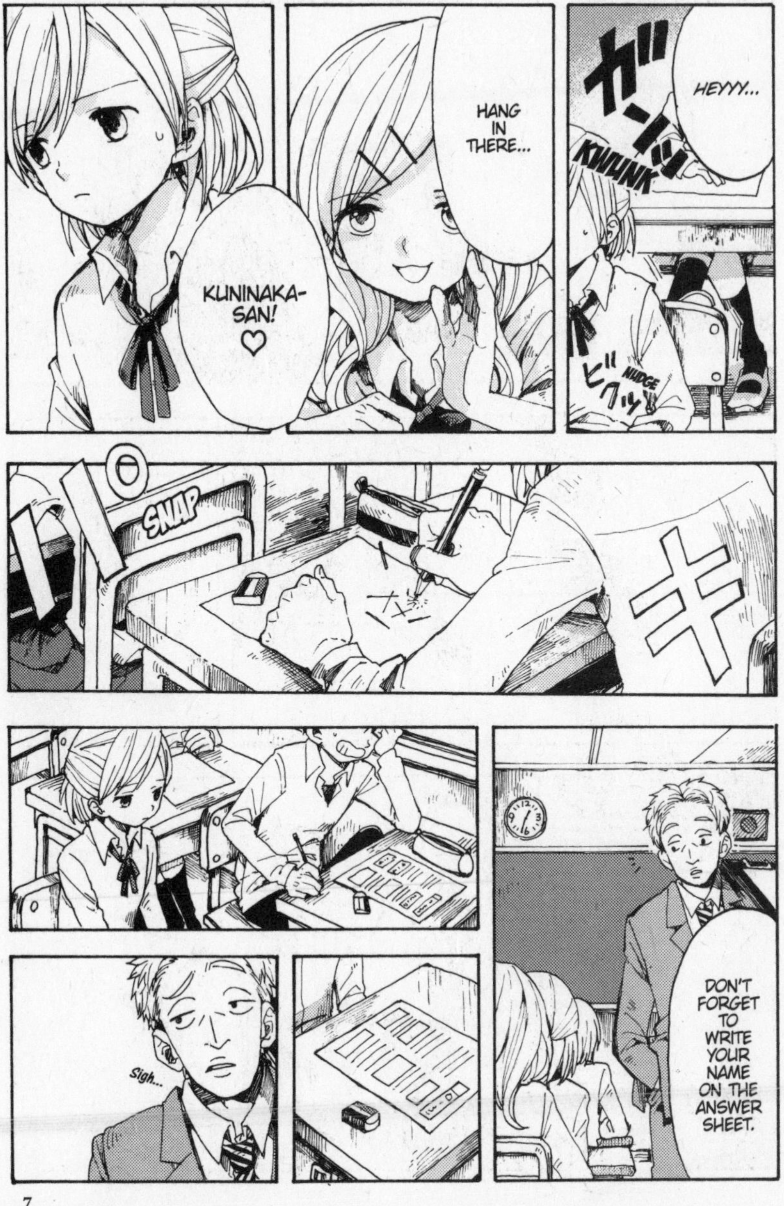
HEYYY...
KWUNK
NUDGE
HANG IN THERE...
KUNINAKA-SAN! ♡
SNAP
DON'T FORGET TO WRITE YOUR NAME ON THE ANSWER SHEET.
Sigh...

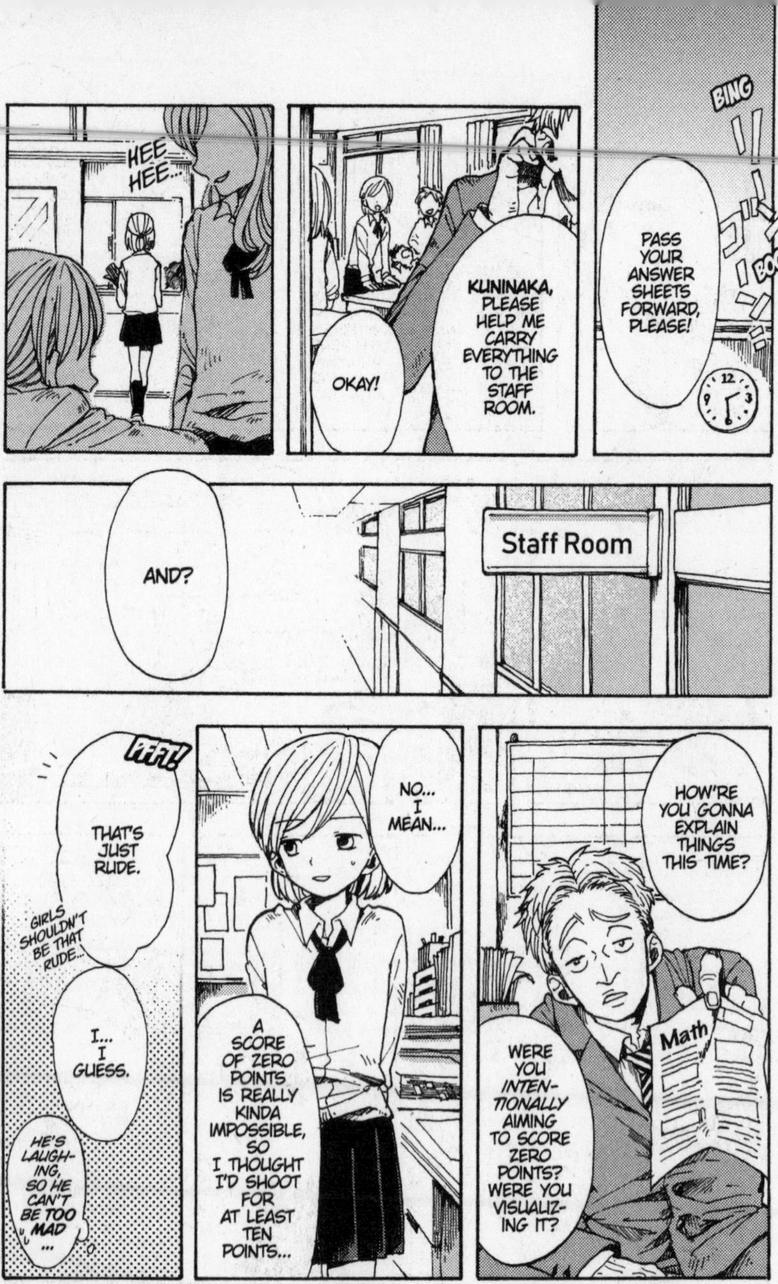
BING
BOONG...
PASS YOUR ANSWER SHEETS FORWARD, PLEASE!
KUNINAKA, PLEASE HELP ME CARRY EVERYTHING TO THE STAFF ROOM.
OKAY!
HEE HEE...
Staff Room
AND?
HOW'RE YOU GONNA EXPLAIN THINGS THIS TIME?
Math
WERE YOU INTENTIONALLY AIMING TO SCORE ZERO POINTS? WERE YOU VISUALIZING IT?
NO... I MEAN...
A SCORE OF ZERO POINTS IS REALLY KINDA IMPOSSIBLE, SO I THOUGHT I'D SHOOT FOR AT LEAST TEN POINTS...
PFFT!
THAT'S JUST RUDE.
GIRLS SHOULDN'T BE THAT RUDE...
I... I GUESS.
HE'S LAUGHING, SO HE CAN'T BE TOO MAD...

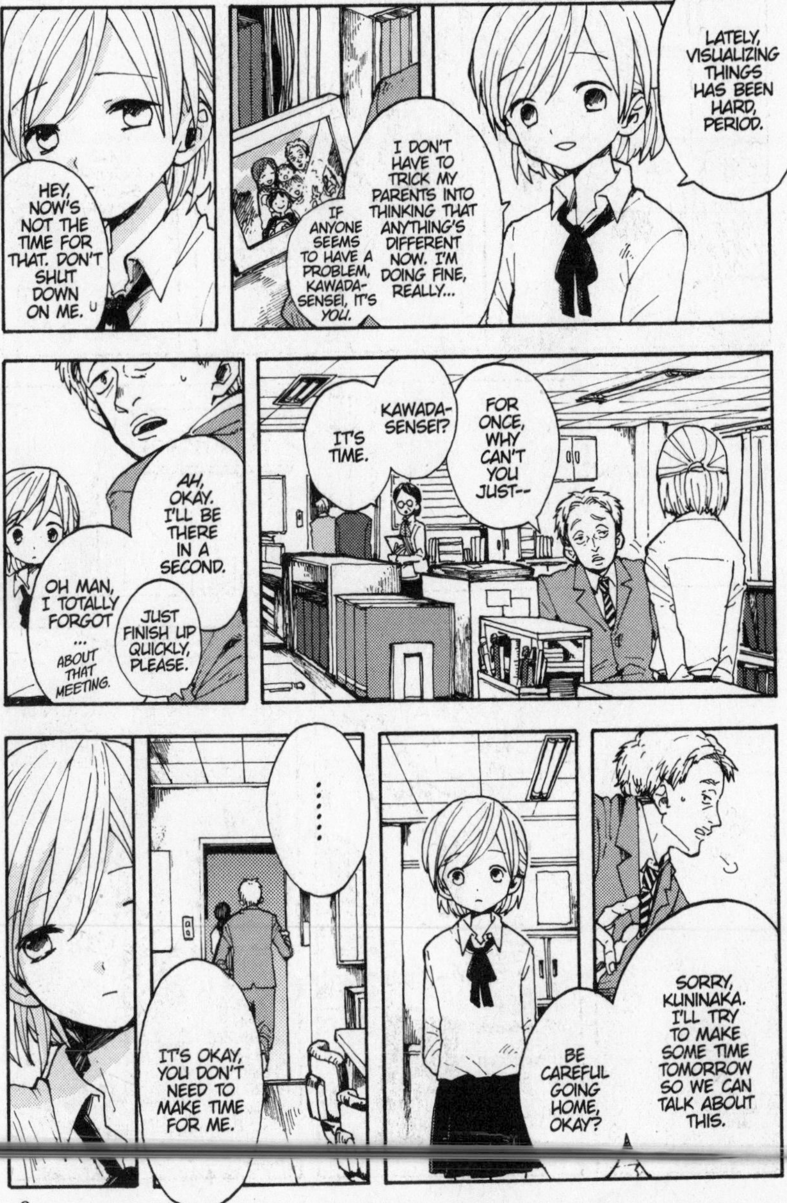
LATELY, VISUALIZING THINGS HAS BEEN HARD, PERIOD.
I DON'T HAVE TO TRICK MY PARENTS INTO THINKING THAT ANYTHING'S DIFFERENT NOW. I'M DOING FINE, REALLY...
IF ANYONE SEEMS TO HAVE A PROBLEM, KAWADA-SENSEI, IT'S YOU.
HEY, NOW'S NOT THE TIME FOR THAT. DON'T SHUT DOWN ON ME.
FOR ONCE, WHY CAN'T YOU JUST--
KAWADA-SENSEI?
IT'S TIME.
AH, OKAY. I'LL BE THERE IN A SECOND.
JUST FINISH UP QUICKLY, PLEASE.
OH MAN, I TOTALLY FORGOT ... ABOUT THAT MEETING.
SORRY, KUNINAKA. I'LL TRY TO MAKE SOME TIME TOMORROW SO WE CAN TALK ABOUT THIS.
BE CAREFUL GOING HOME, OKAY?
......
IT'S OKAY, YOU DON'T NEED TO MAKE TIME FOR ME.

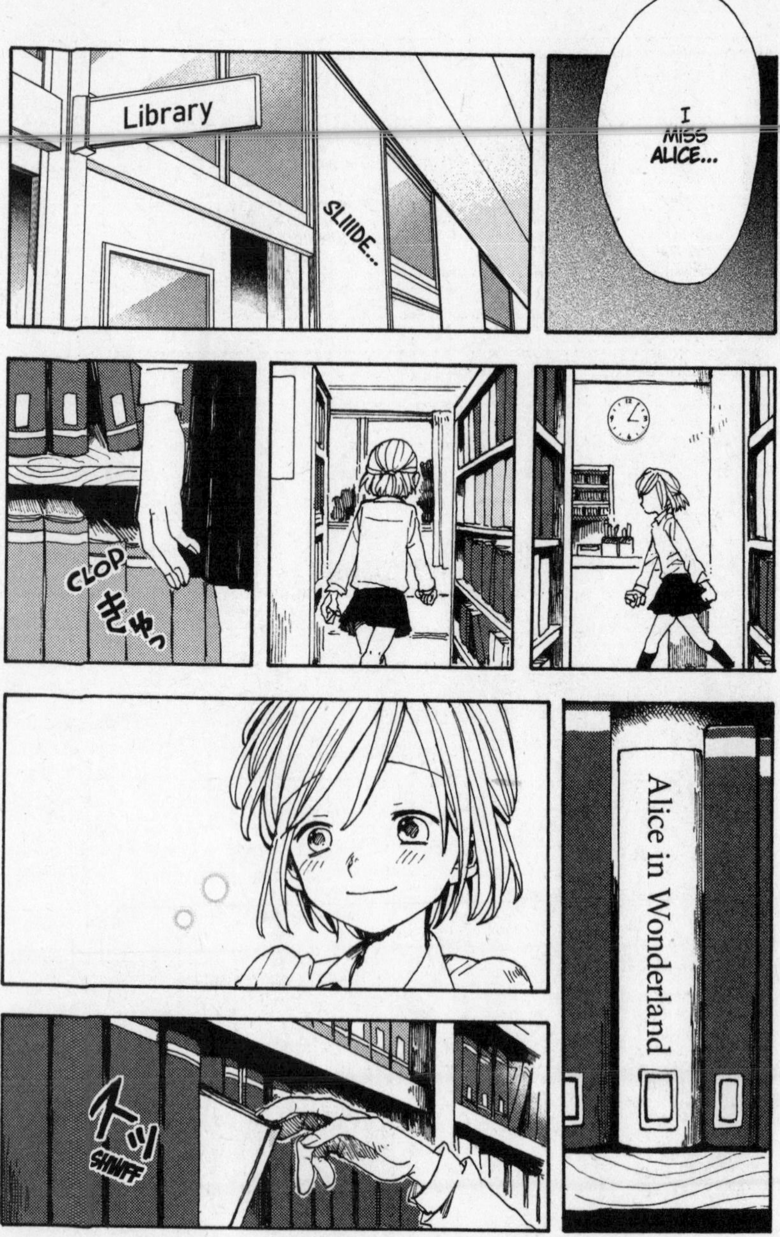
I MISS ALICE...
Library
SLIIIDE...
CLOP
きゅっ
Alice in Wonderland
スッ
SHWFF

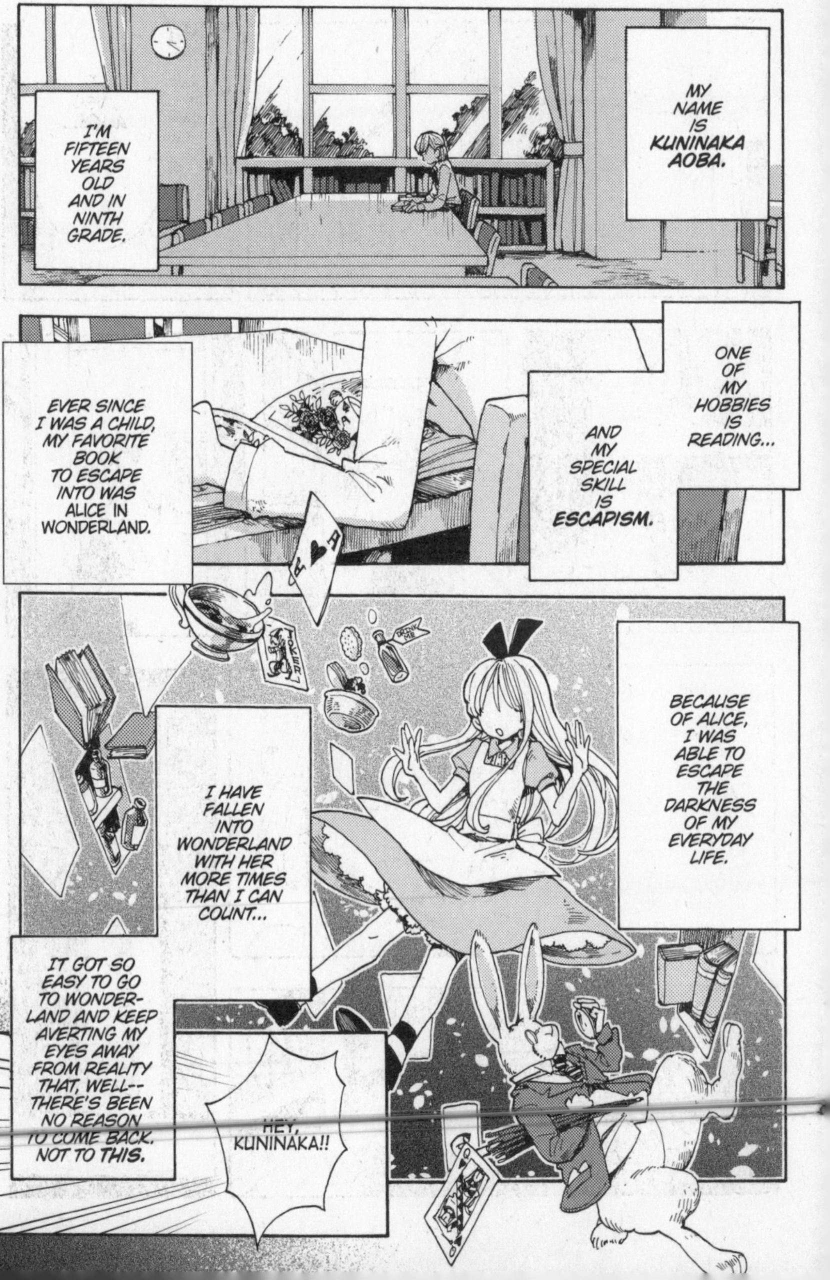
MY NAME IS KUNINAKA AOBA.
I'M FIFTEEN YEARS OLD AND IN NINTH GRADE.
ONE OF MY HOBBIES IS READING...
AND MY SPECIAL SKILL IS ESCAPISM.
EVER SINCE I WAS A CHILD, MY FAVORITE BOOK TO ESCAPE INTO WAS ALICE IN WONDERLAND.
BECAUSE OF ALICE, I WAS ABLE TO ESCAPE THE DARKNESS OF MY EVERYDAY LIFE.
I HAVE FALLEN INTO WONDERLAND WITH HER MORE TIMES THAN I CAN COUNT...
IT GOT SO EASY TO GO TO WONDER-LAND AND KEEP AVERTING MY EYES AWAY FROM REALITY THAT, WELL-- THERE'S BEEN NO REASON TO COME BACK. NOT TO THIS.
HEY, KUNINAKA!!

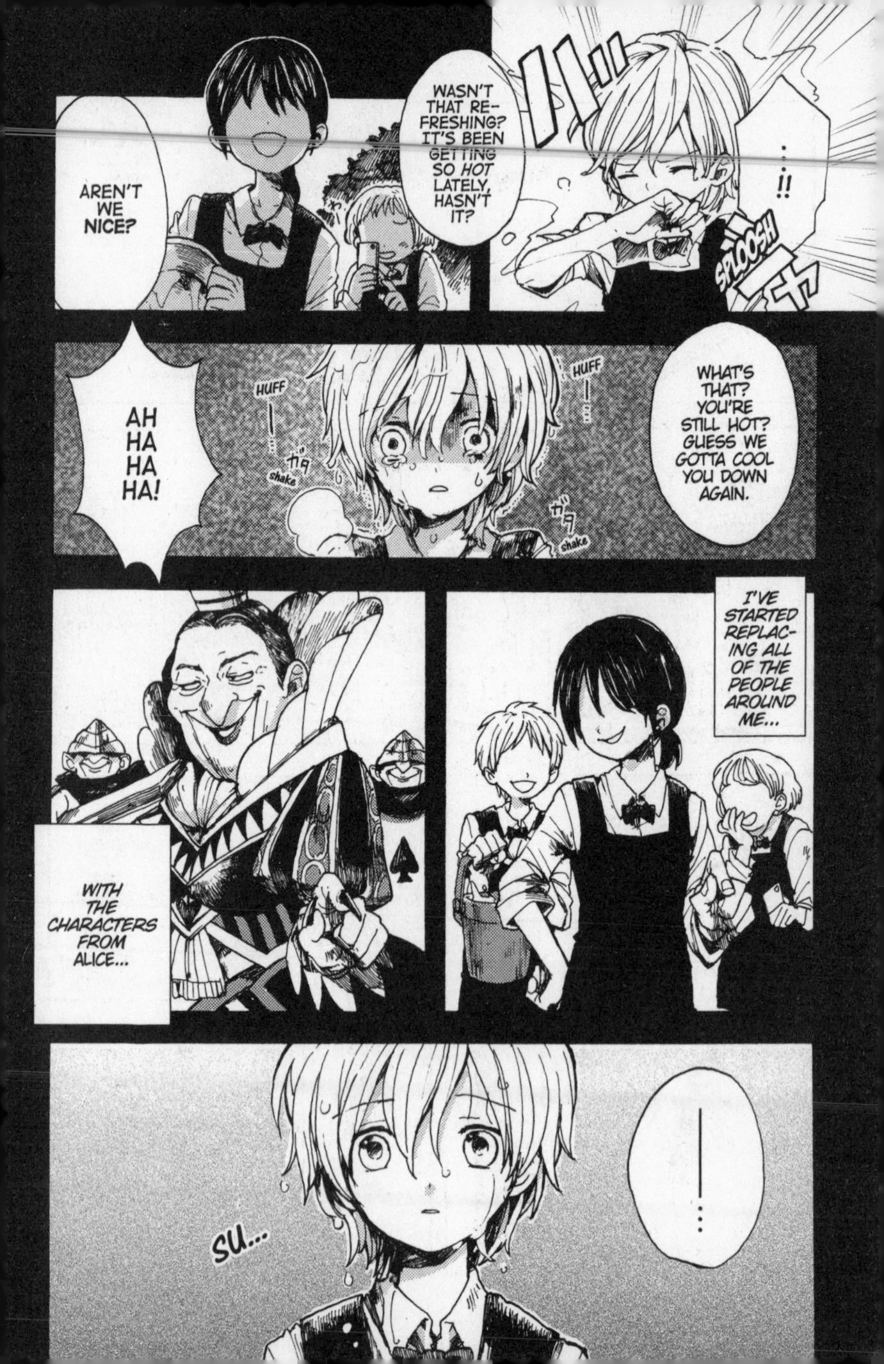
...!!
SPLOOSH
WASN'T THAT RE-FRESHING? IT'S BEEN GETTING SO *HOT* LATELY, HASN'T IT?
AREN'T WE NICE?
WHAT'S THAT? YOU'RE STILL HOT? GUESS WE GOTTA COOL YOU DOWN AGAIN.
HUFF
HUFF
shake
shake
AH HA HA HA!
I'VE STARTED REPLACING ALL OF THE PEOPLE AROUND ME...
WITH THE CHARACTERS FROM ALICE...
...
SU...

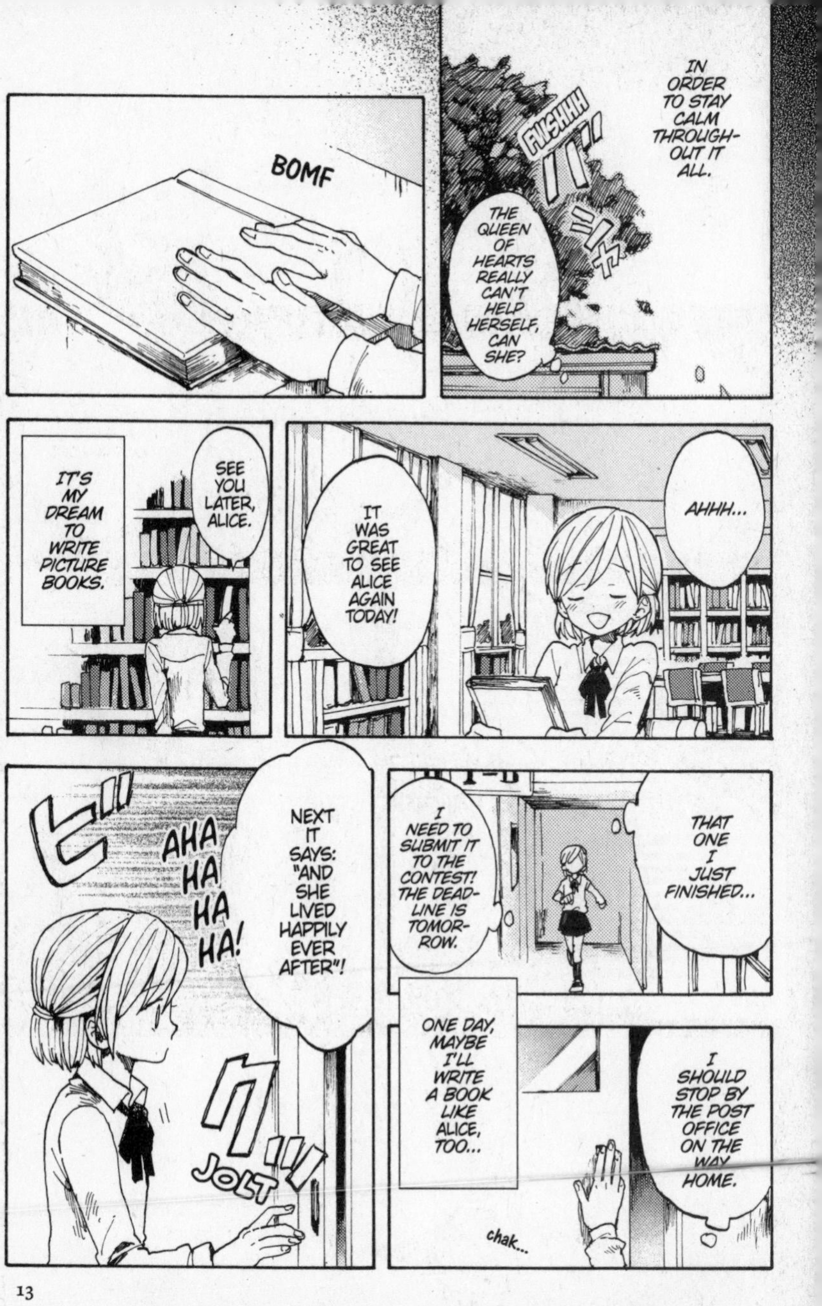
IN ORDER TO STAY CALM THROUGH-OUT IT ALL.
FWSHHH
THE QUEEN OF HEARTS REALLY CAN'T HELP HERSELF, CAN SHE?
BOMF
AHHH...
IT WAS GREAT TO SEE ALICE AGAIN TODAY!
SEE YOU LATER, ALICE.
IT'S MY DREAM TO WRITE PICTURE BOOKS.
THAT ONE I JUST FINISHED...
I NEED TO SUBMIT IT TO THE CONTEST! THE DEAD-LINE IS TOMOR-ROW.
I SHOULD STOP BY THE POST OFFICE ON THE WAY HOME.
ONE DAY, MAYBE I'LL WRITE A BOOK LIKE ALICE, TOO...
chak...
NEXT IT SAYS: "AND SHE LIVED HAPPILY EVER AFTER"!
AHA HA HA HA!
JOLT

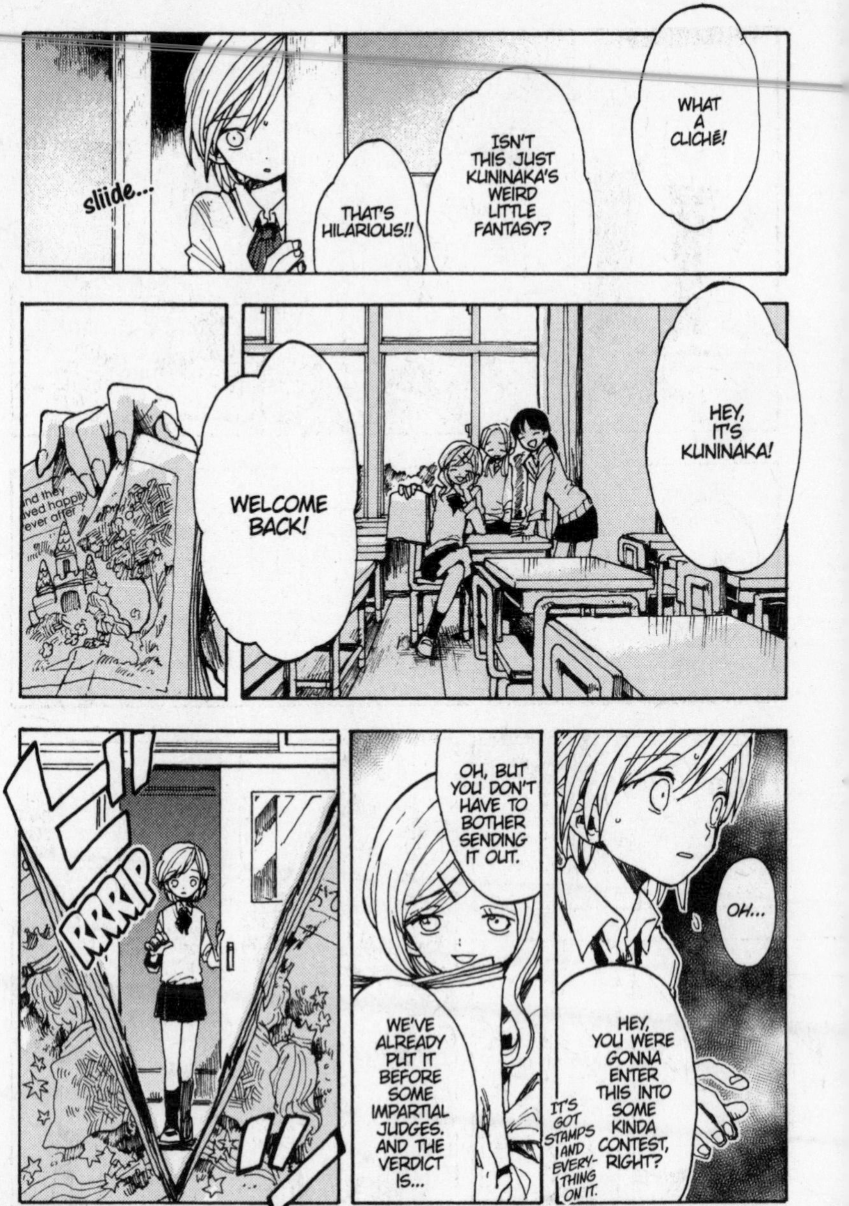
WHAT A CLICHÉ!
ISN'T THIS JUST KUNINAKA'S WEIRD LITTLE FANTASY?
THAT'S HILARIOUS!!
sliide...
HEY, IT'S KUNINAKA!
WELCOME BACK!
OH...
HEY, YOU WERE GONNA ENTER THIS INTO SOME KINDA CONTEST, RIGHT?
IT'S GOT STAMPS AND EVERY-THING ON IT.
OH, BUT YOU DON'T HAVE TO BOTHER SENDING IT OUT.
WE'VE ALREADY PUT IT BEFORE SOME IMPARTIAL JUDGES. AND THE VERDICT IS...
RRRIP

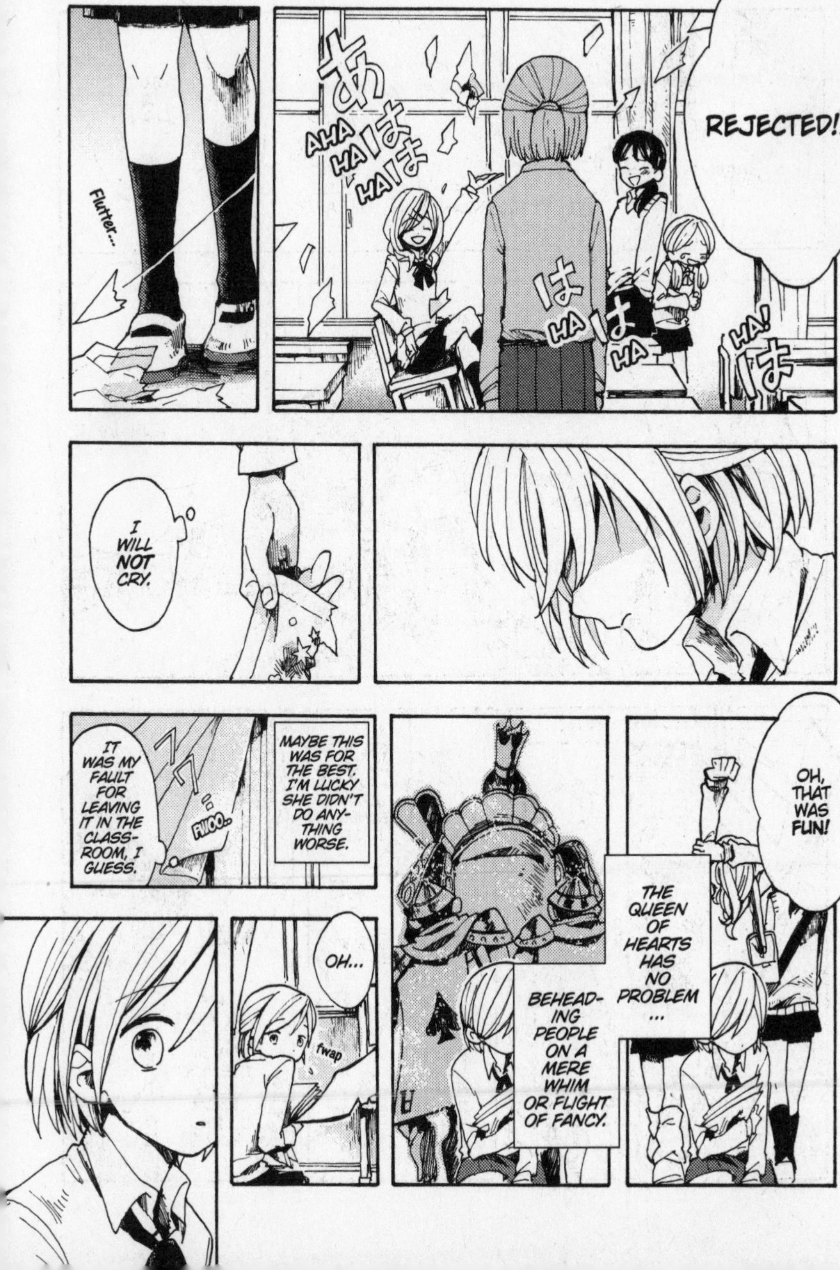
REJECTED!!
AHA HA HA
あはは
は HA は HA
HA! は
Flutter...
I WILL NOT CRY.
OH, THAT WAS FUN!
THE QUEEN OF HEARTS HAS NO PROBLEM ...
BEHEADING PEOPLE ON A MERE WHIM OR FLIGHT OF FANCY.
MAYBE THIS WAS FOR THE BEST. I'M LUCKY SHE DIDN'T DO ANYTHING WORSE.
IT WAS MY FAULT FOR LEAVING IT IN THE CLASSROOM, I GUESS.
FWOO..
OH...
fwap

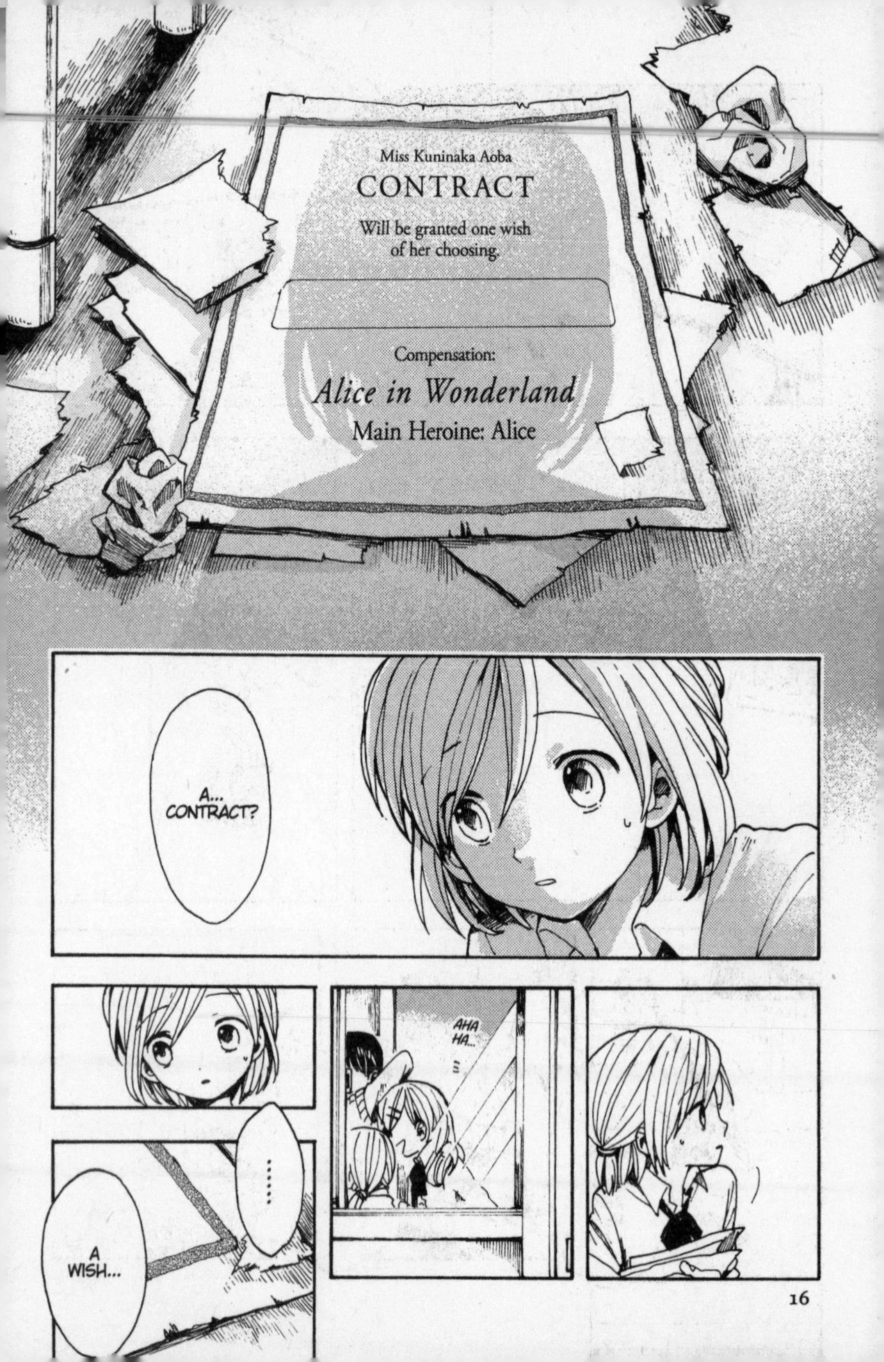
Miss Kuninaka Aoba
CONTRACT
Will be granted one wish of her choosing.
Compensation:
Alice in Wonderland
Main Heroine: Alice
A... CONTRACT?
AHA HA...
......
A WISH...

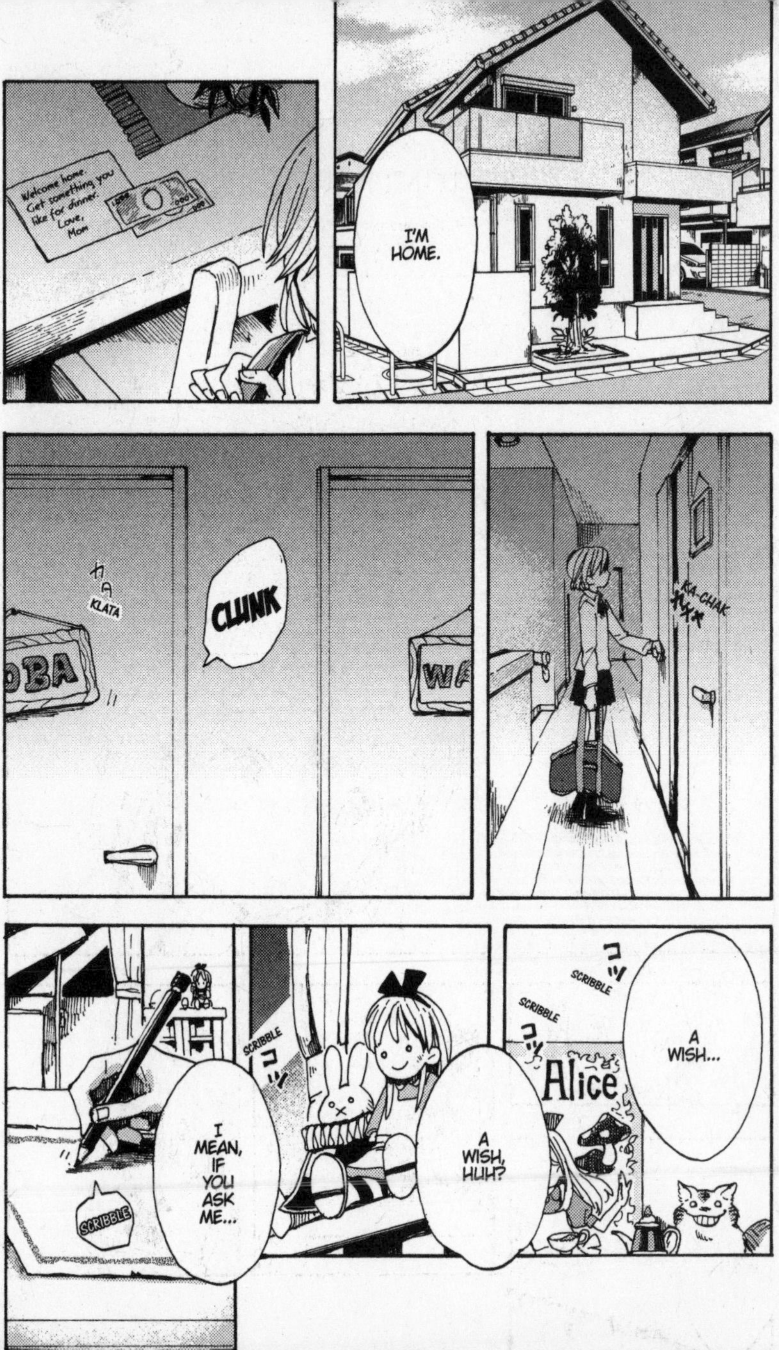
I'M HOME.
Welcome home.
Get something you like for dinner.
Love,
Mom
KA-CHAK
CLUNK
KLATA
A WISH...
SCRIBBLE
SCRIBBLE
Alice
A WISH, HUH?
I MEAN, IF YOU ASK ME...
SCRIBBLE
SCRIBBLE

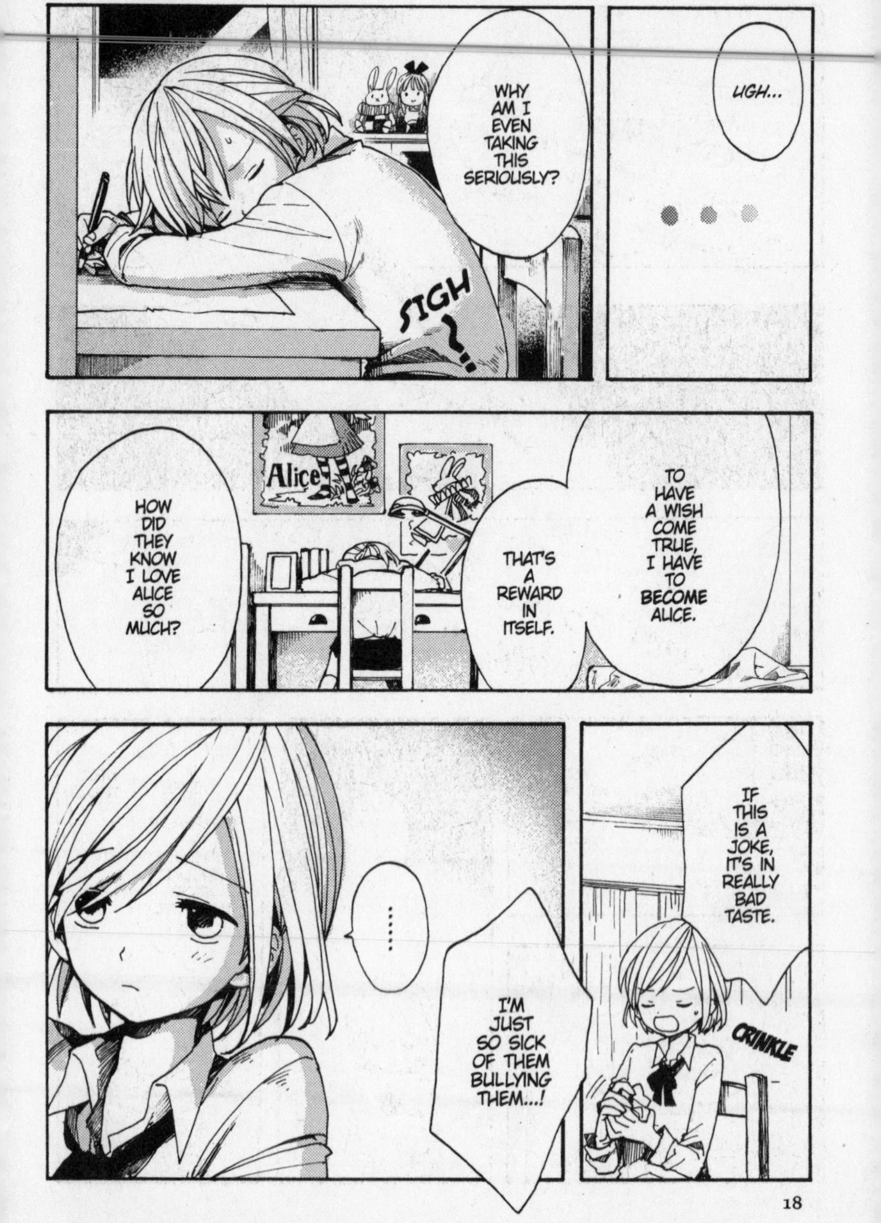
UGH...
WHY AM I EVEN TAKING THIS SERIOUSLY?
SIGH
TO HAVE A WISH COME TRUE, I HAVE TO BECOME ALICE.
THAT'S A REWARD IN ITSELF.
Alice
HOW DID THEY KNOW I LOVE ALICE SO MUCH?
IF THIS IS A JOKE, IT'S IN REALLY BAD TASTE.
CRINKLE
I'M JUST SO SICK OF THEM BULLYING THEM...!
......

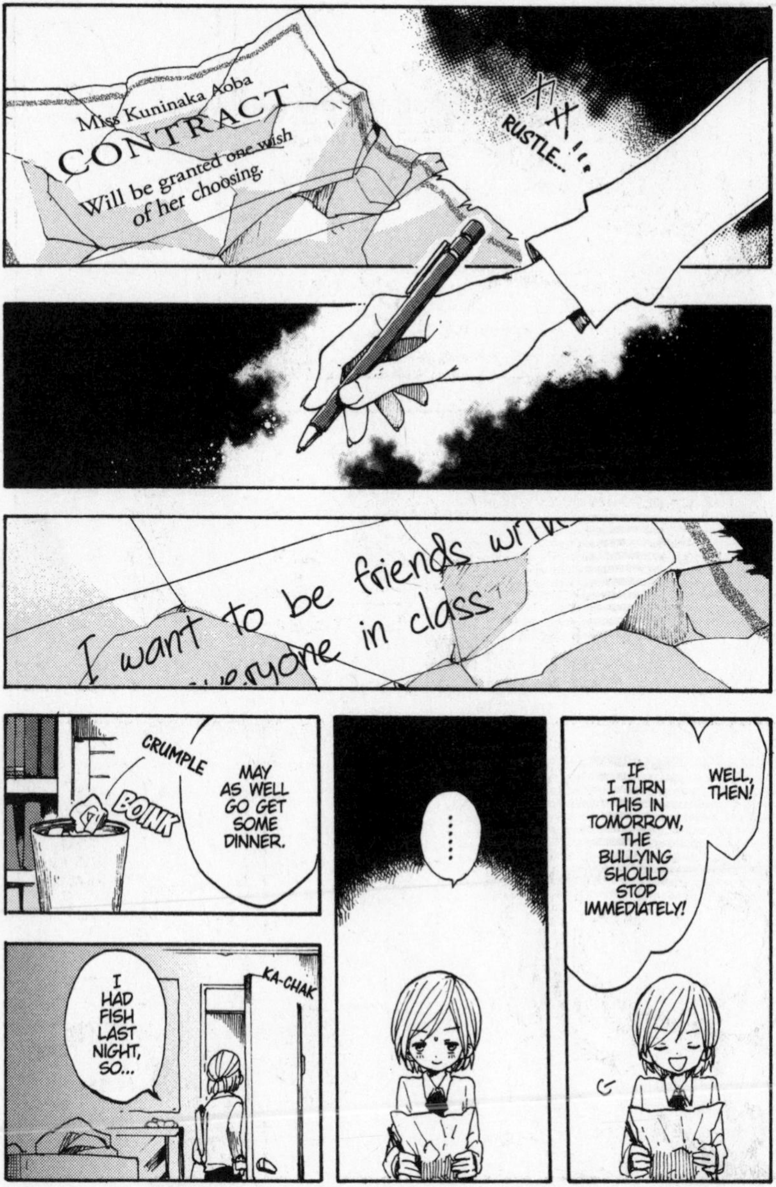
Miss Kuninaka Aoba
CONTRACT
Will be granted one wish of her choosing.
RUSTLE...
I want to be friends
in class
WELL, THEN!
IF I TURN THIS IN TOMORROW, THE BULLYING SHOULD STOP IMMEDIATELY!
......
CRUMPLE
BOINK
MAY AS WELL GO GET SOME DINNER.
KA-CHAK
I HAD FISH LAST NIGHT, SO...

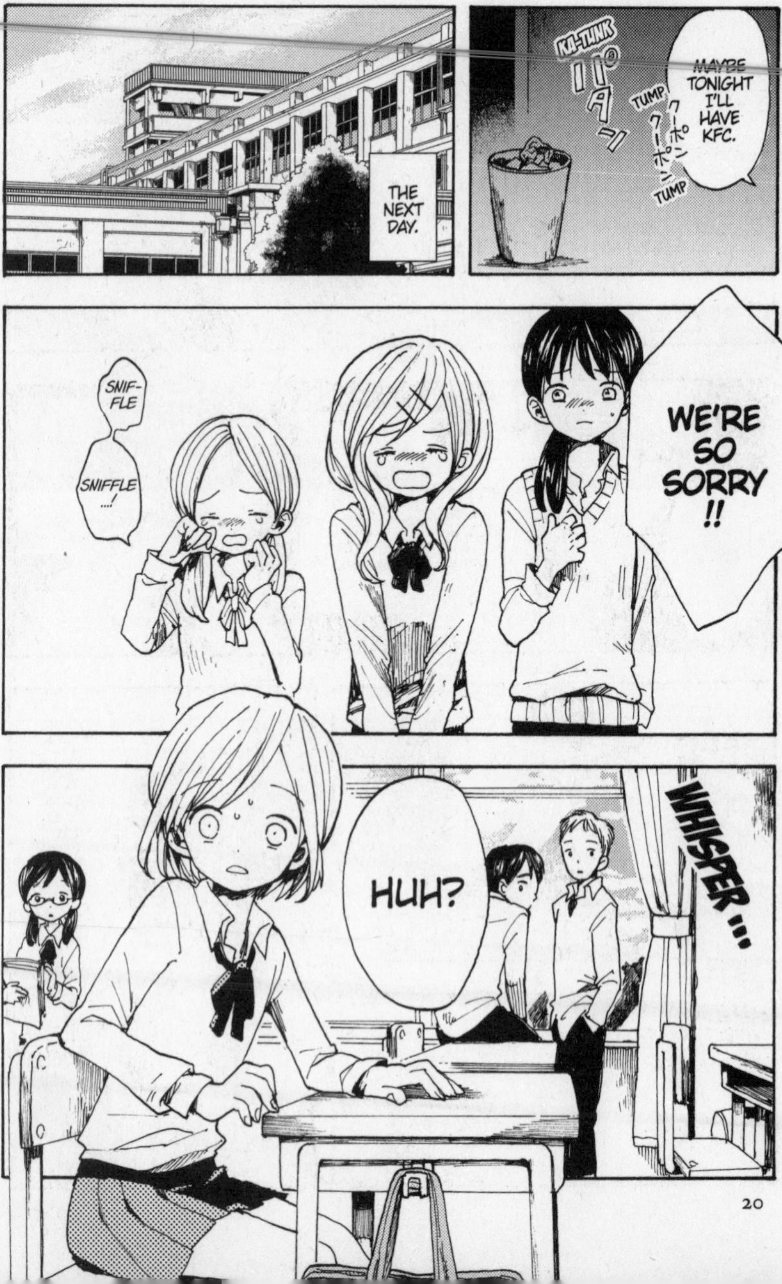
THE NEXT DAY.
MAYBE TONIGHT I'LL HAVE KFC.
TUMP クーポン
TUMP クーポン
KA-THUNK パタッ
WE'RE SO SORRY !!
SNIF-FLE
SNIFFLE ...!
HUH?
WHISPER ...

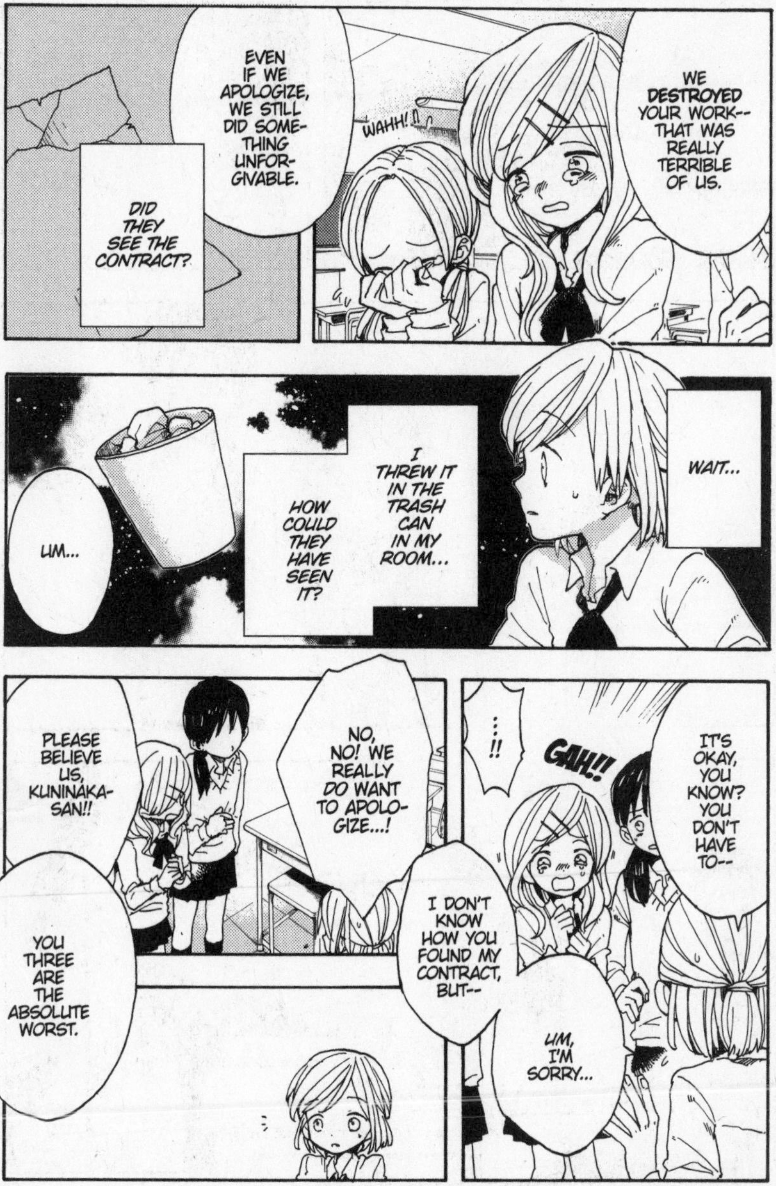
WE DESTROYED YOUR WORK--THAT WAS REALLY TERRIBLE OF US.
WAHH!
EVEN IF WE APOLOGIZE, WE STILL DID SOME-THING UNFOR-GIVABLE.
DID THEY SEE THE CONTRACT?
WAIT...
I THREW IT IN THE TRASH CAN IN MY ROOM...
HOW COULD THEY HAVE SEEN IT?
UM...
...!!
GAH!!
IT'S OKAY, YOU KNOW? YOU DON'T HAVE TO--
I DON'T KNOW HOW YOU FOUND MY CONTRACT, BUT--
UM, I'M SORRY...
NO, NO! WE REALLY DO WANT TO APOLO-GIZE...!
PLEASE BELIEVE US, KUNINAKA-SAN!!
YOU THREE ARE THE ABSOLUTE WORST.

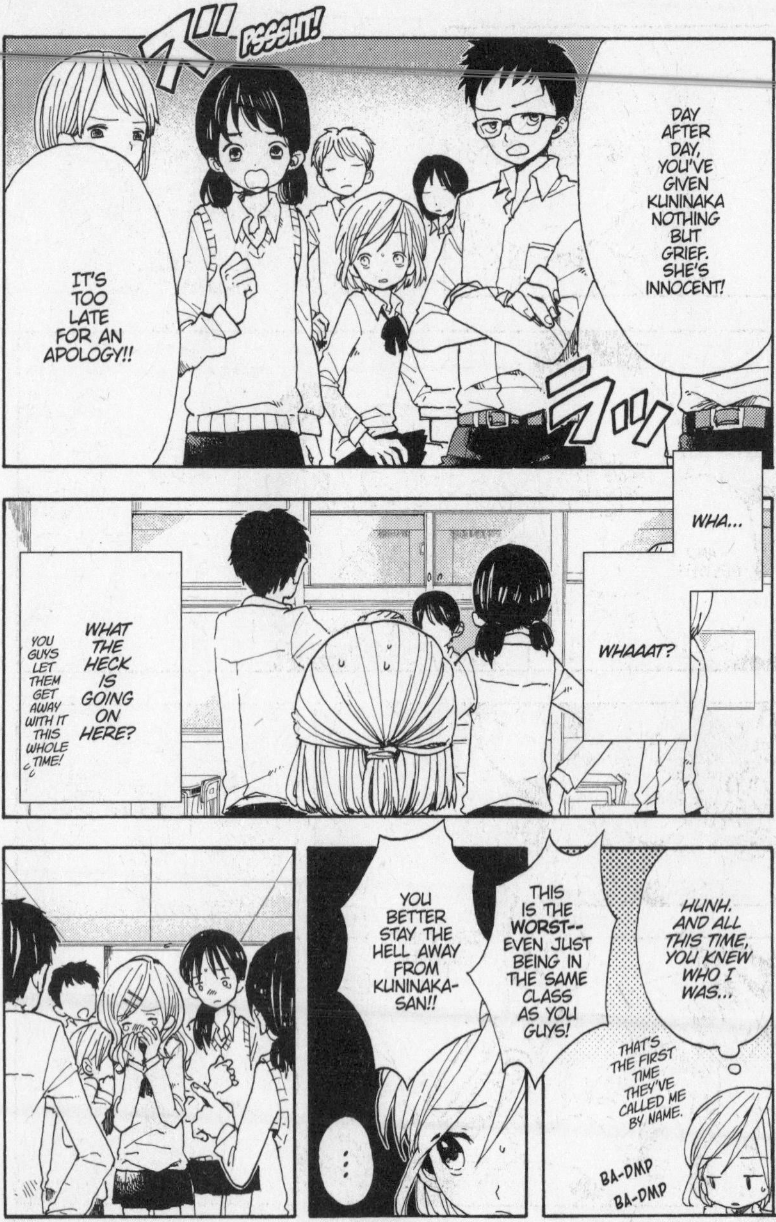
PSSSHT!
DAY AFTER DAY, YOU'VE GIVEN KUNINAKA NOTHING BUT GRIEF. SHE'S INNOCENT!
IT'S TOO LATE FOR AN APOLOGY!!
WHA...
WHAAAT?
WHAT THE HECK IS GOING ON HERE?
YOU GUYS LET THEM GET AWAY WITH IT THIS WHOLE TIME!
HUNH. AND ALL THIS TIME, YOU KNEW WHO I WAS...
THAT'S THE FIRST TIME THEY'VE CALLED ME BY NAME.
BA-DMP
BA-DMP
THIS IS THE WORST-- EVEN JUST BEING IN THE SAME CLASS AS YOU GUYS!
YOU BETTER STAY THE HELL AWAY FROM KUNINAKA-SAN!!
...

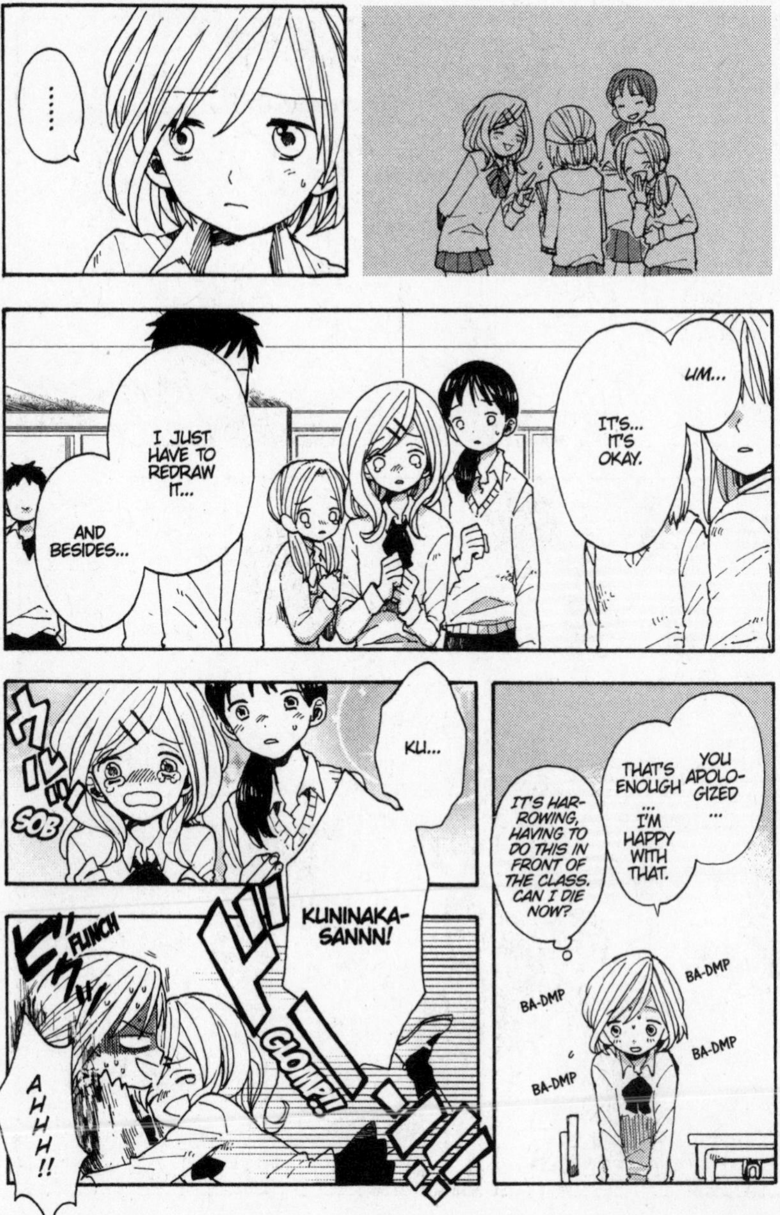
......
UM...
IT'S... IT'S OKAY.
I JUST HAVE TO REDRAW IT...
AND BESIDES...
YOU APOLOGIZED...
THAT'S ENOUGH... I'M HAPPY WITH THAT.
IT'S HARROWING, HAVING TO DO THIS IN FRONT OF THE CLASS. CAN I DIE NOW?
BA-DMP
BA-DMP
BA-DMP
BA-DMP
KU...
SOB
KUNINAKA-SANNN!
GLOMP!!
FLINCH
AHHHH!!

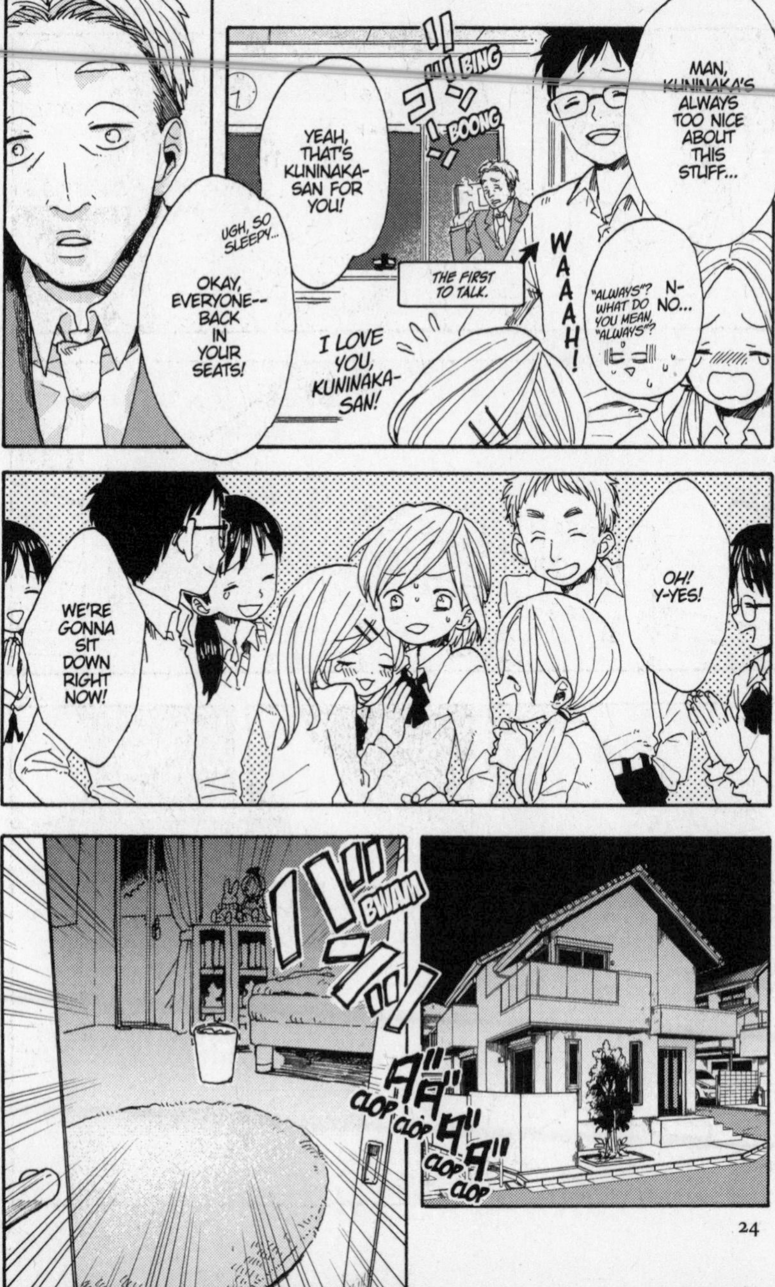
MAN, KUNINAKA'S ALWAYS TOO NICE ABOUT THIS STUFF...
N- NO...
"ALWAYS"? WHAT DO YOU MEAN, "ALWAYS"?
WAAAH!
THE FIRST TO TALK.
BING
BOONG
YEAH, THAT'S KUNINAKA-SAN FOR YOU!
I LOVE YOU, KUNINAKA-SAN!
UGH, SO SLEEPY...
OKAY, EVERYONE-- BACK IN YOUR SEATS!
OH! Y-YES!
WE'RE GONNA SIT DOWN RIGHT NOW!
CLOP CLOP CLOP CLOP
BWAM

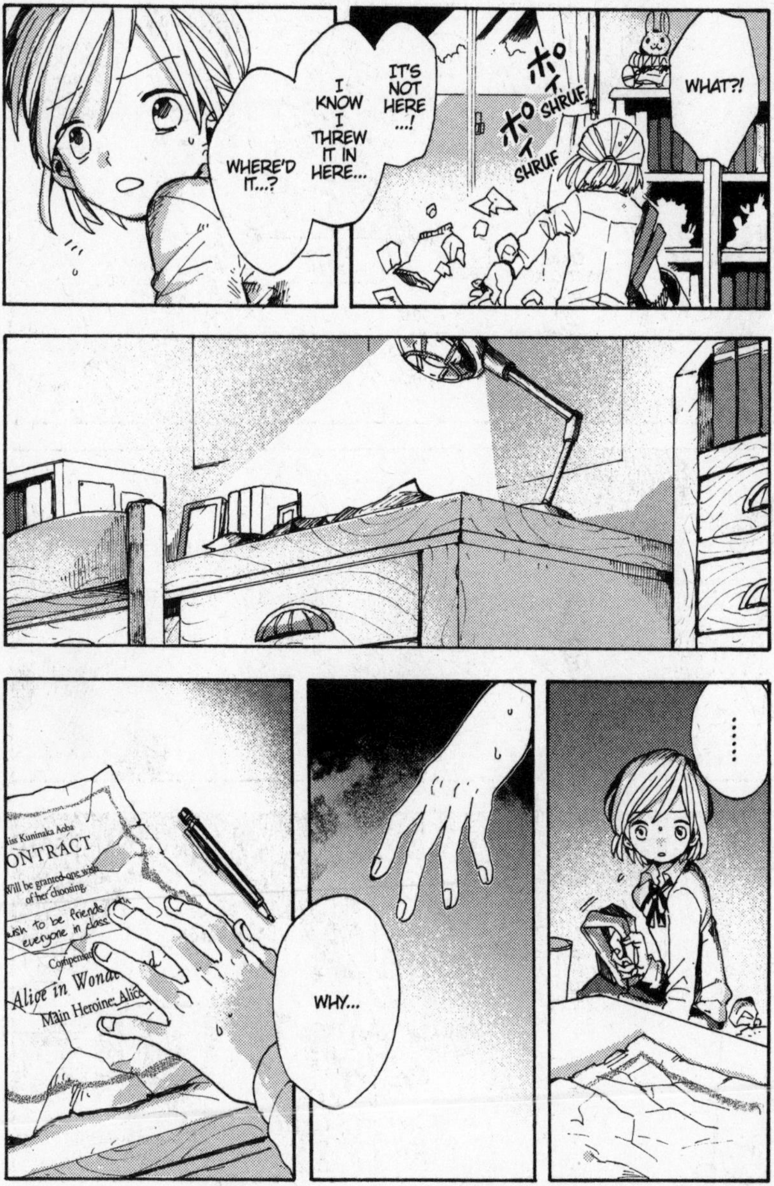
WHAT?!
ホイ SHRUF
ホイ SHRUF
IT'S NOT HERE ...!
I KNOW I THREW IT IN HERE...
WHERE'D IT...?
......
WHY...
iss Kuninaka Aoba
ONTRACT
Will be granted one wish of her choosing
wish to be friends everyone in class
Compensati
Alice in Wond
Main Heroine: Alice

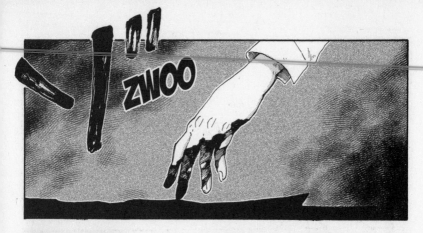

ZU ZU ZU...

WH...

WHAT IS...

THIS?

ZU ZU ZU

?!

WSH

OH NO!

ZU ZU...

IT WON'T... IT WON'T COME OFF!

AHH...!

SCRUB SCRUB SCRUB

26

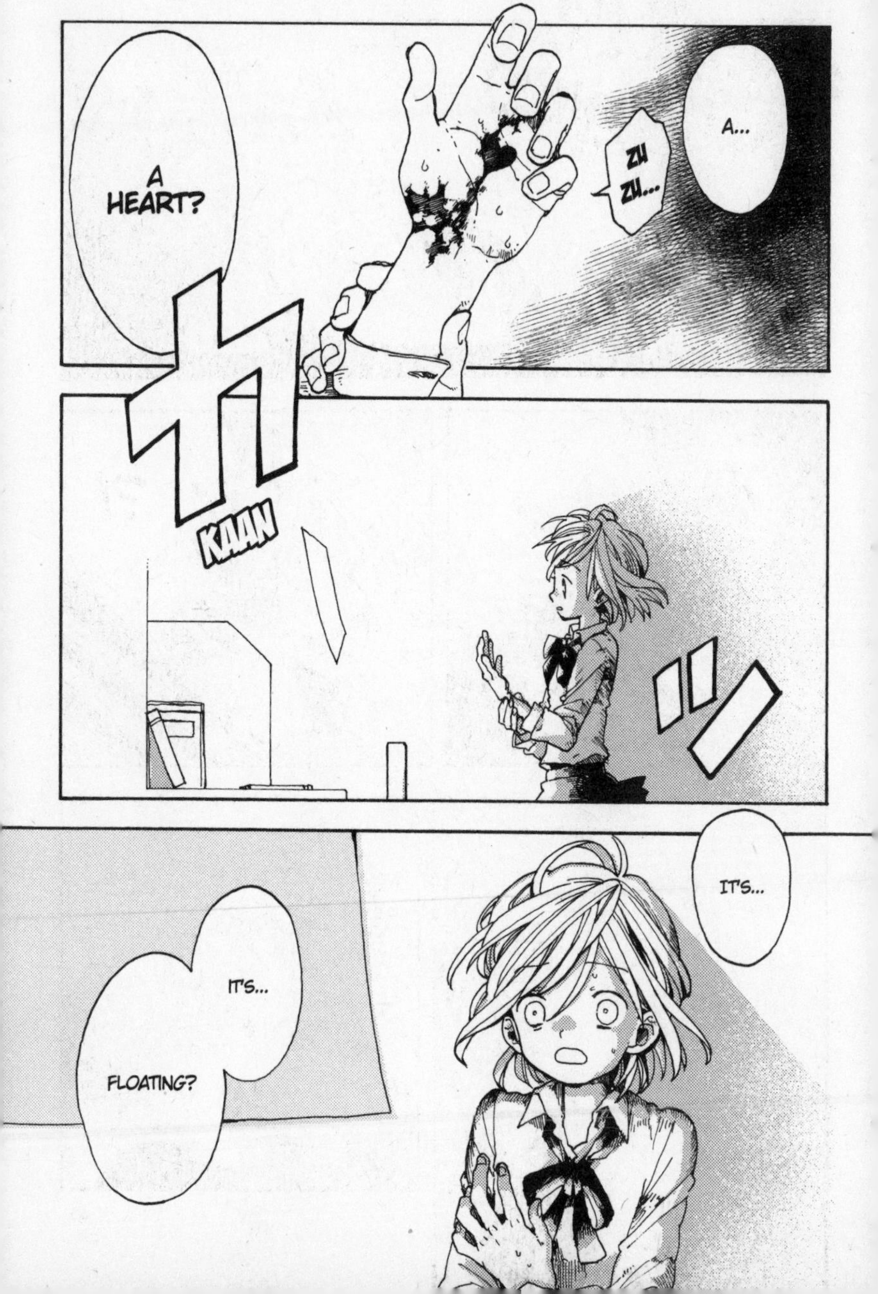
A...
ZU ZU...
A HEART?
KAAN
IT'S...
IT'S... FLOATING?

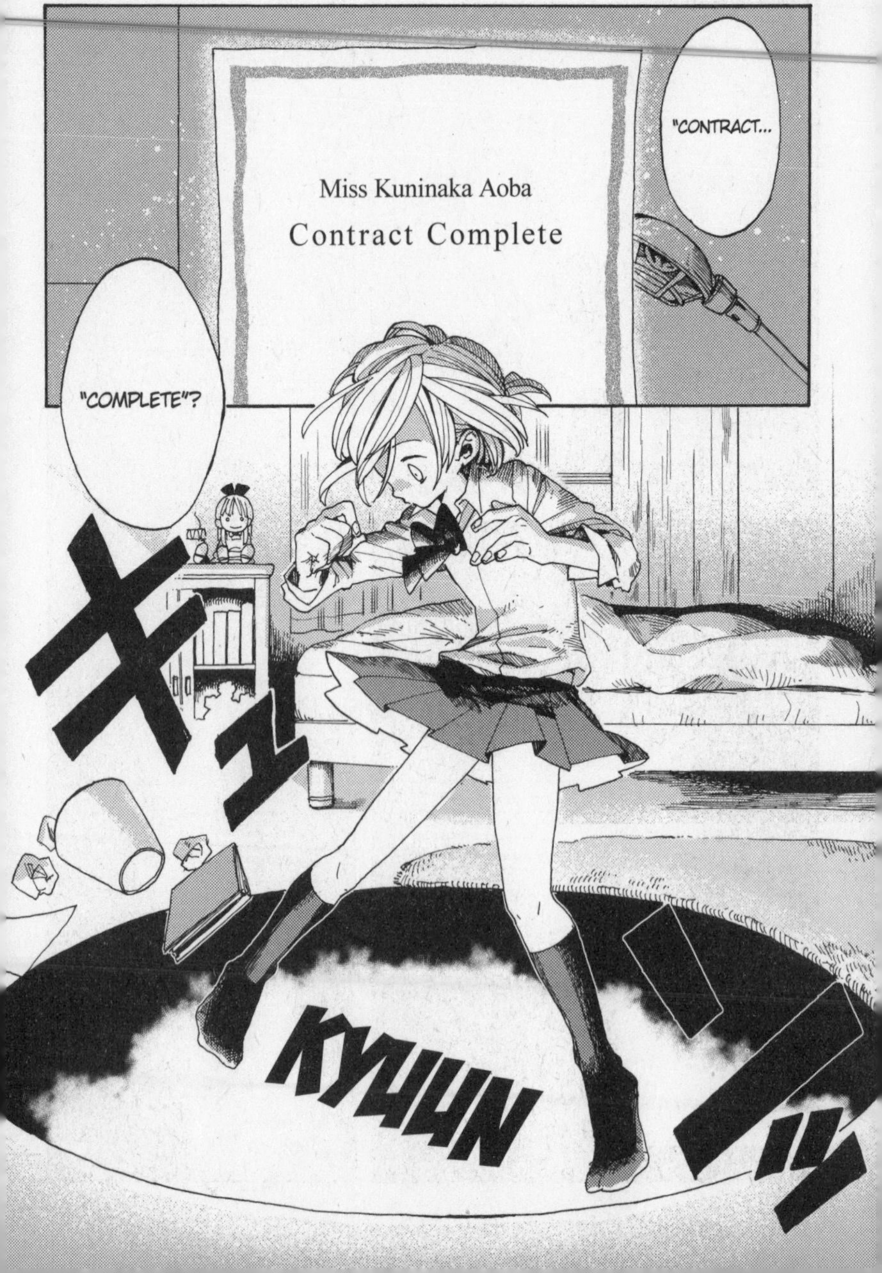
"CONTRACT...
Miss Kuninaka Aoba
Contract Complete
"COMPLETE"?
KYUUN

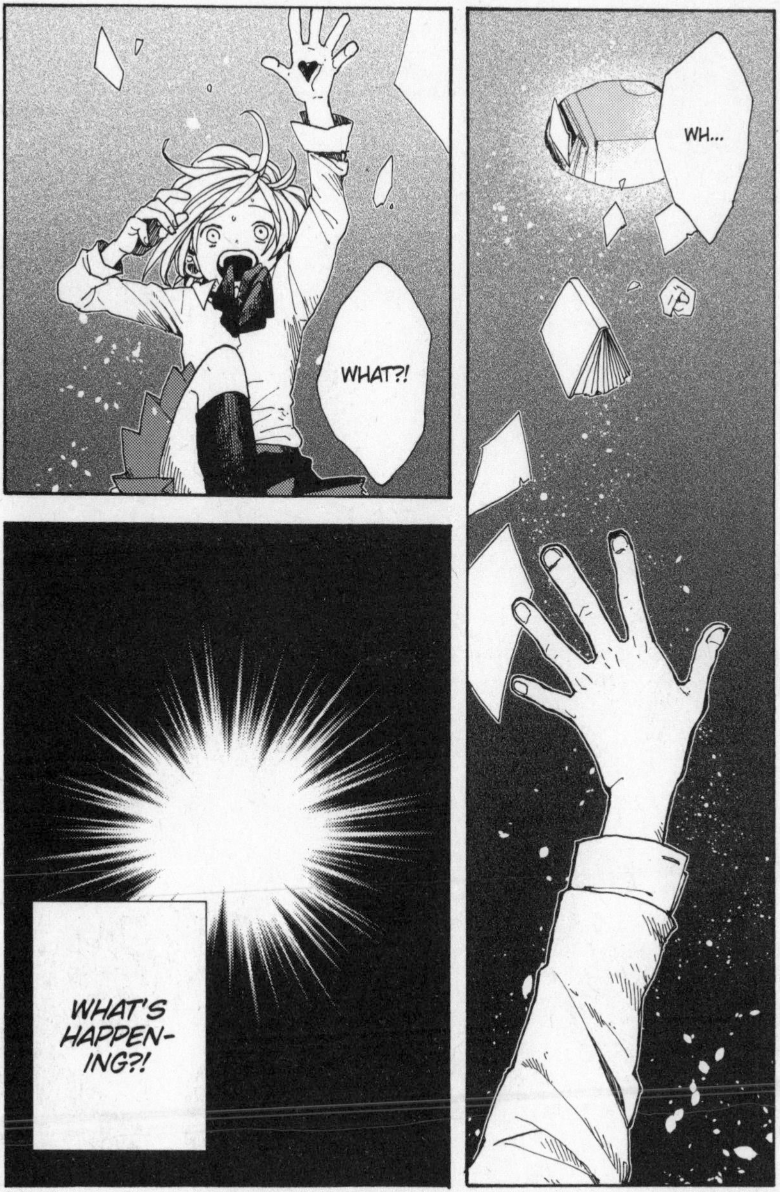
WH...
WHAT?!
WHAT'S HAPPEN-ING?!

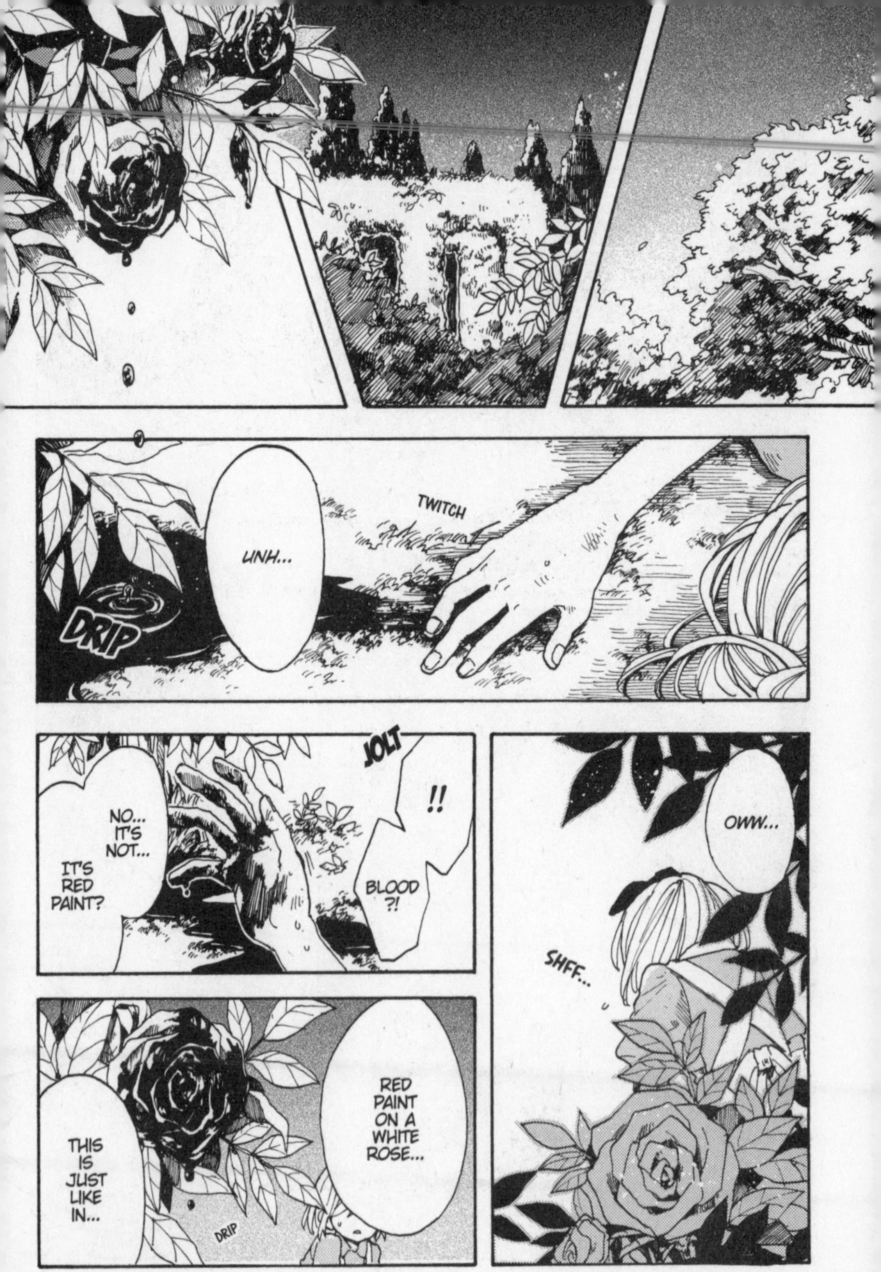
TWITCH
UNH...
DRIP
OWW...
SHFF...
JOLT
!!
BLOOD?!
NO... IT'S NOT...
IT'S RED PAINT?
RED PAINT ON A WHITE ROSE...
THIS IS JUST LIKE IN...
DRIP

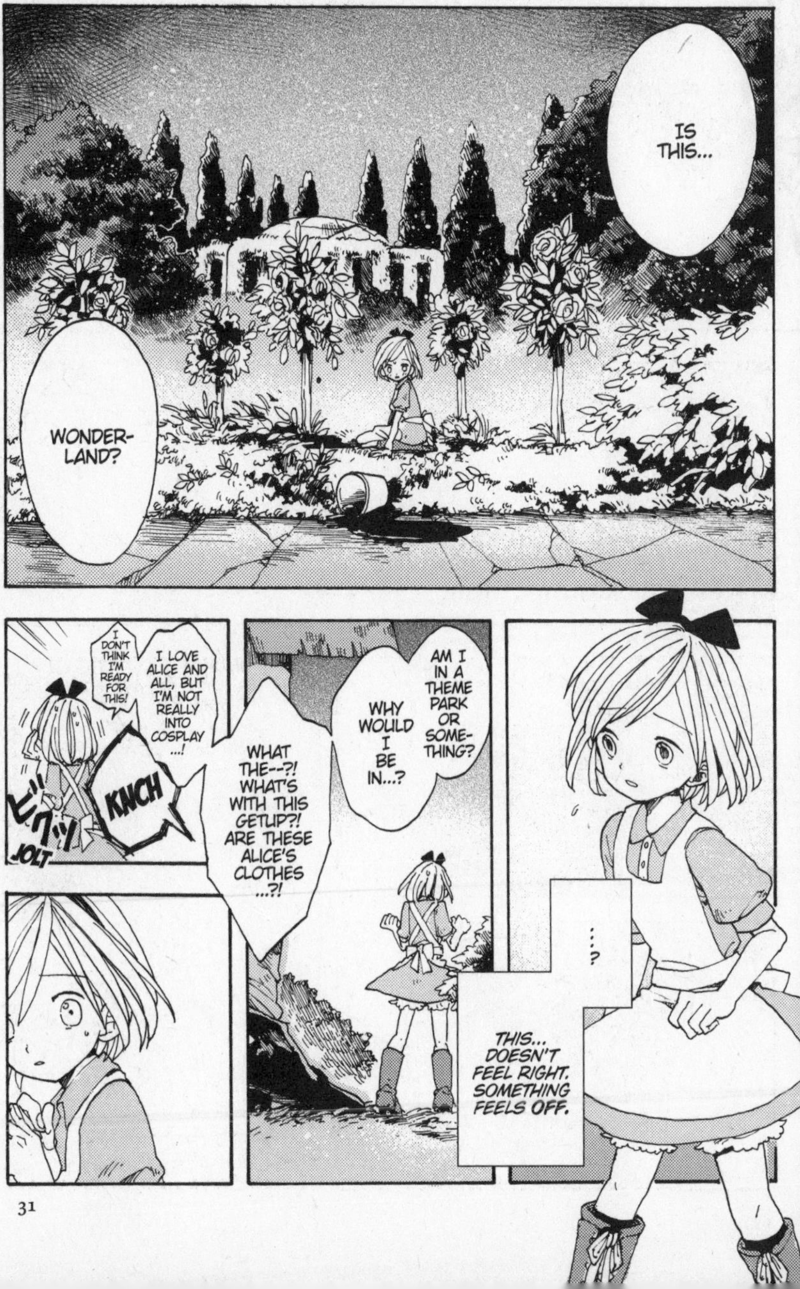
IS THIS...
WONDERLAND?
...?
THIS... DOESN'T FEEL RIGHT. SOMETHING FEELS OFF.
AM I IN A THEME PARK OR SOMETHING?
WHY WOULD I BE IN...?
WHAT THE--?! WHAT'S WITH THIS GETUP?! ARE THESE ALICE'S CLOTHES ...?!
KNCH
I LOVE ALICE AND ALL, BUT I'M NOT REALLY INTO COSPLAY ...!
I DON'T THINK I'M READY FOR THIS!
JOLT

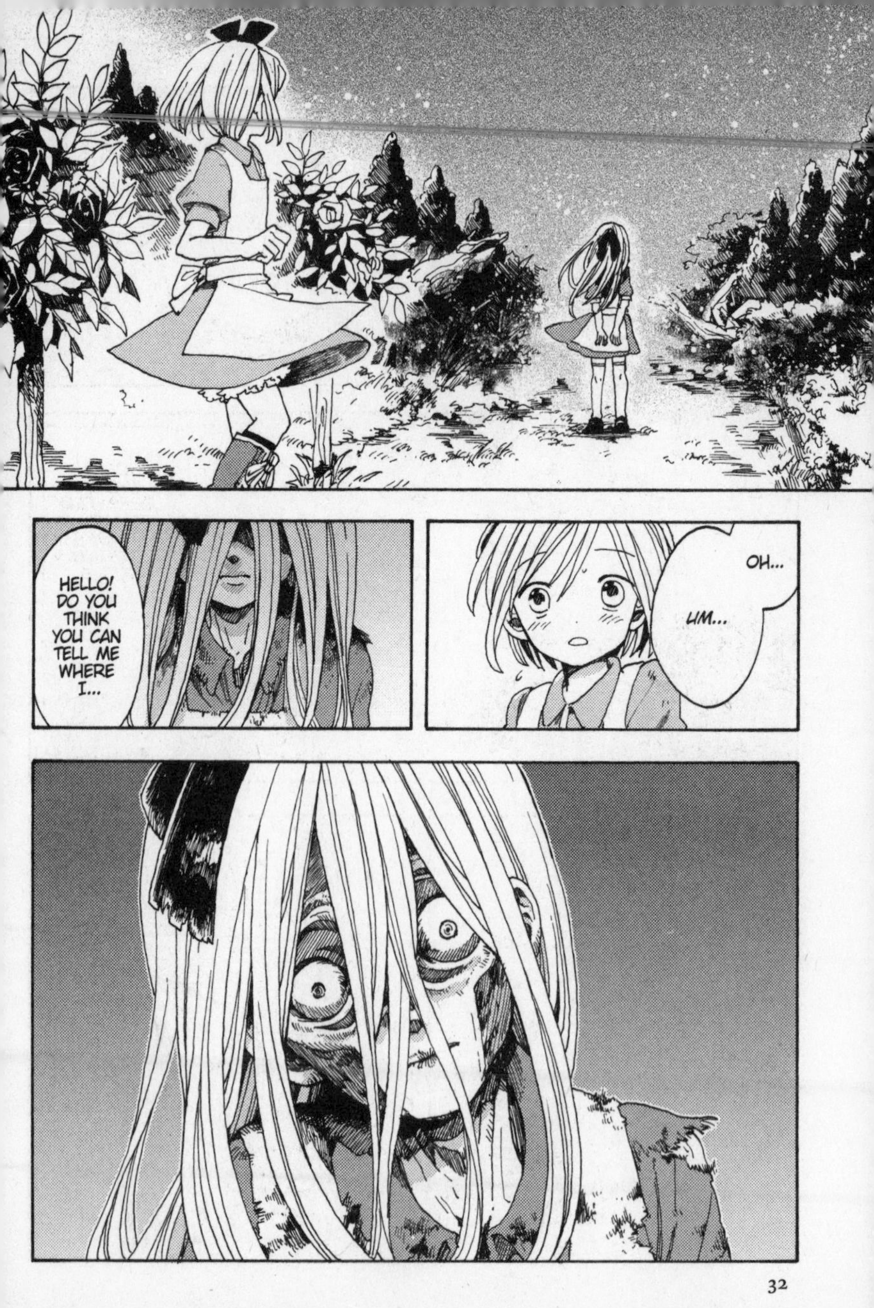

HELLO! DO YOU THINK YOU CAN TELL ME WHERE I...
OH...
UM...

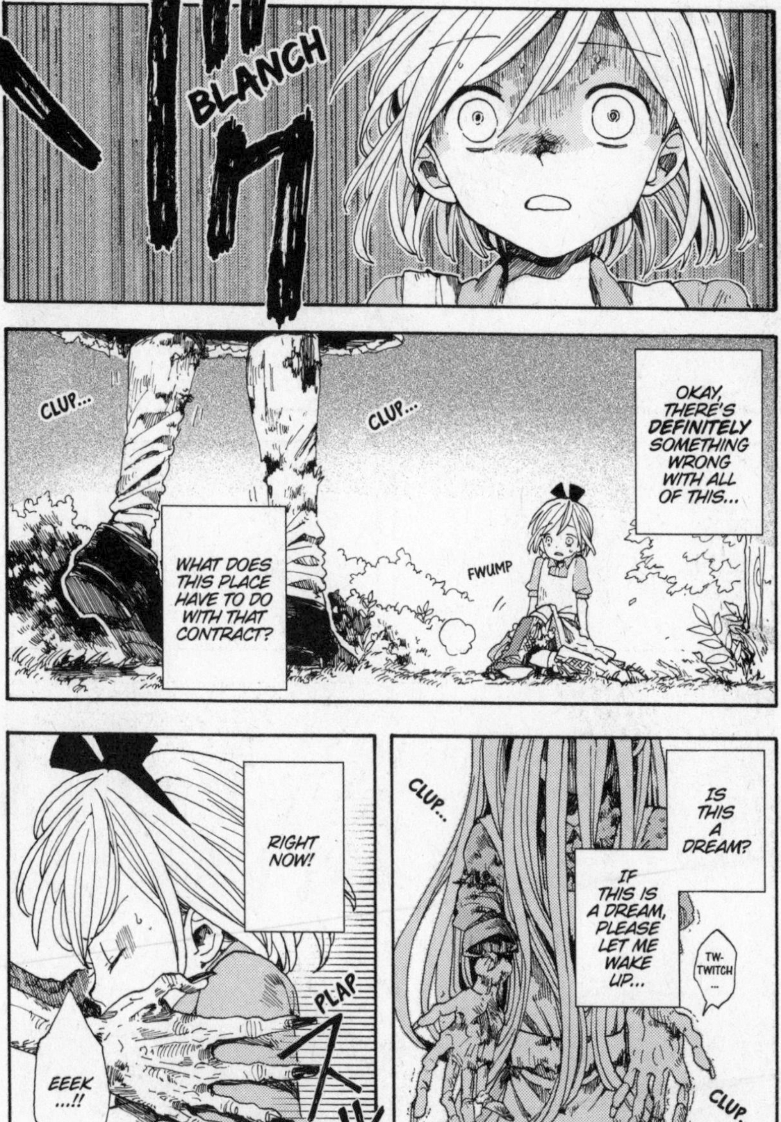
BLANCH
OKAY, THERE'S DEFINITELY SOMETHING WRONG WITH ALL OF THIS...
FWUMP
CLUP...
CLUP...
WHAT DOES THIS PLACE HAVE TO DO WITH THAT CONTRACT?
IS THIS A DREAM?
IF THIS IS A DREAM, PLEASE LET ME WAKE UP...
TW-TWITCH...
CLUP...
CLUP...
RIGHT NOW!
PLAP
EEEK...!!

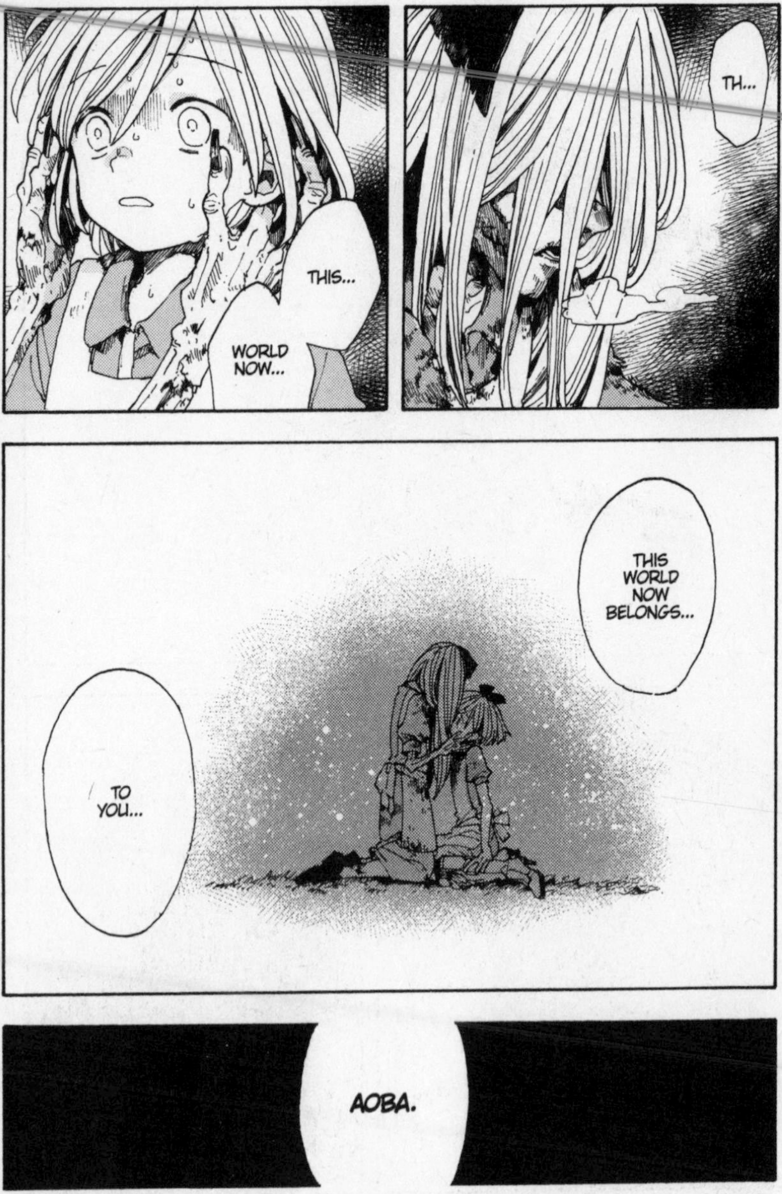
TH...
THIS...
WORLD NOW...
THIS WORLD NOW BELONGS...
TO YOU...
AOBA.

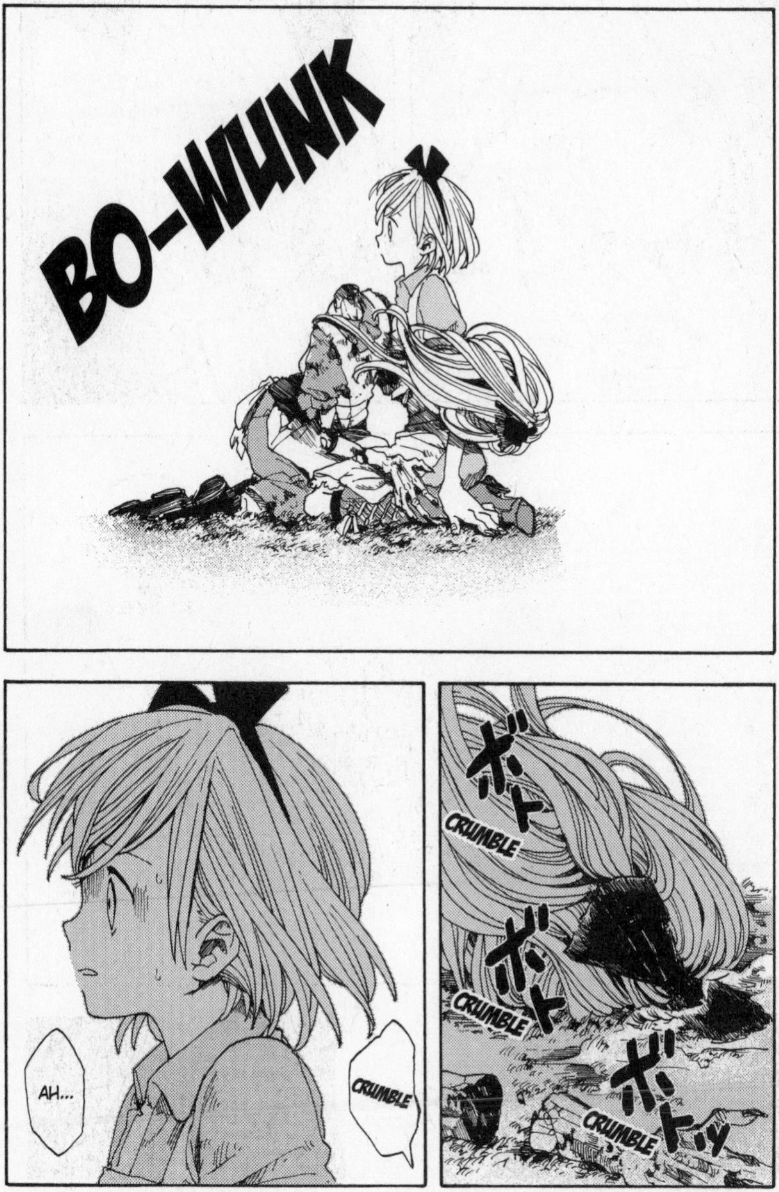
BO-WUNK
ボトッ
CRUMBLE
ボトッ
CRUMBLE
ボトッ
CRUMBLE
CRUMBLE
AH...

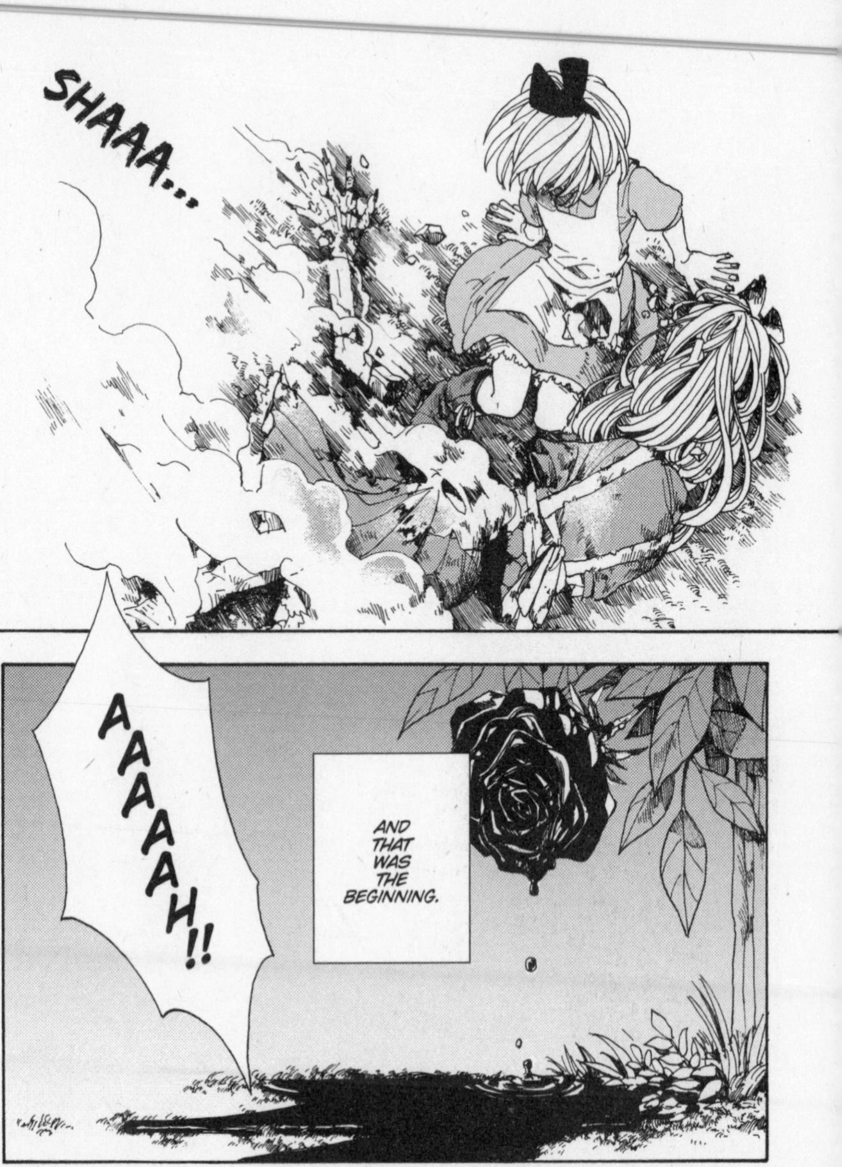
SHAAA...
AAAAAH!!
AND THAT WAS THE BEGINNING.

Alice in Wonderland

First published: 1865.
Author: Lewis Carroll.

Lewis Carroll
based *Alice* off a book
he drew by hand for his
friend's daughter, *Alice's
Adventures Under
Ground.*

FAIRY
TALE
BATTLE
ROYALE

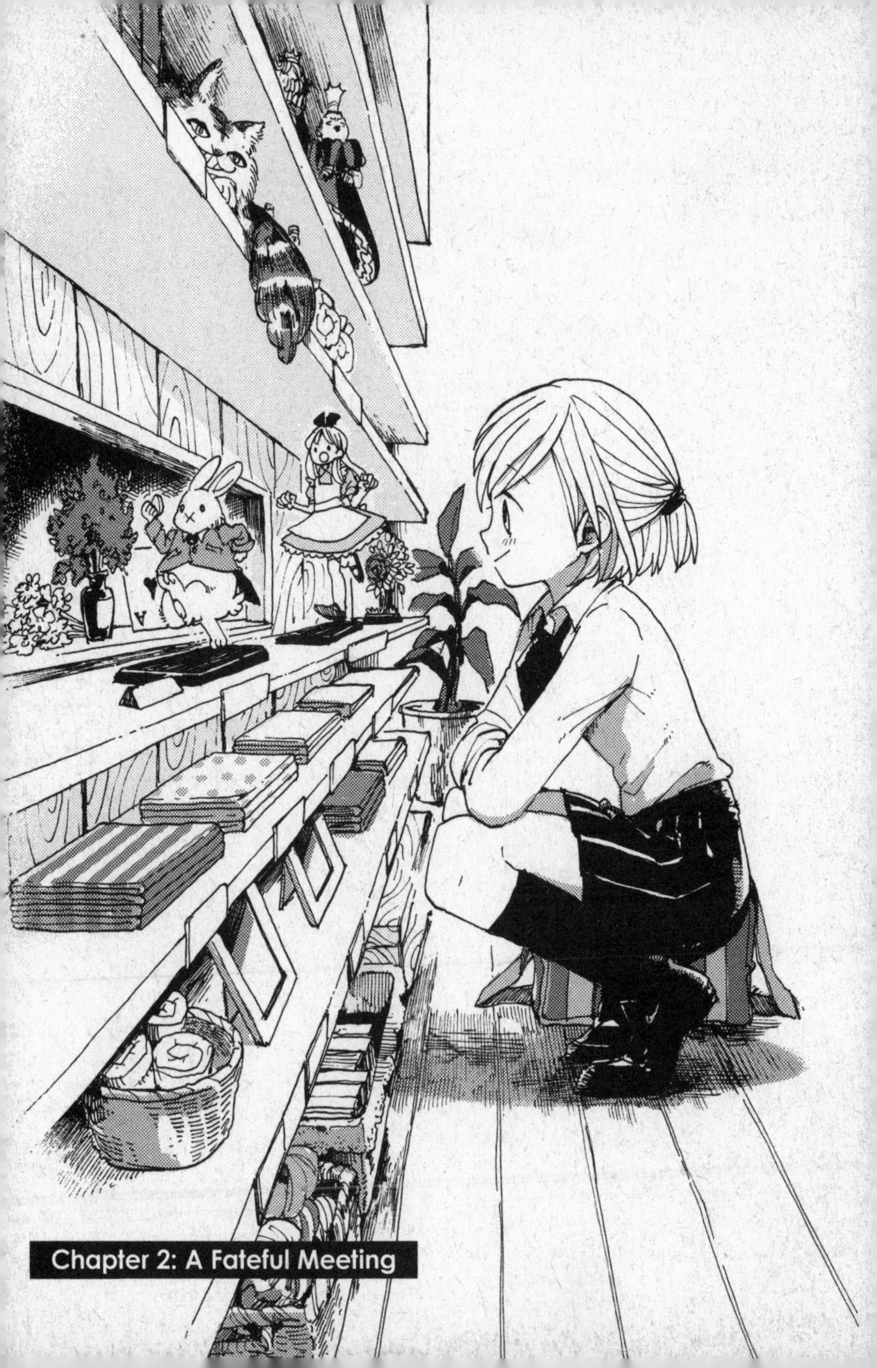

Chapter 2: A Fateful Meeting

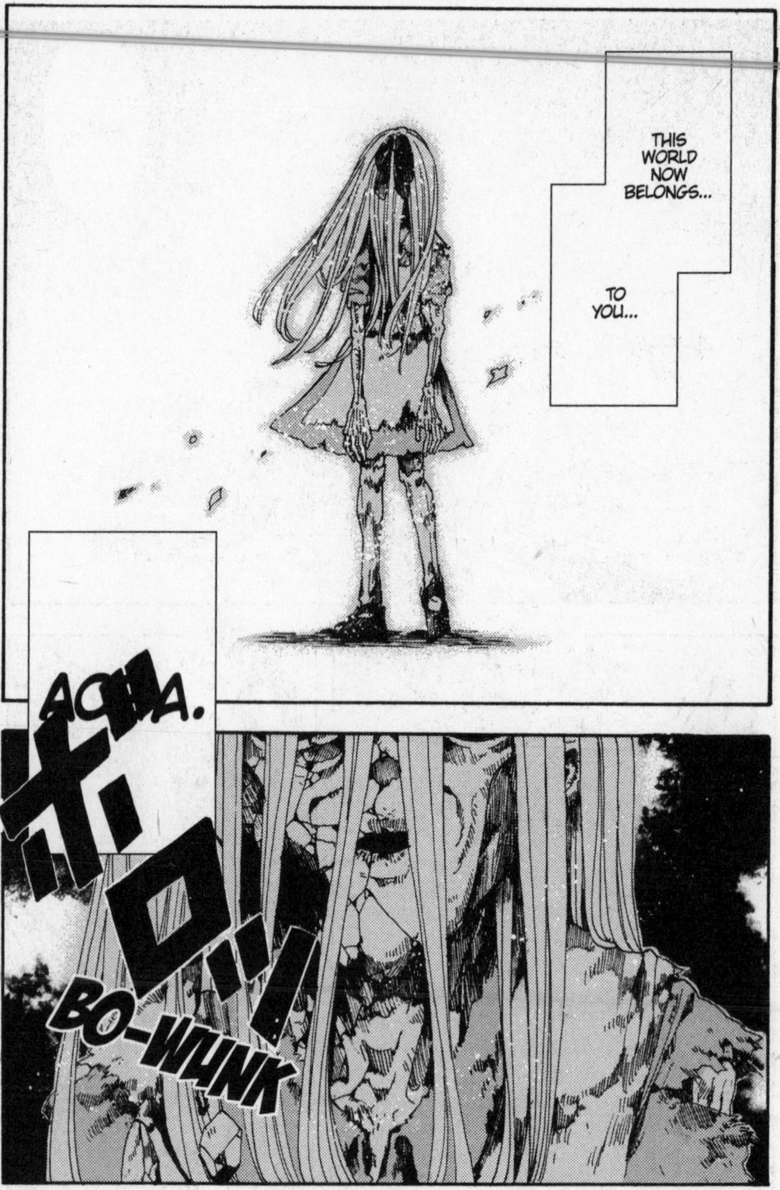
THIS WORLD NOW BELONGS...
TO YOU...
BO-WUNK

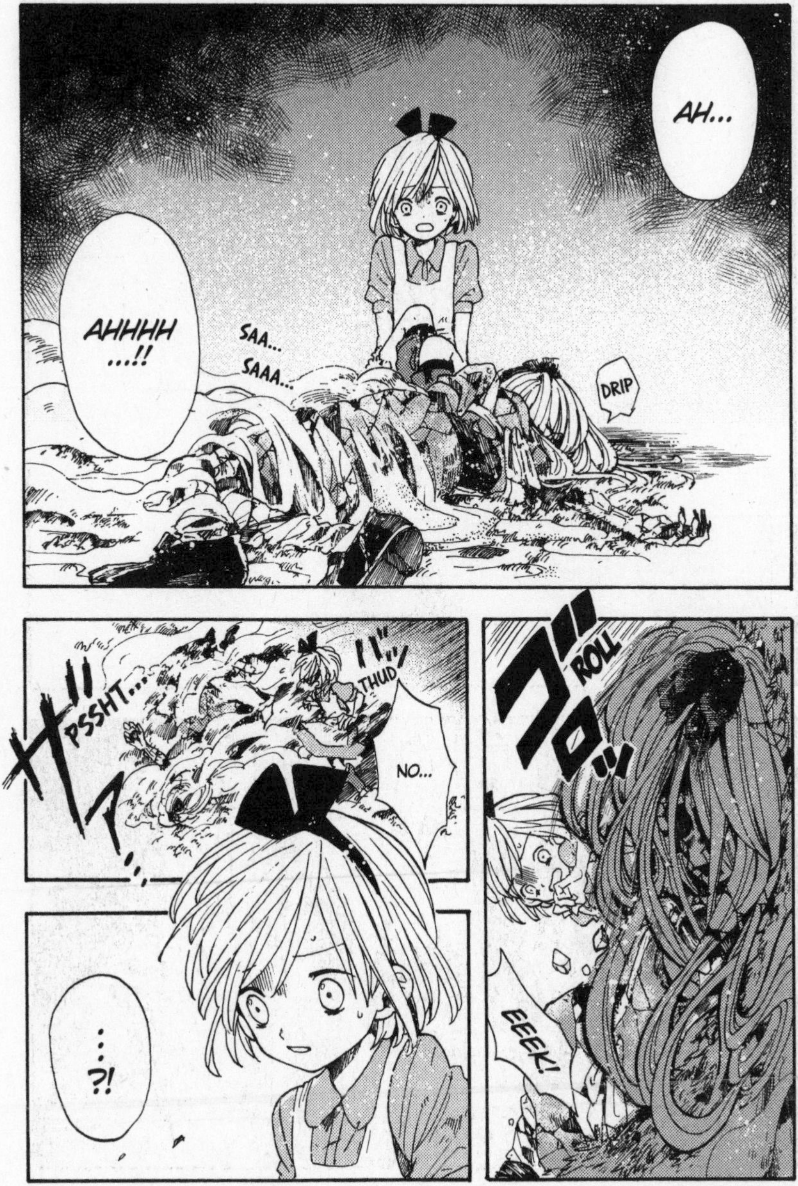
AH...
DRIP
AHHHH ...!!
SAA...
SAAA...
ROLL
EEEK!
THUD
NO...
PSSHT...
...?!

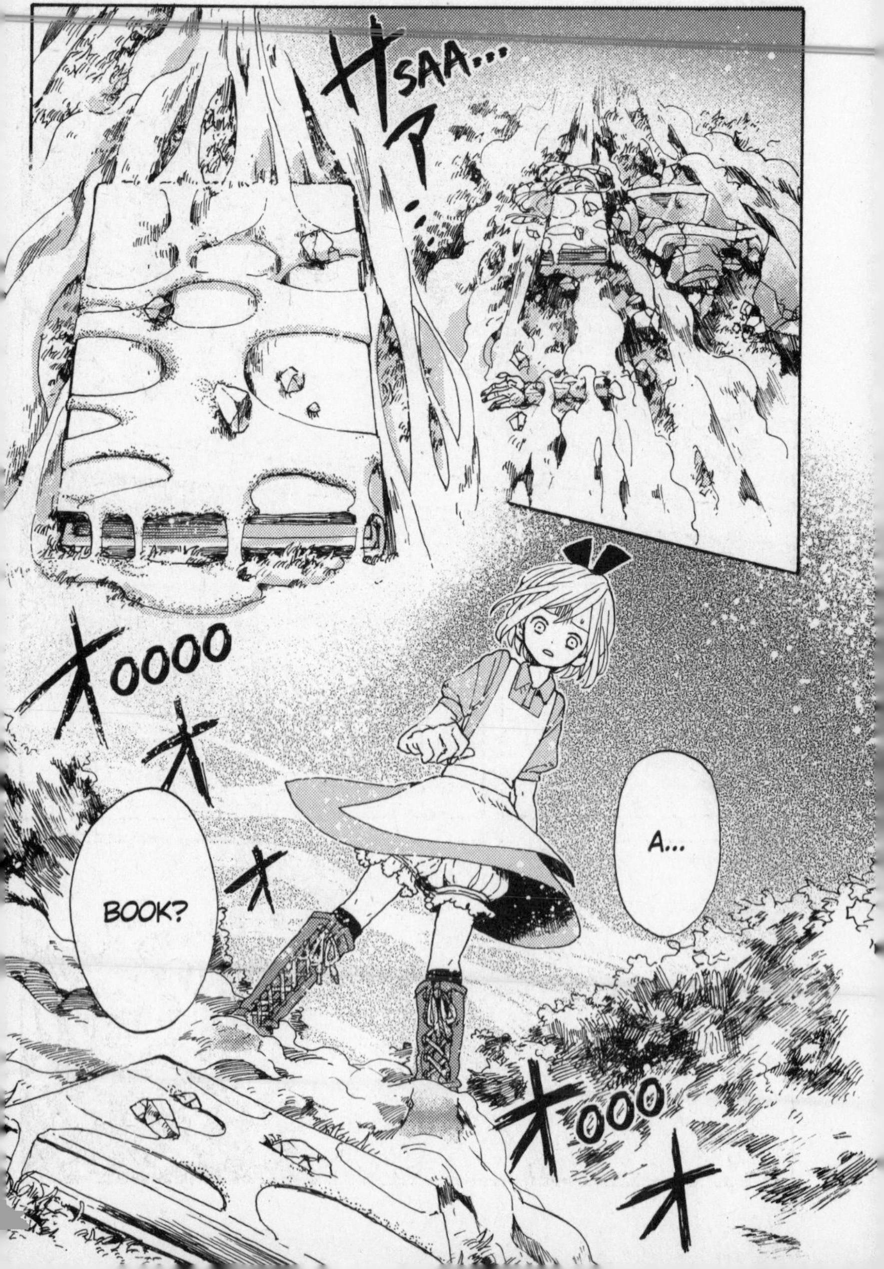
サア…
SAA...
A...
BOOK?
OOOO
OOO

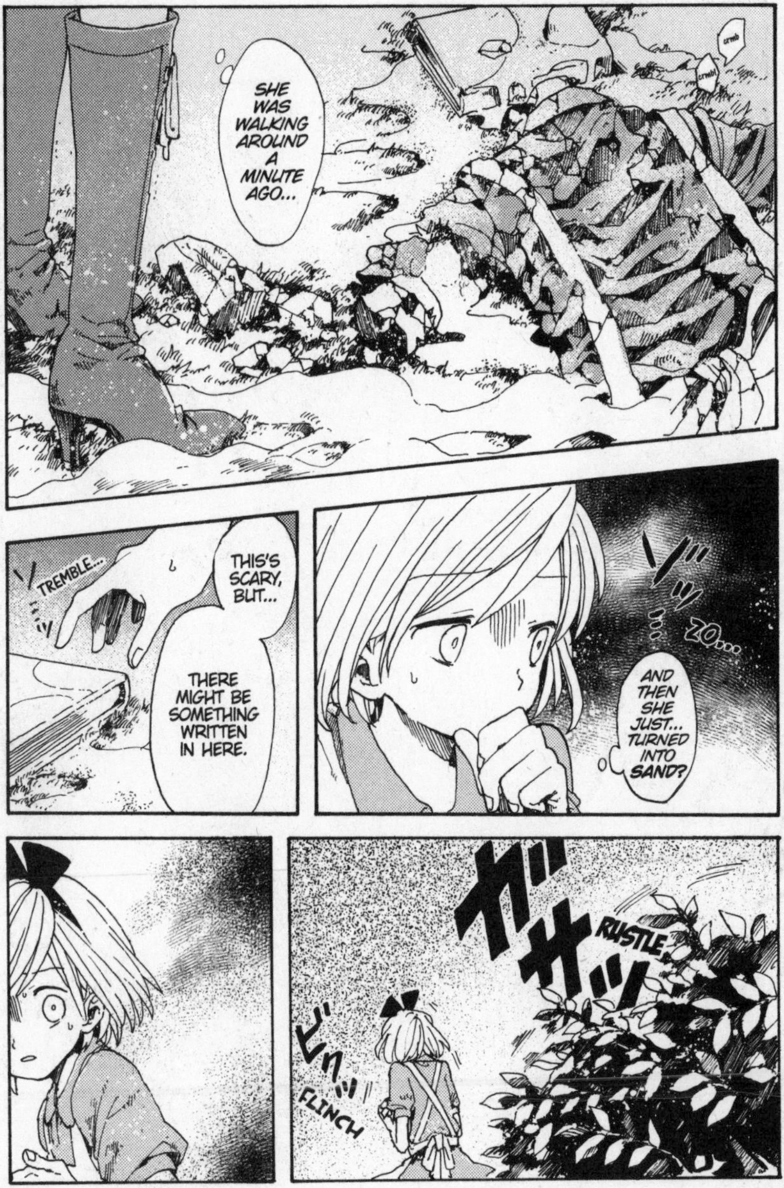
crmb
crmbl
SHE WAS WALKING AROUND A MINUTE AGO...
ZO...
AND THEN SHE JUST... TURNED INTO SAND?
TREMBLE...
THIS'S SCARY, BUT...
THERE MIGHT BE SOMETHING WRITTEN IN HERE.
RUSTLE
FLINCH

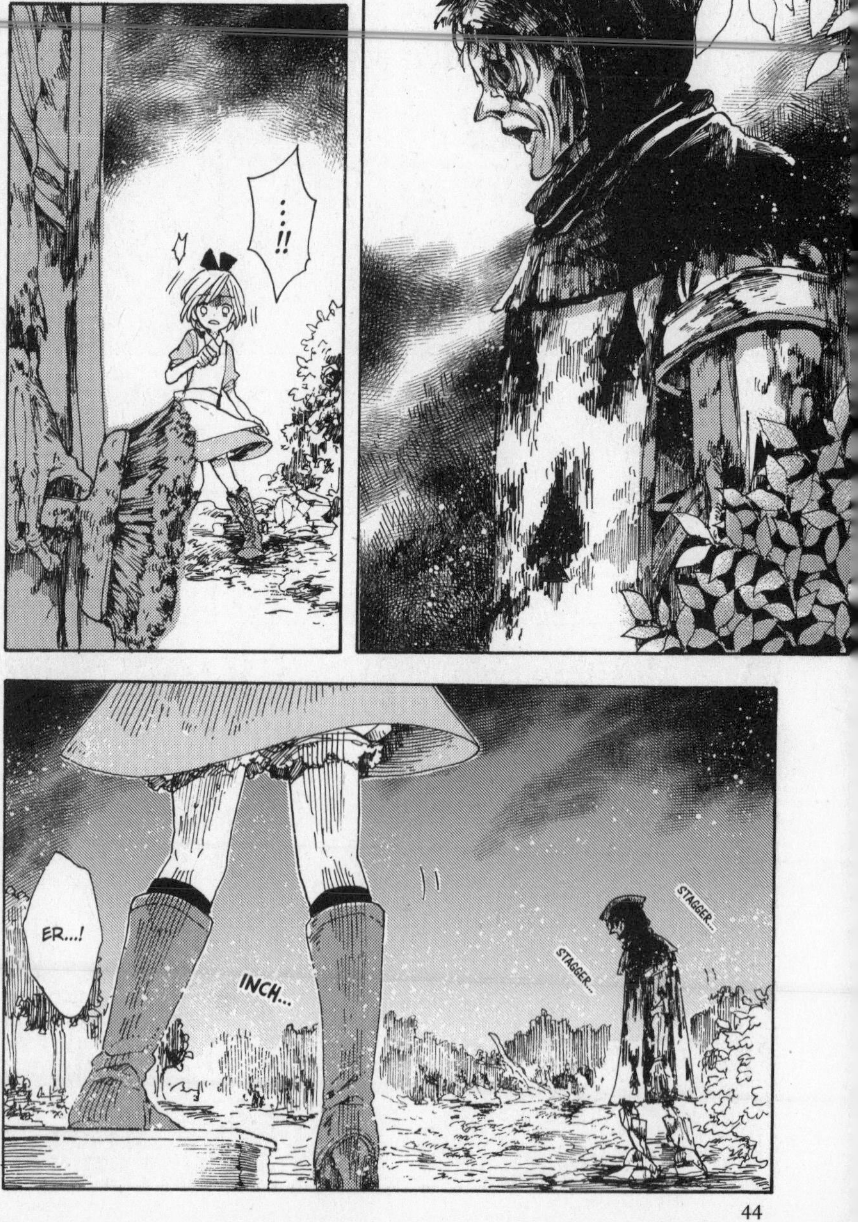
...!!
STAGGER...
STAGGER...
INCH...
ER...!

KREEEK
AHHH...
AHH...
AHHHH...
...!!
CLOMP

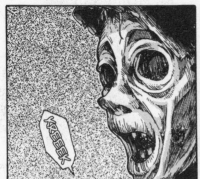

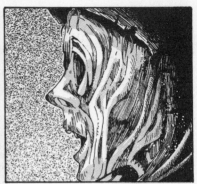

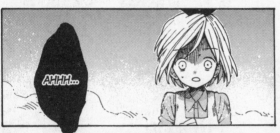

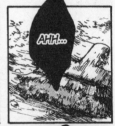

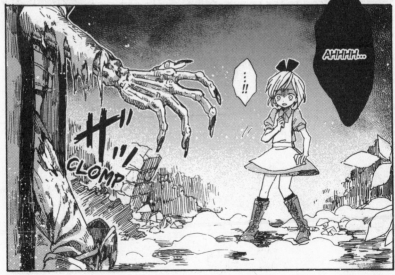

GASP!

AHH...

THWUMP

CLOM...

ONE
OF
THE
TRUMP
CARD
SOLDIERS?

SSST...

AHH
...

AHHH...

CLOM...

AHH...

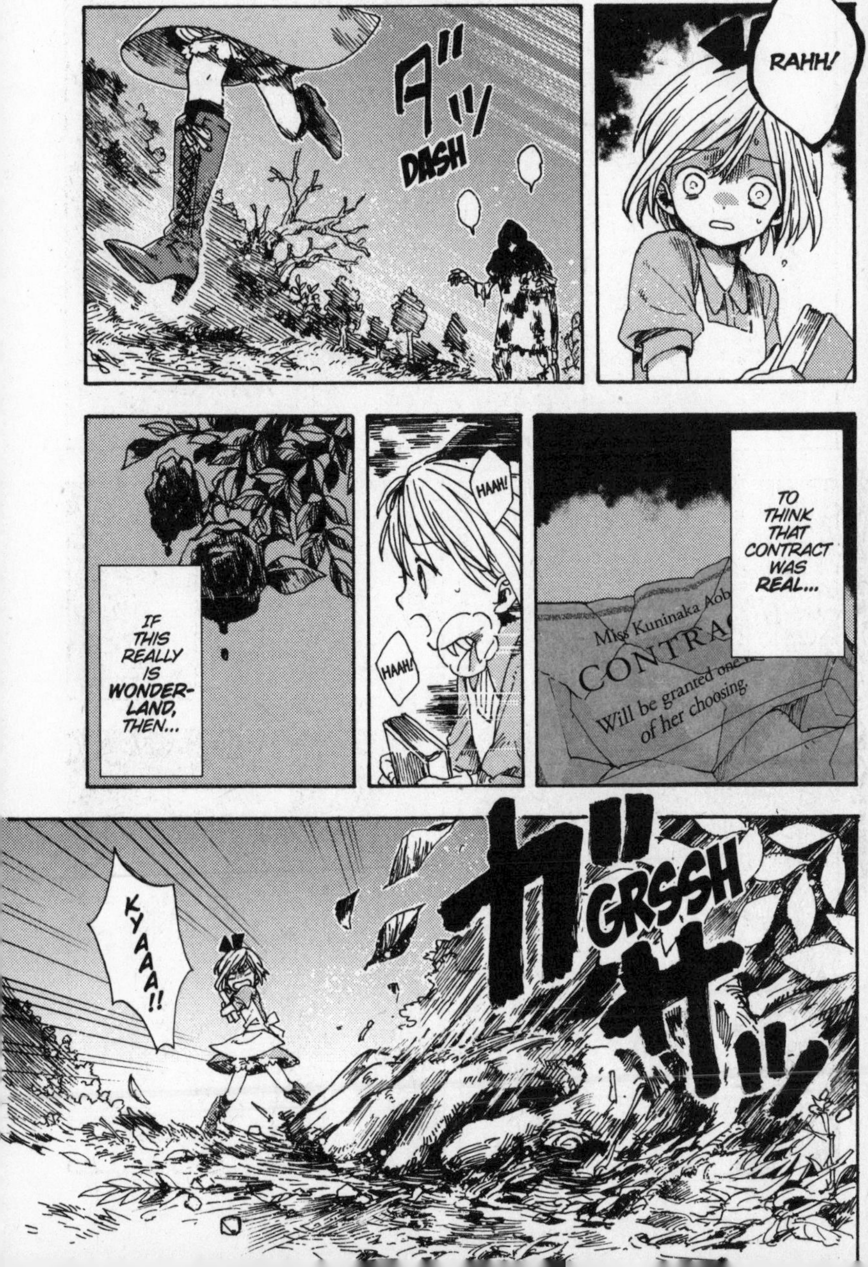

RAHH!
ダッ
DASH
TO THINK THAT CONTRACT WAS REAL...
Miss Kuninaka Aob
CONTRAC
Will be granted one
of her choosing.
HAAH!
HAAH!
IF THIS REALLY IS WONDER-LAND, THEN...
ガサッ
GRSSH
KYAAA!!

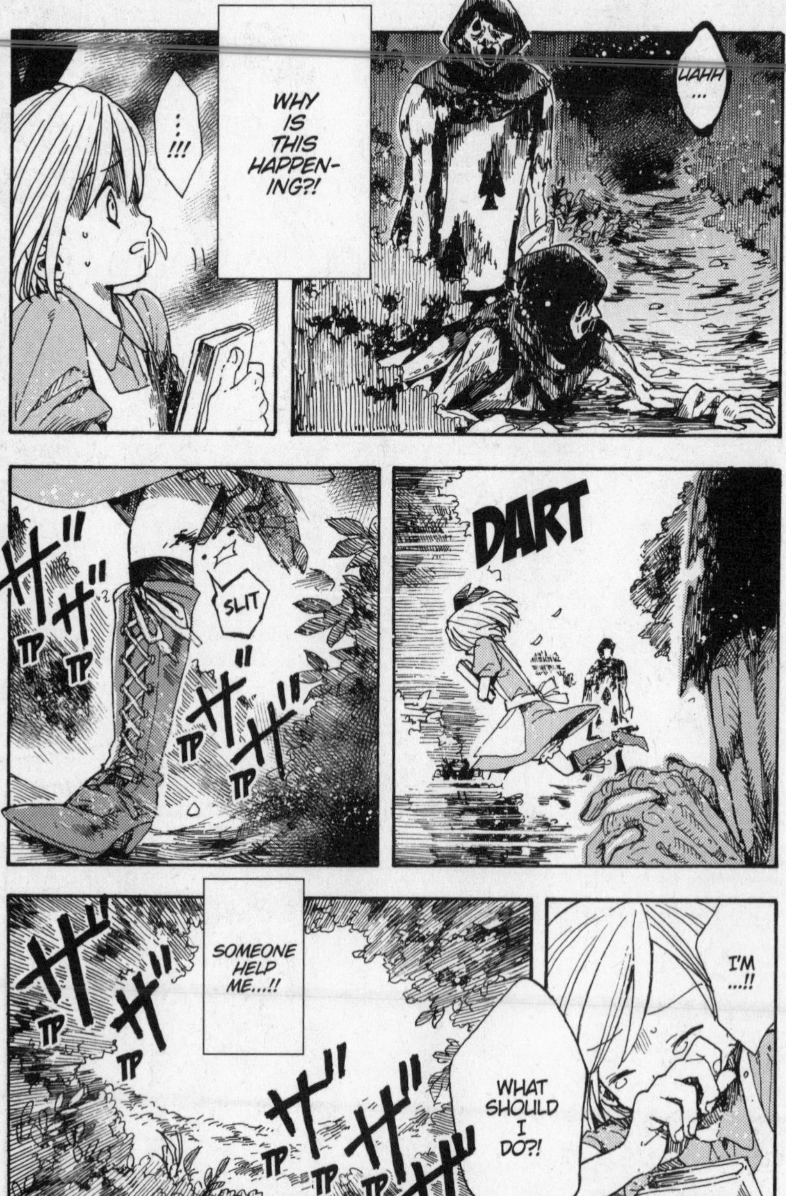
UAHH ...
WHY IS THIS HAPPENING?!
... !!!
DART
SLIT
TP TP
TP TP
I'M ...!!
WHAT SHOULD I DO?!
SOMEONE HELP ME...!!
TP TP
TP TP TP

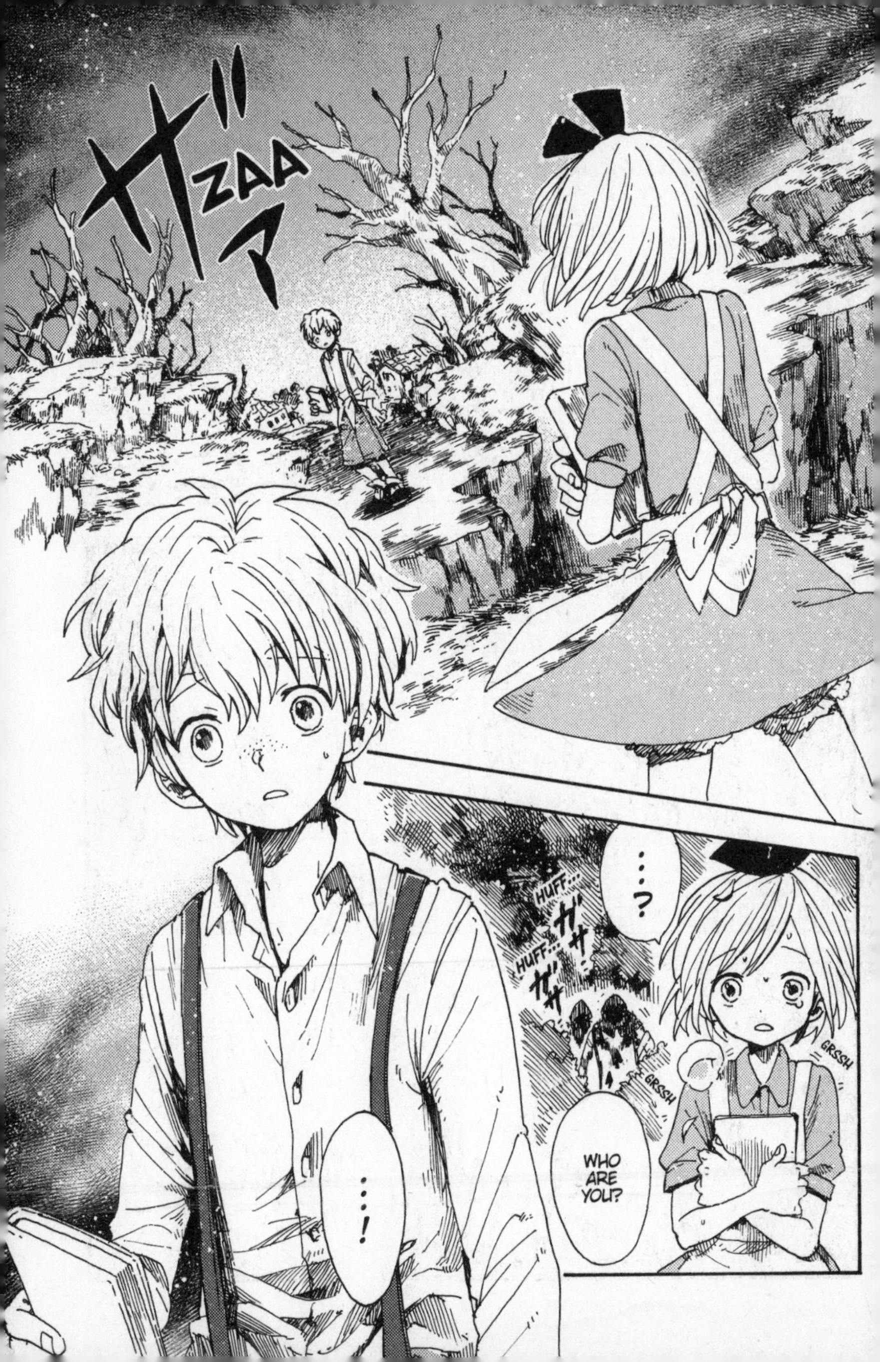
ZAA
...?
HUFF...
HUFF...
GRSSH
GRSSH
WHO ARE YOU?
...!

COME
WITH
ME!

CLOM...

HAH?!

OVER
HERE!!

CLOM...

QUICK!!

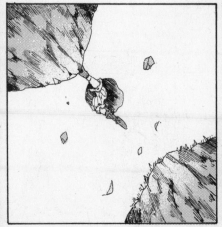

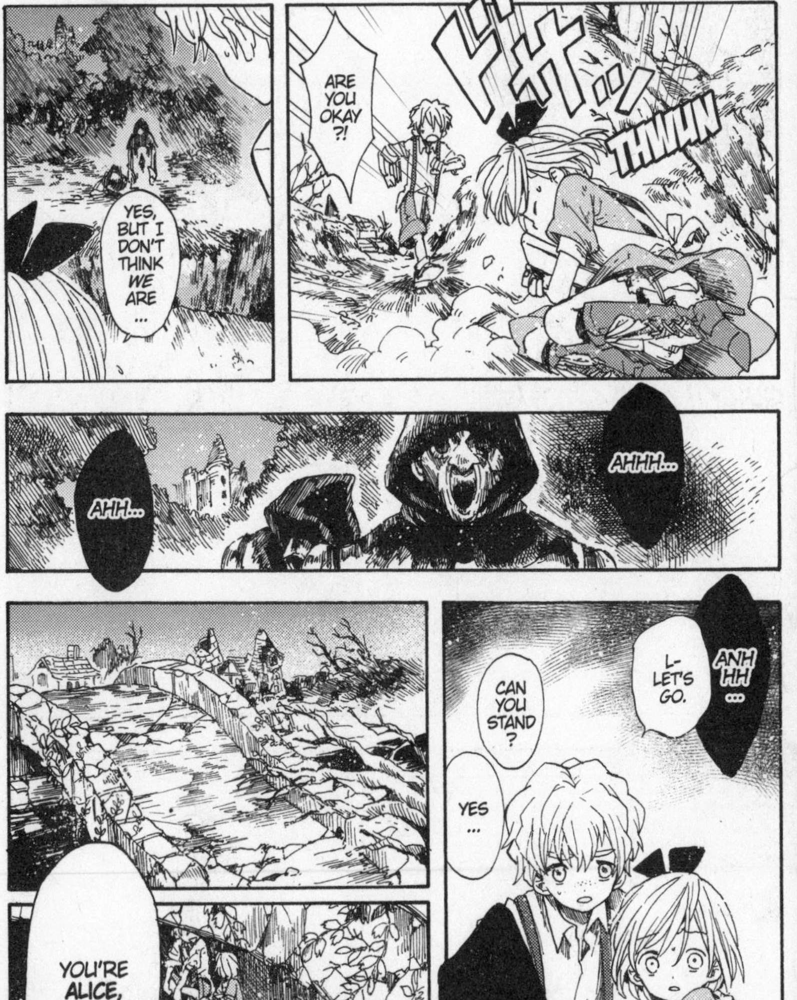
ARE YOU OKAY ?!
THWUN
YES, BUT I DON'T THINK WE ARE ...
AHHHH...
AHH...
ANH HH ...
L- LET'S GO.
CAN YOU STAND ?
YES ...
RAHHHH...
YOU'RE ALICE, RIGHT?
CREEAK

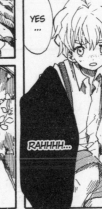

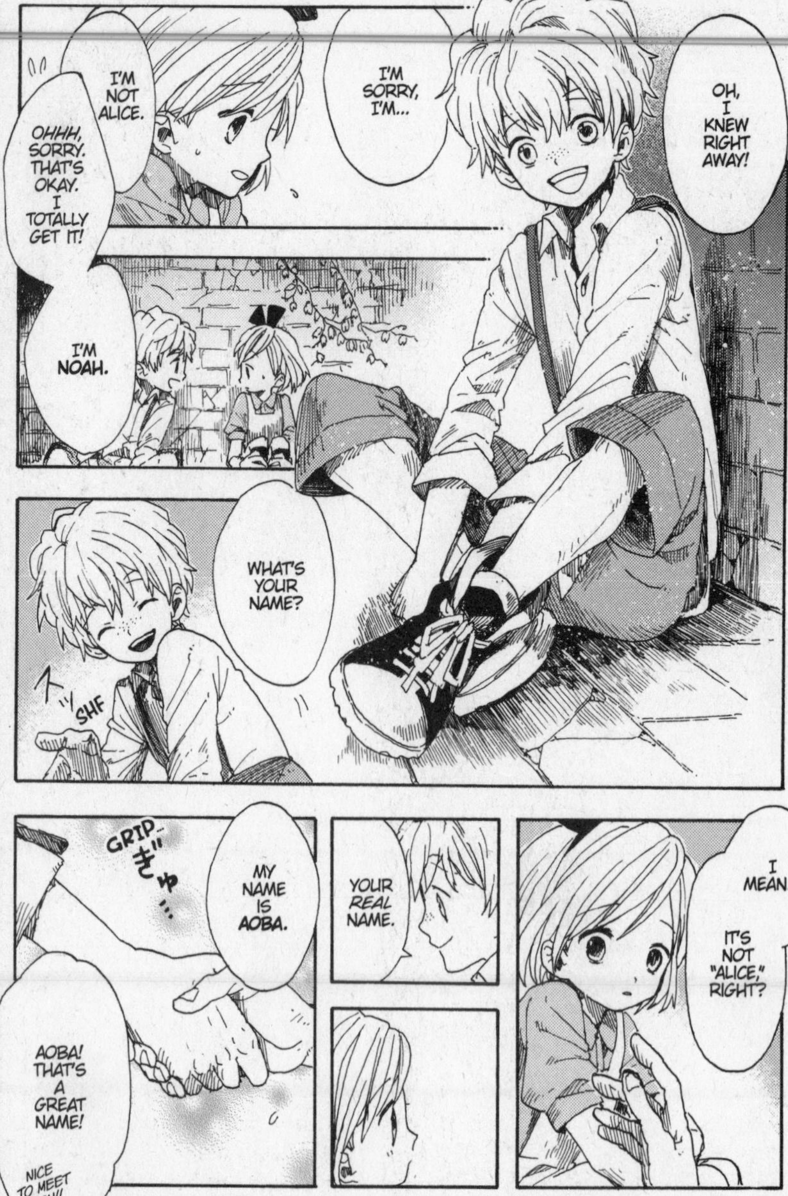
OH, I KNEW RIGHT AWAY!
I'M SORRY, I'M...
I'M NOT ALICE.
OHHH, SORRY. THAT'S OKAY. I TOTALLY GET IT!
I'M NOAH.
WHAT'S YOUR NAME?
SHF
I MEAN...
IT'S NOT "ALICE," RIGHT?
YOUR REAL NAME.
MY NAME IS AOBA.
GRIP
ぎゅ
AOBA! THAT'S A GREAT NAME!
NICE TO MEET YOU!!

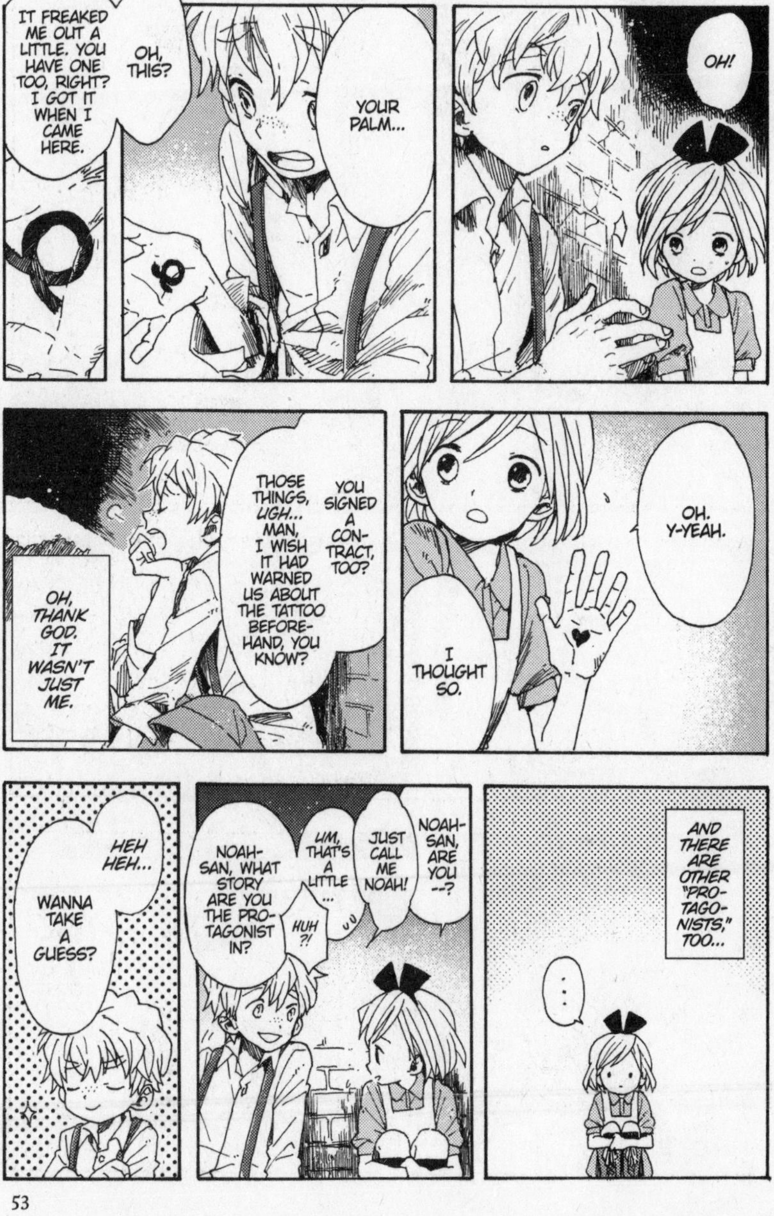
OH!
YOUR PALM...
OH, THIS?
IT FREAKED ME OUT A LITTLE. YOU HAVE ONE TOO, RIGHT? I GOT IT WHEN I CAME HERE.
OH. Y-YEAH.
I THOUGHT SO.
YOU SIGNED A CONTRACT, TOO?
THOSE THINGS, UGH... MAN, I WISH IT HAD WARNED US ABOUT THE TATTOO BEFOREHAND, YOU KNOW?
OH, THANK GOD. IT WASN'T JUST ME.
AND THERE ARE OTHER "PROTAGONISTS," TOO...
...
NOAH-SAN, ARE YOU--?
JUST CALL ME NOAH!
UM, THAT'S A LITTLE ...
HUH?!
NOAH-SAN, WHAT STORY ARE YOU THE PROTAGONIST IN?
HEH HEH...
WANNA TAKE A GUESS?

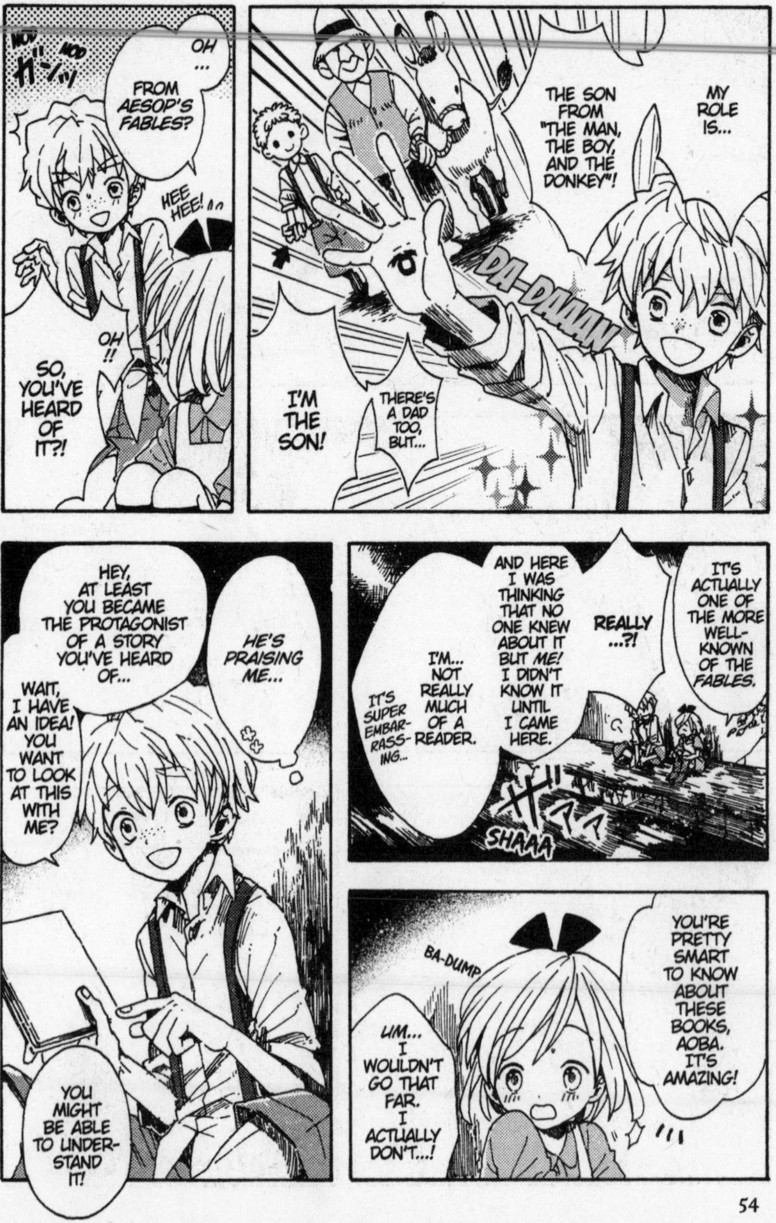
MY ROLE IS...
THE SON FROM "THE MAN, THE BOY, AND THE DONKEY"!
DA-DAAAN
THERE'S A DAD TOO, BUT...
I'M THE SON!
OH ... FROM AESOP'S FABLES?
NOD NOD
HEE HEE!
OH!!
SO, YOU'VE HEARD OF IT?!
IT'S ACTUALLY ONE OF THE MORE WELL-KNOWN OF THE FABLES.
REALLY ...?!
AND HERE I WAS THINKING THAT NO ONE KNEW ABOUT IT BUT ME! I DIDN'T KNOW IT UNTIL I CAME HERE.
I'M... NOT REALLY MUCH OF A READER.
IT'S SUPER EMBARRASSING...
SHAAA
YOU'RE PRETTY SMART TO KNOW ABOUT THESE BOOKS, AOBA. IT'S AMAZING!
BA-DUMP
UM... I WOULDN'T GO THAT FAR. I ACTUALLY DON'T...!
HEY, AT LEAST YOU BECAME THE PROTAGONIST OF A STORY YOU'VE HEARD OF...
HE'S PRAISING ME...
WAIT, I HAVE AN IDEA! YOU WANT TO LOOK AT THIS WITH ME?
YOU MIGHT BE ABLE TO UNDERSTAND IT!

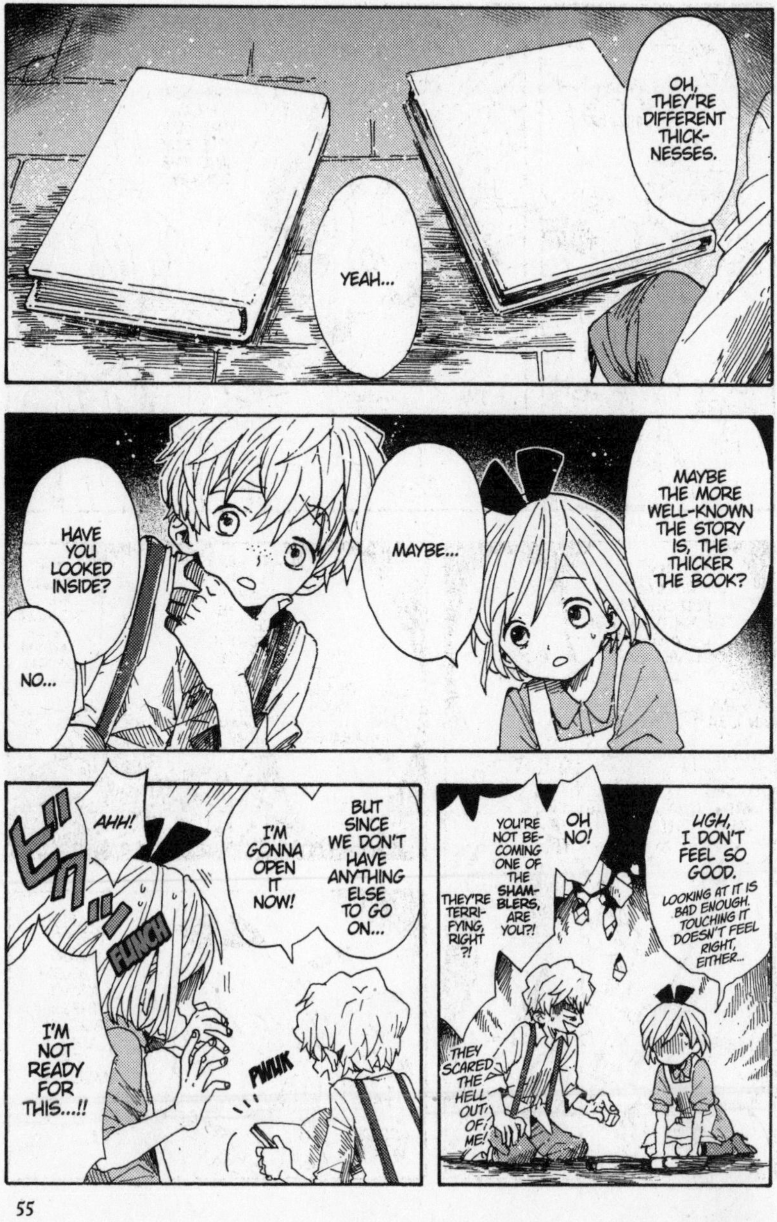
OH, THEY'RE DIFFERENT THICK-NESSES.
YEAH...
MAYBE THE MORE WELL-KNOWN THE STORY IS, THE THICKER THE BOOK?
MAYBE...
HAVE YOU LOOKED INSIDE?
NO...
UGH, I DON'T FEEL SO GOOD.
LOOKING AT IT IS BAD ENOUGH. TOUCHING IT DOESN'T FEEL RIGHT, EITHER...
OH NO!
YOU'RE NOT BE-COMING ONE OF THE SHAM-BLERS, ARE YOU?!
THEY'RE TERRI-FYING, RIGHT ?!
THEY SCARED THE HELL OUT OF ME!
BUT SINCE WE DON'T HAVE ANYTHING ELSE TO GO ON...
I'M GONNA OPEN IT NOW!
AHH!
FLINCH
PWUK
I'M NOT READY FOR THIS...!!

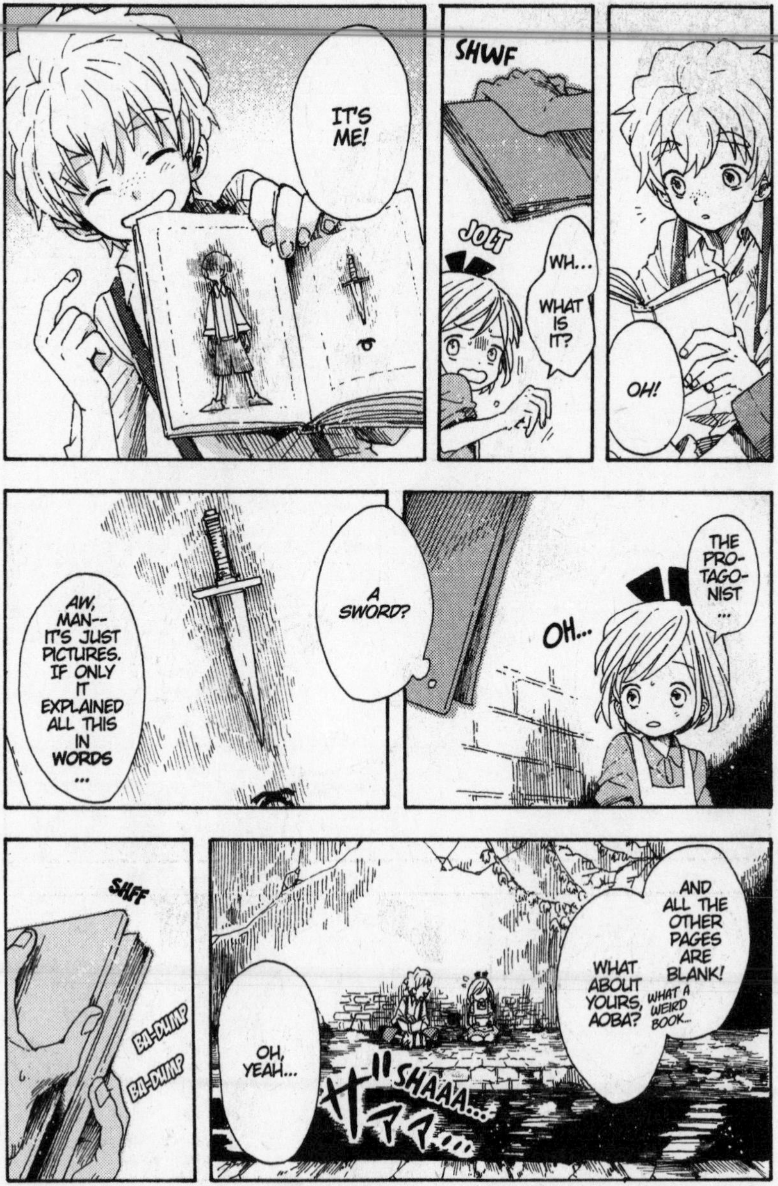
OH!
SHWF
JOLT
WH... WHAT IS IT?
IT'S ME!
THE PROTAGONIST ...
OH...
A SWORD?
AW, MAN-- IT'S JUST PICTURES. IF ONLY IT EXPLAINED ALL THIS IN WORDS ...
AND ALL THE OTHER PAGES ARE BLANK!
WHAT A WEIRD BOOK...
WHAT ABOUT YOURS, AOBA?
SHAAA...
OH, YEAH...
SHFF
BA-DUMP
BA-DUMP

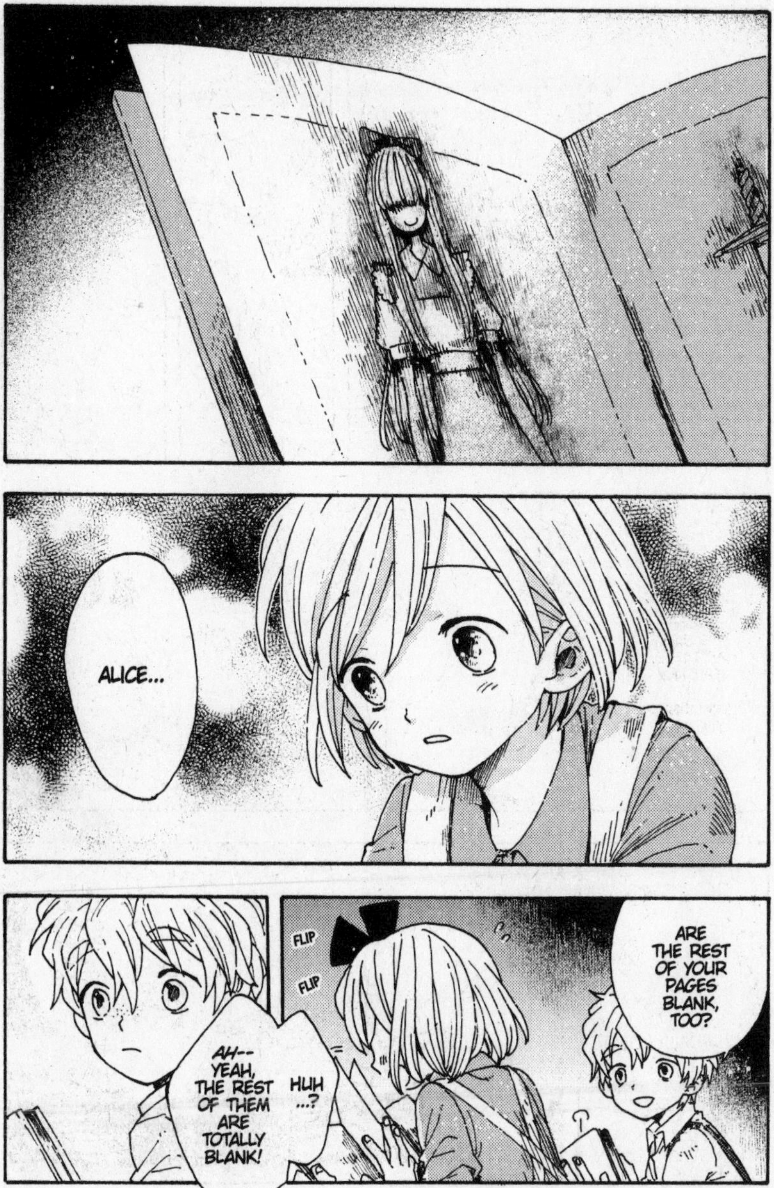
ALICE...
ARE THE REST OF YOUR PAGES BLANK, TOO?
FLIP
FLIP
HUH ...?
AH-- YEAH, THE REST OF THEM ARE TOTALLY BLANK!

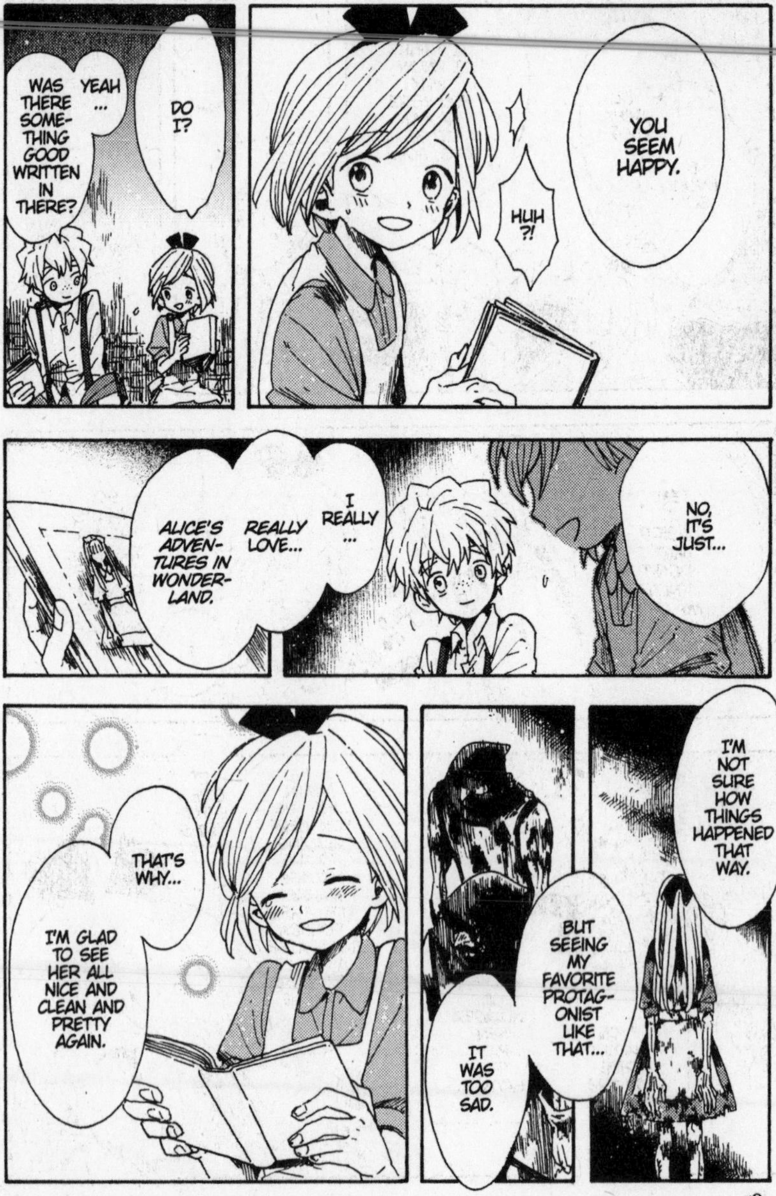
YOU SEEM HAPPY.
HUH ?!
DO I?
YEAH ...
WAS THERE SOMETHING GOOD WRITTEN IN THERE?
NO, IT'S JUST...
I REALLY ...
REALLY LOVE...
ALICE'S ADVENTURES IN WONDERLAND.
I'M NOT SURE HOW THINGS HAPPENED THAT WAY.
BUT SEEING MY FAVORITE PROTAGONIST LIKE THAT...
IT WAS TOO SAD.
THAT'S WHY...
I'M GLAD TO SEE HER ALL NICE AND CLEAN AND PRETTY AGAIN.

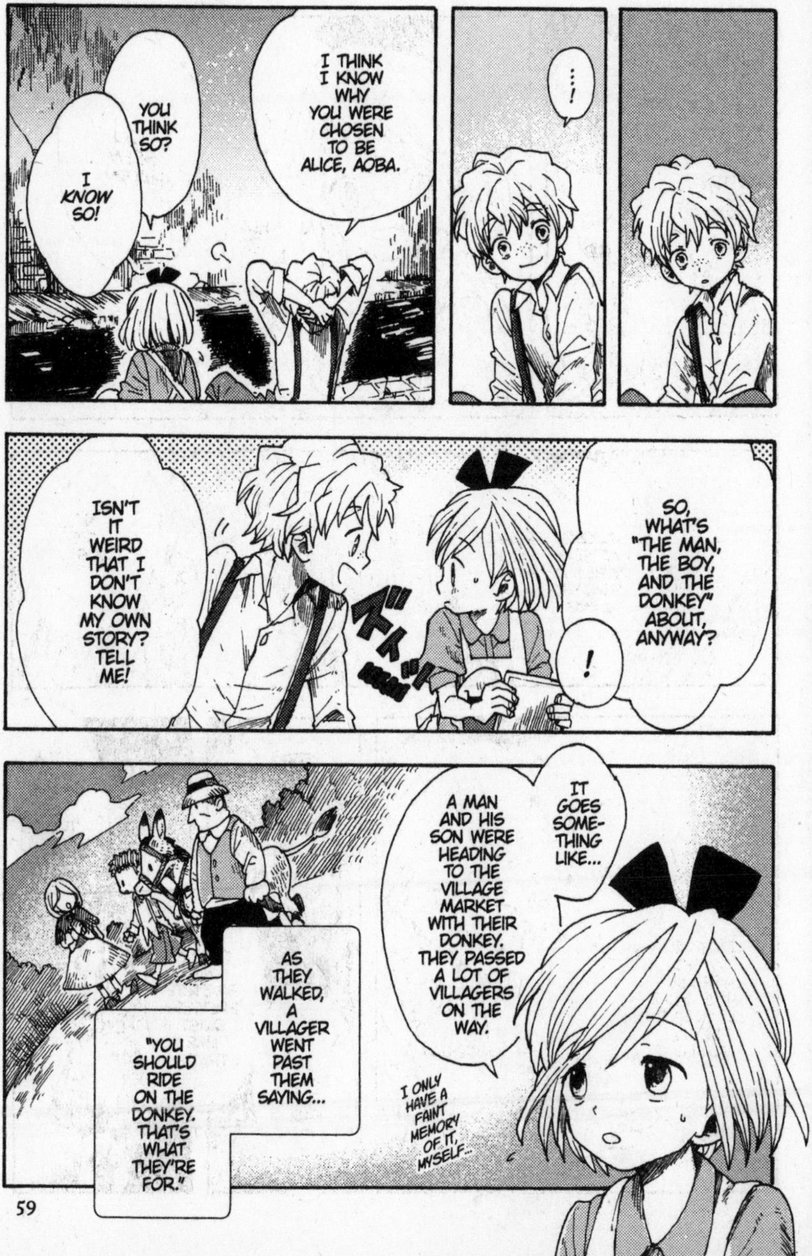
I THINK I KNOW WHY YOU WERE CHOSEN TO BE ALICE, AOBA.
YOU THINK SO?
I KNOW SO!
...!
SO, WHAT'S "THE MAN, THE BOY, AND THE DONKEY" ABOUT, ANYWAY?
!
ISN'T IT WEIRD THAT I DON'T KNOW MY OWN STORY? TELL ME!
IT GOES SOME-THING LIKE...
A MAN AND HIS SON WERE HEADING TO THE VILLAGE MARKET WITH THEIR DONKEY. THEY PASSED A LOT OF VILLAGERS ON THE WAY.
I ONLY HAVE A FAINT MEMORY OF IT, MYSELF...
AS THEY WALKED, A VILLAGER WENT PAST THEM SAYING...
"YOU SHOULD RIDE ON THE DONKEY. THAT'S WHAT THEY'RE FOR."

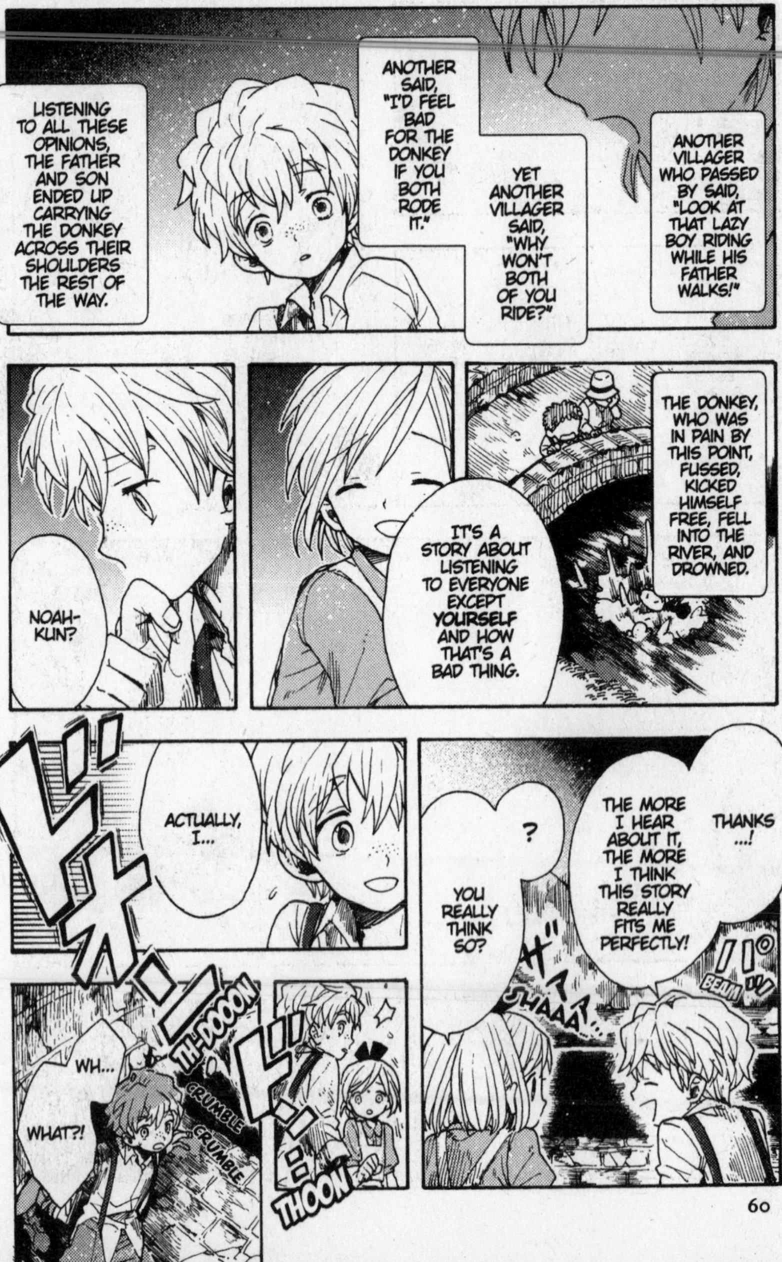
ANOTHER VILLAGER WHO PASSED BY SAID, "LOOK AT THAT LAZY BOY RIDING WHILE HIS FATHER WALKS!"
YET ANOTHER VILLAGER SAID, "WHY WON'T BOTH OF YOU RIDE?"
ANOTHER SAID, "I'D FEEL BAD FOR THE DONKEY IF YOU BOTH RODE IT."
LISTENING TO ALL THESE OPINIONS, THE FATHER AND SON ENDED UP CARRYING THE DONKEY ACROSS THEIR SHOULDERS THE REST OF THE WAY.
THE DONKEY, WHO WAS IN PAIN BY THIS POINT, FUSSED, KICKED HIMSELF FREE, FELL INTO THE RIVER, AND DROWNED.
IT'S A STORY ABOUT LISTENING TO EVERYONE EXCEPT **YOURSELF** AND HOW THAT'S A BAD THING.
NOAH-KUN?
THANKS ...!
THE MORE I HEAR ABOUT IT, THE MORE I THINK THIS STORY REALLY FITS ME PERFECTLY!
BEAM
SHAAA...
?
YOU REALLY THINK SO?
ACTUALLY, I...
TH-DOOON
CRUMBLE CRUMBLE
WH...
WHAT?!
THOON

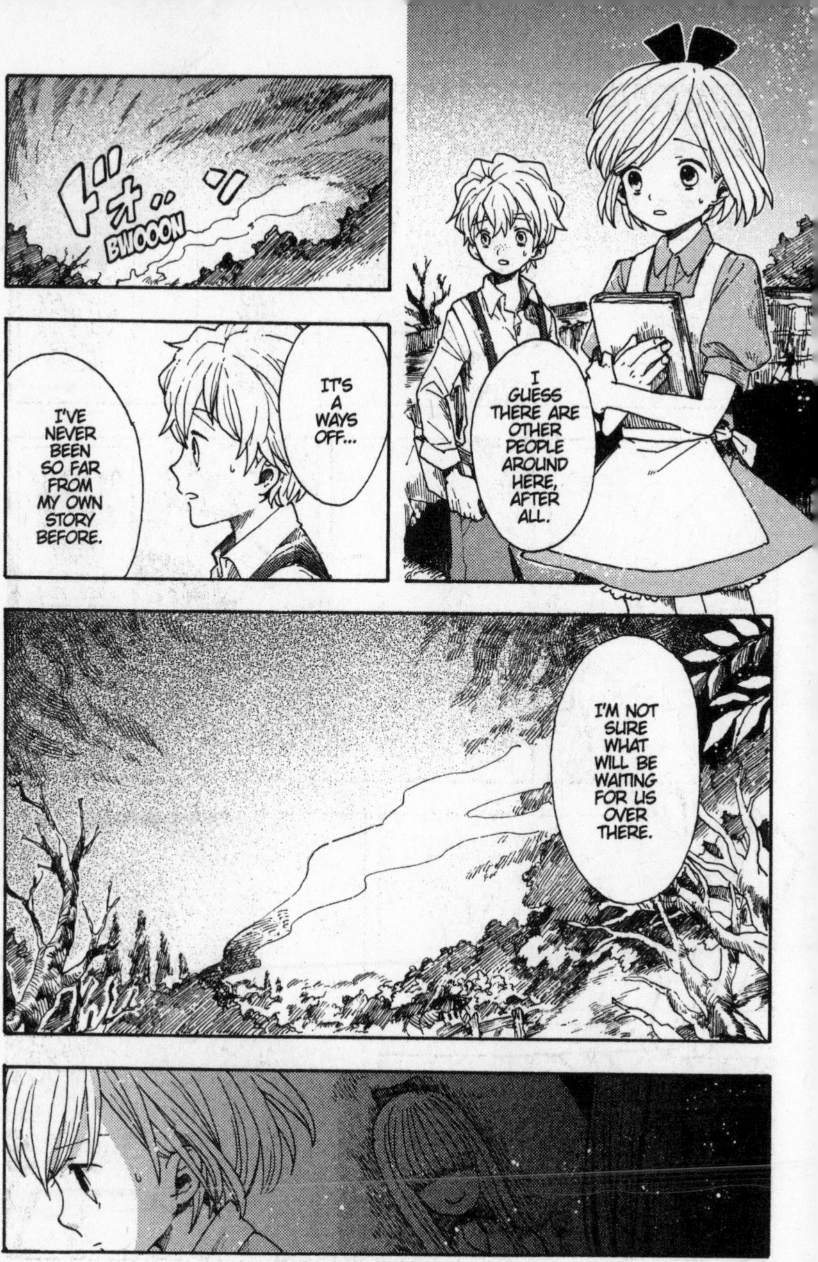
ドォォン
BWOOOON
IT'S A WAYS OFF...
I'VE NEVER BEEN SO FAR FROM MY OWN STORY BEFORE.
I GUESS THERE ARE OTHER PEOPLE AROUND HERE, AFTER ALL.
I'M NOT SURE WHAT WILL BE WAITING FOR US OVER THERE.

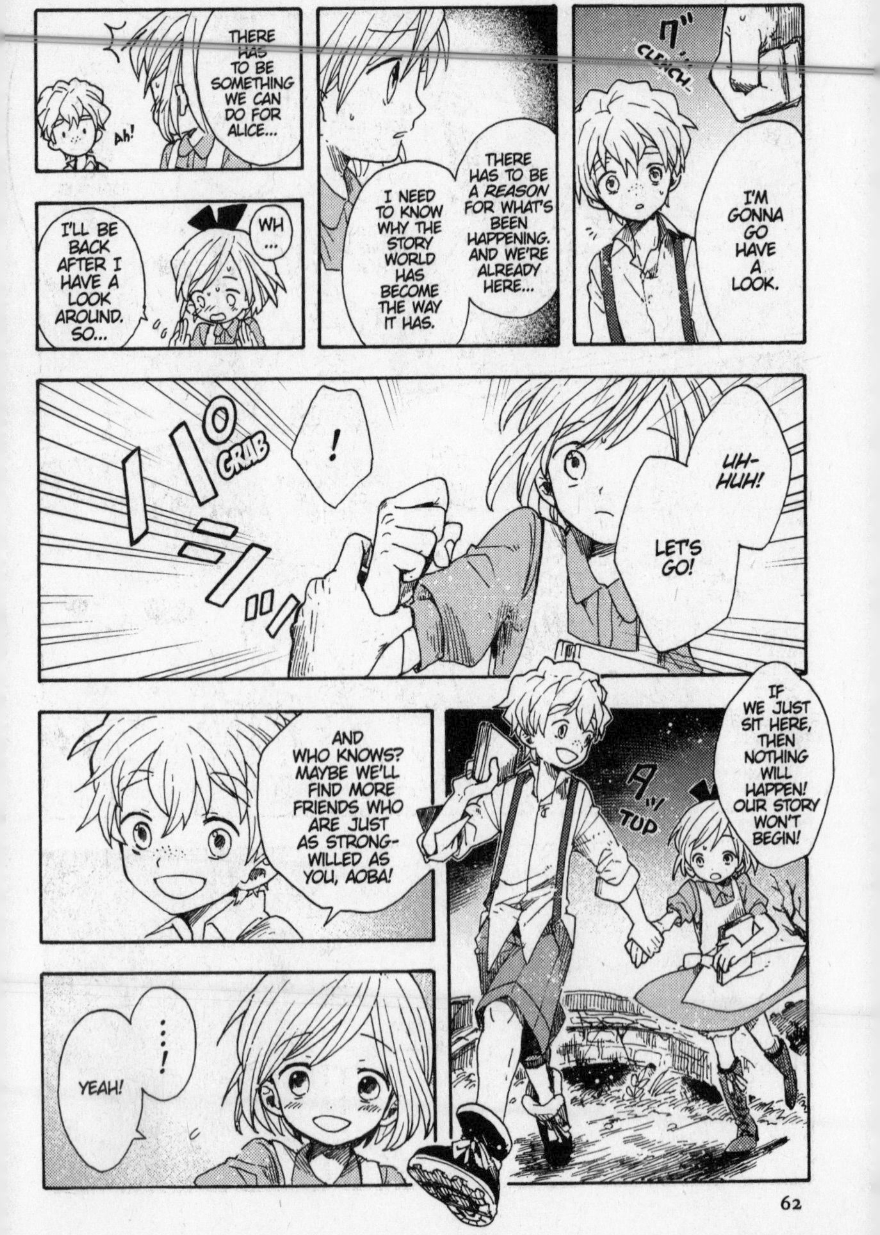
CLENCH
I'M GONNA GO HAVE A LOOK.
THERE HAS TO BE A *REASON* FOR WHAT'S BEEN HAPPENING. AND WE'RE ALREADY HERE...
I NEED TO KNOW WHY THE STORY WORLD HAS BECOME THE WAY IT HAS.
THERE HAS TO BE SOMETHING WE CAN DO FOR ALICE...
Ah!
WH...
I'LL BE BACK AFTER I HAVE A LOOK AROUND. SO...
UH-HUH!
LET'S GO!
!
GRAB
IF WE JUST SIT HERE, THEN NOTHING WILL HAPPEN! OUR STORY WON'T BEGIN!
TUP
AND WHO KNOWS? MAYBE WE'LL FIND MORE FRIENDS WHO ARE JUST AS STRONG-WILLED AS YOU, AOBA!
...!
YEAH!

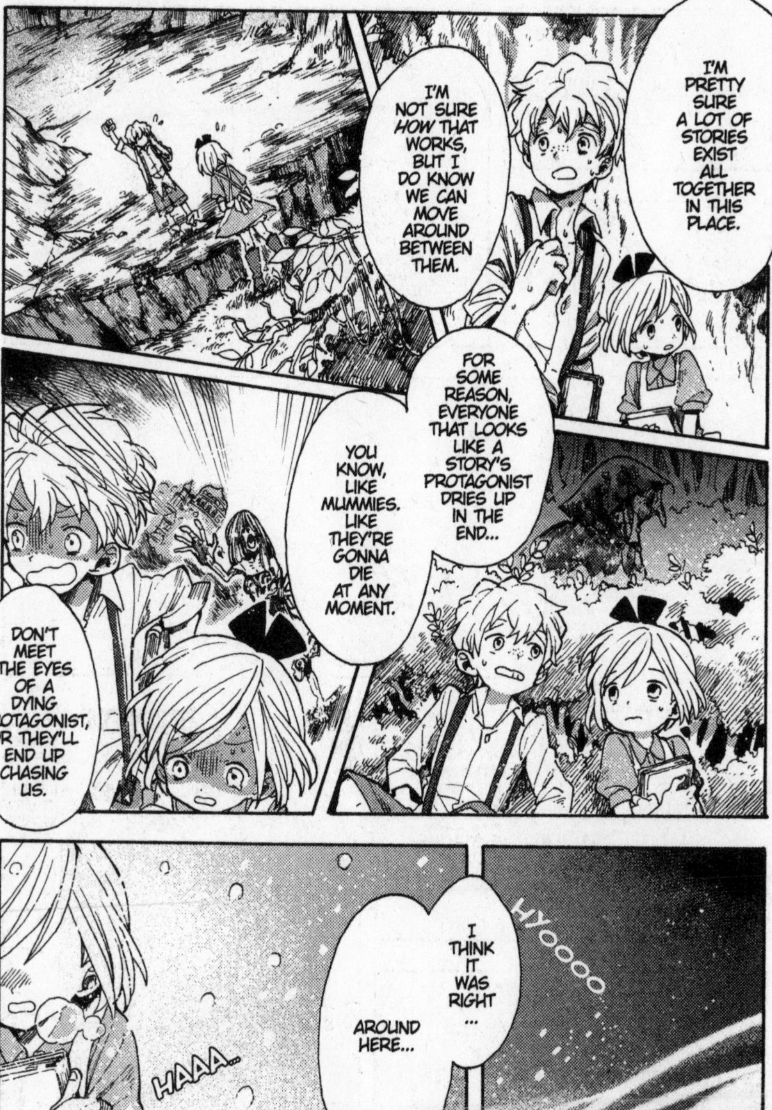
I'M PRETTY SURE A LOT OF STORIES EXIST ALL TOGETHER IN THIS PLACE.
I'M NOT SURE *HOW* THAT WORKS, BUT I DO KNOW WE CAN MOVE AROUND BETWEEN THEM.
FOR SOME REASON, EVERYONE THAT LOOKS LIKE A STORY'S PROTAGONIST DRIES UP IN THE END...
YOU KNOW, LIKE MUMMIES. LIKE THEY'RE GONNA DIE AT ANY MOMENT.
DON'T MEET THE EYES OF A DYING PROTAGONIST, OR THEY'LL END UP CHASING US.
HYOOOO...
I THINK IT WAS RIGHT ...
AROUND HERE...
HAAA...

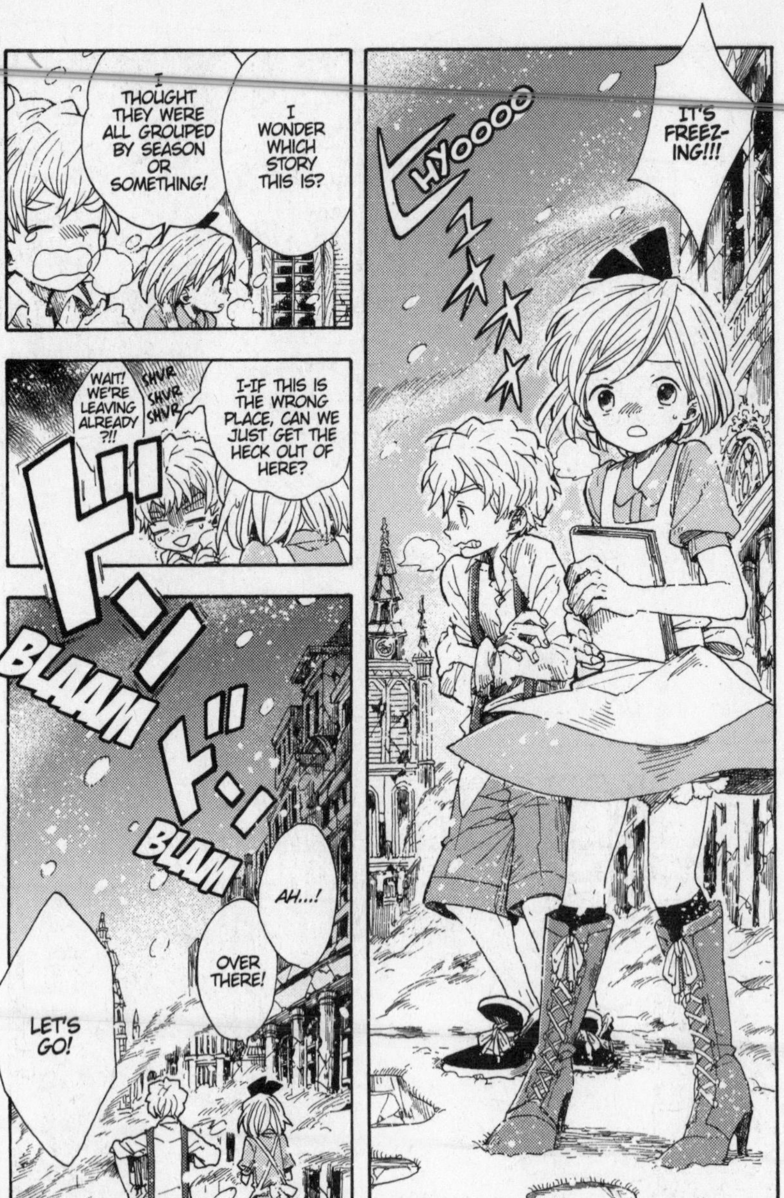
IT'S FREEZING!!!
HYOOOOO
I WONDER WHICH STORY THIS IS?
I THOUGHT THEY WERE ALL GROUPED BY SEASON OR SOMETHING!
I-IF THIS IS THE WRONG PLACE, CAN WE JUST GET THE HECK OUT OF HERE?
SHVR SHVR SHVR
WAIT! WE'RE LEAVING ALREADY ?!!
BLAAAM
BLAM
AH...!
OVER THERE!
LET'S GO!

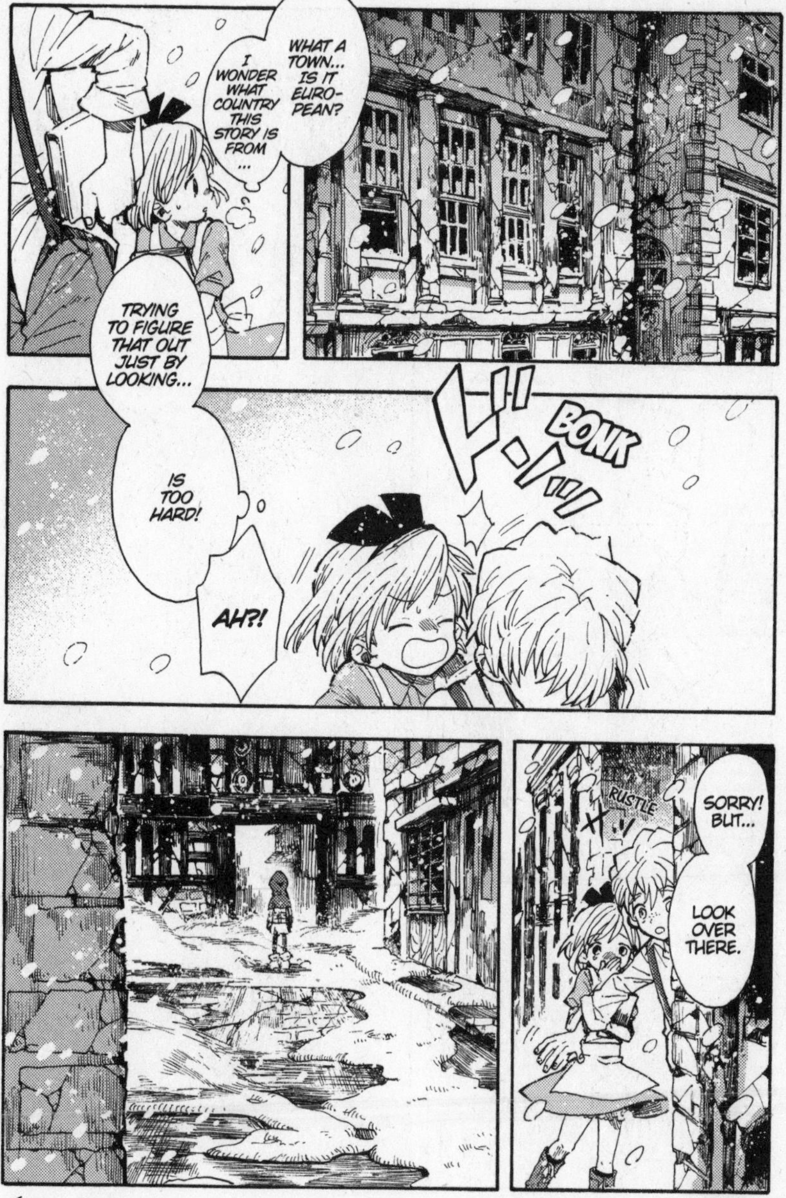
WHAT A TOWN... IS IT EURO-PEAN?
I WONDER WHAT COUNTRY THIS STORY IS FROM ...
TRYING TO FIGURE THAT OUT JUST BY LOOKING...
IS TOO HARD!
BONK
AH?!
SORRY! BUT...
LOOK OVER THERE.
RUSTLE

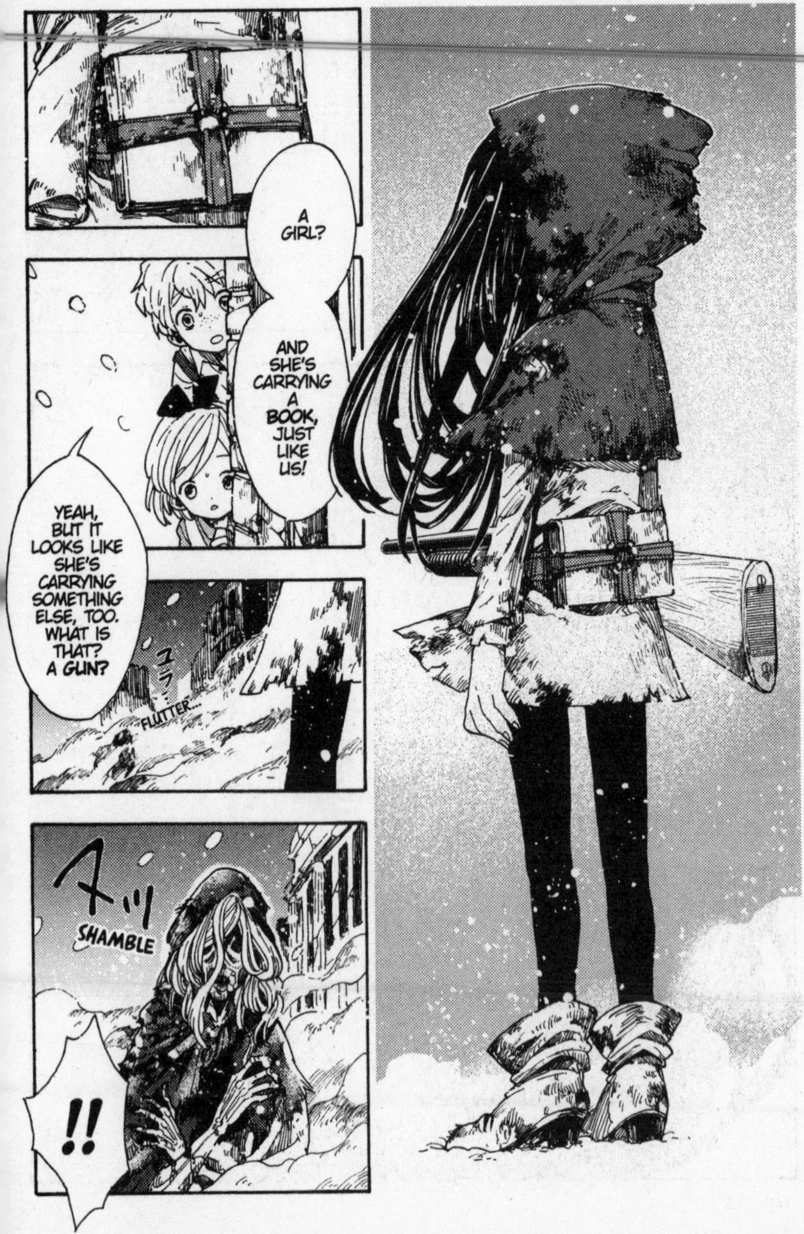
A GIRL?
AND SHE'S CARRYING A BOOK, JUST LIKE US!
YEAH, BUT IT LOOKS LIKE SHE'S CARRYING SOMETHING ELSE, TOO. WHAT IS THAT? A GUN?
ユラ
FLUTTER...
フッ
SHAMBLE
!!

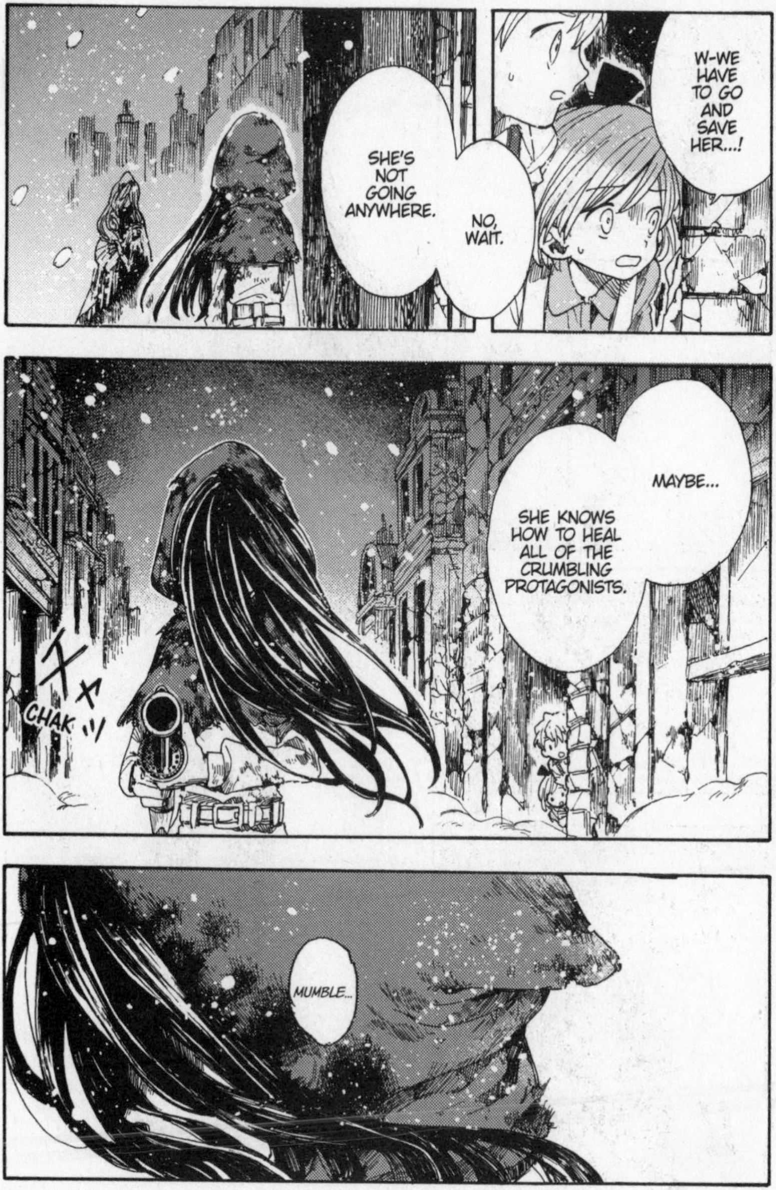
W-WE HAVE TO GO AND SAVE HER...!
NO, WAIT.
SHE'S NOT GOING ANYWHERE.
MAYBE...
SHE KNOWS HOW TO HEAL ALL OF THE CRUMBLING PROTAGONISTS.
CHAK
MUMBLE...

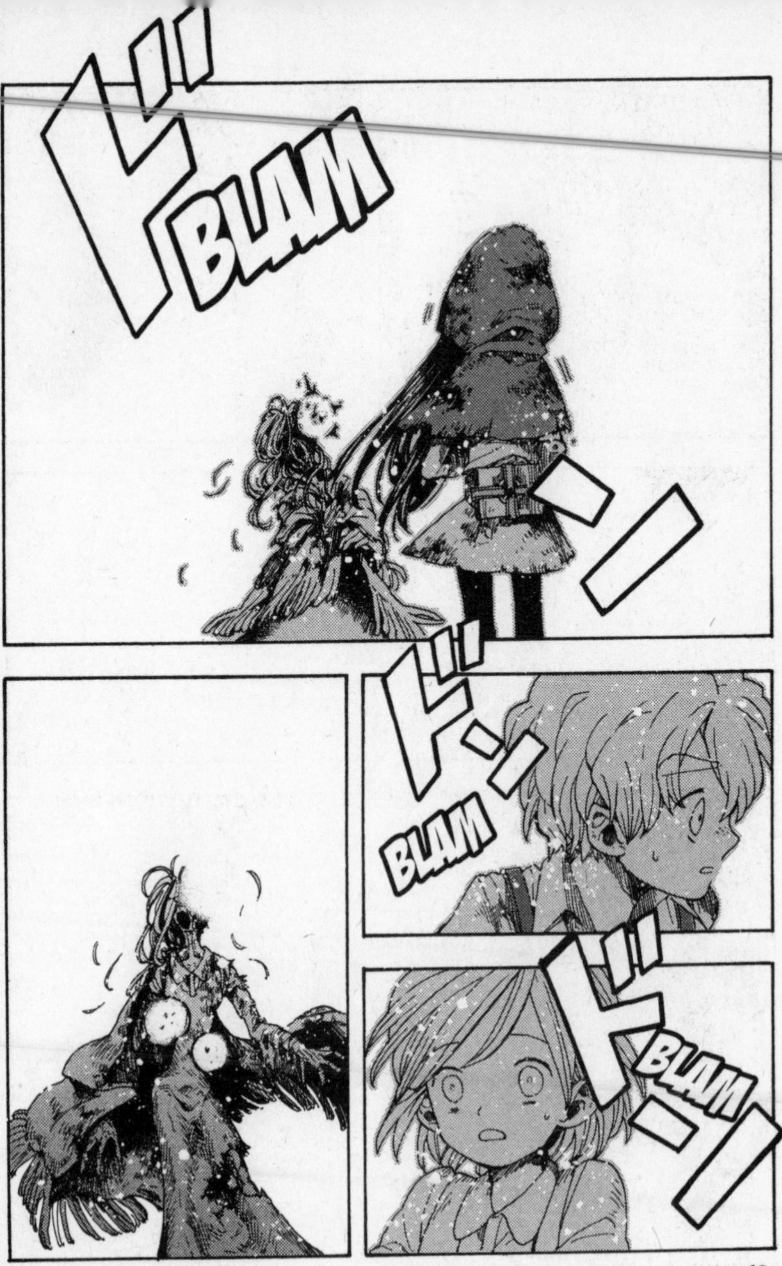
BLAM
BLAM
BLAM

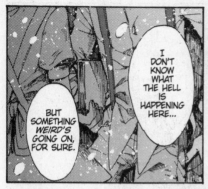

FWUD
I DON'T KNOW WHAT THE HELL IS HAPPENING HERE...
BUT SOMETHING WEIRD'S GOING ON, FOR SURE.
ANYWAY, LET'S GET OUT OF HERE...
WE DON'T HAVE ANY WEAPONS, AND I THINK IT MIGHT BE A BIT EARLY TO START TALKING TO THAT PARTICULAR PROTAGONIST.
THE AREA WE WERE JUST IN HAD A BETTER CLIMATE, SO MAYBE WE SHOULD ...
BLANCH
N...
HAH!
Tremble...
NOAH-SAN...

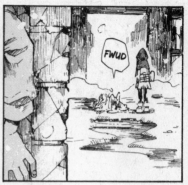

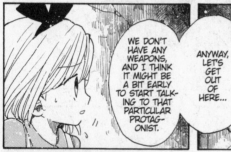

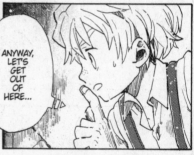

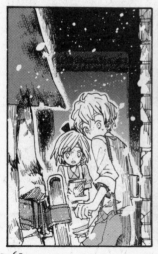

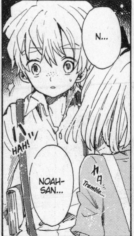

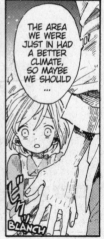

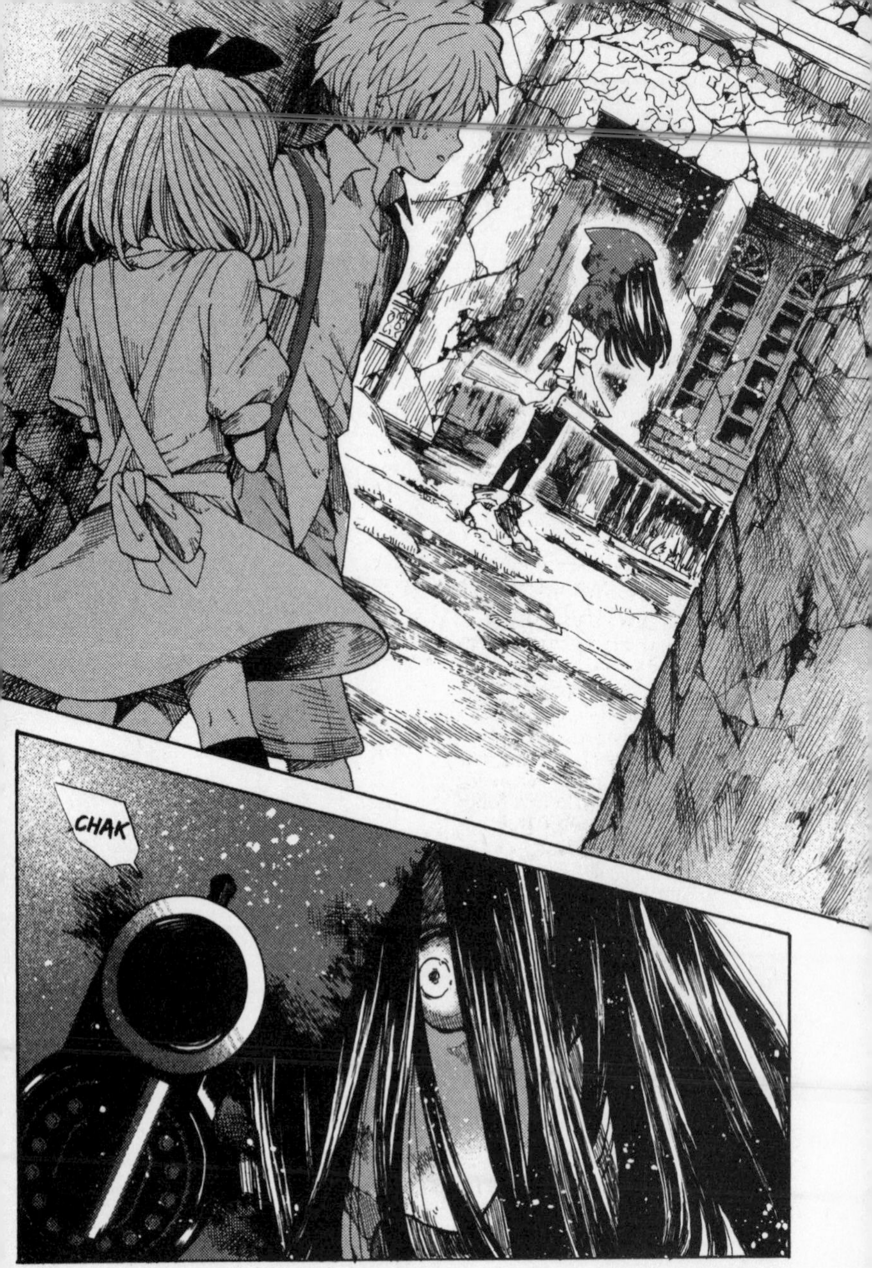
CHAK

"The Man, the Boy, and the Donkey"

First Published:
Unknown. Appears
in *Aesop's Fables*.
It is thought that the
Grecian author Aesop
first wrote this fable
around 6 BCE.

FAIRY TALE BATTLE ROYALE

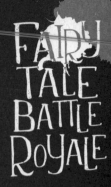

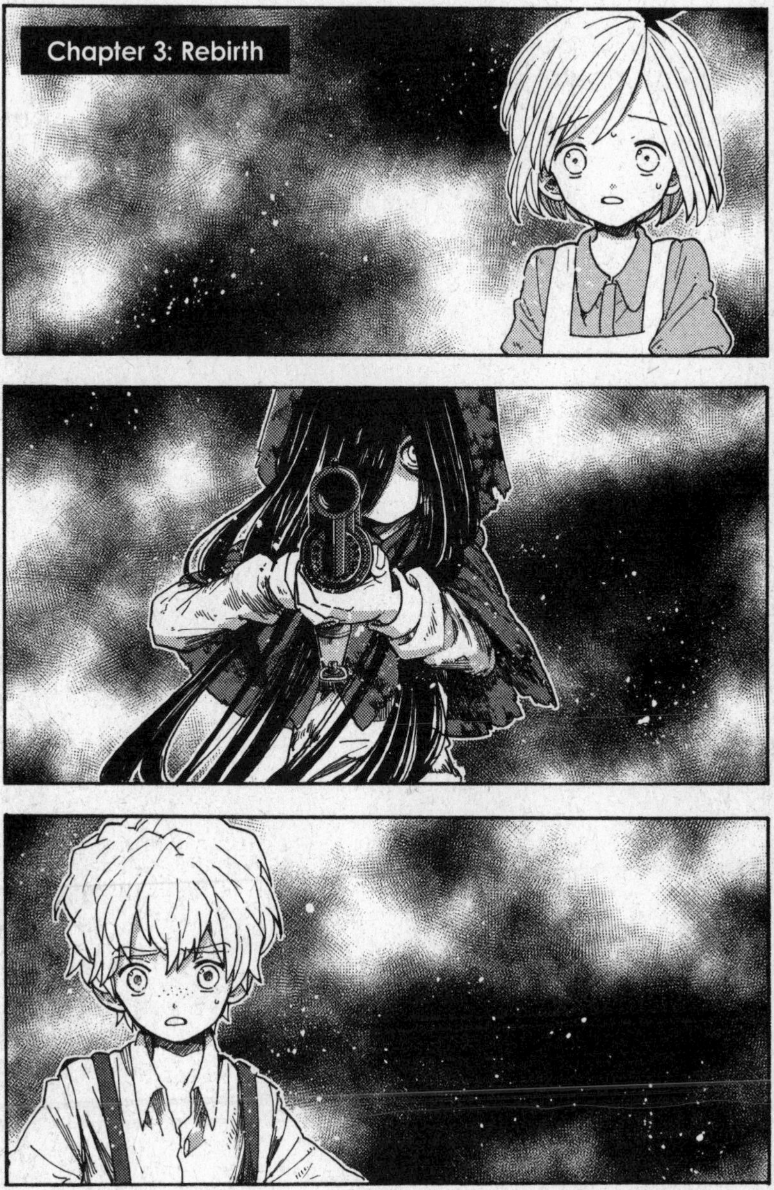
Chapter 3: Rebirth

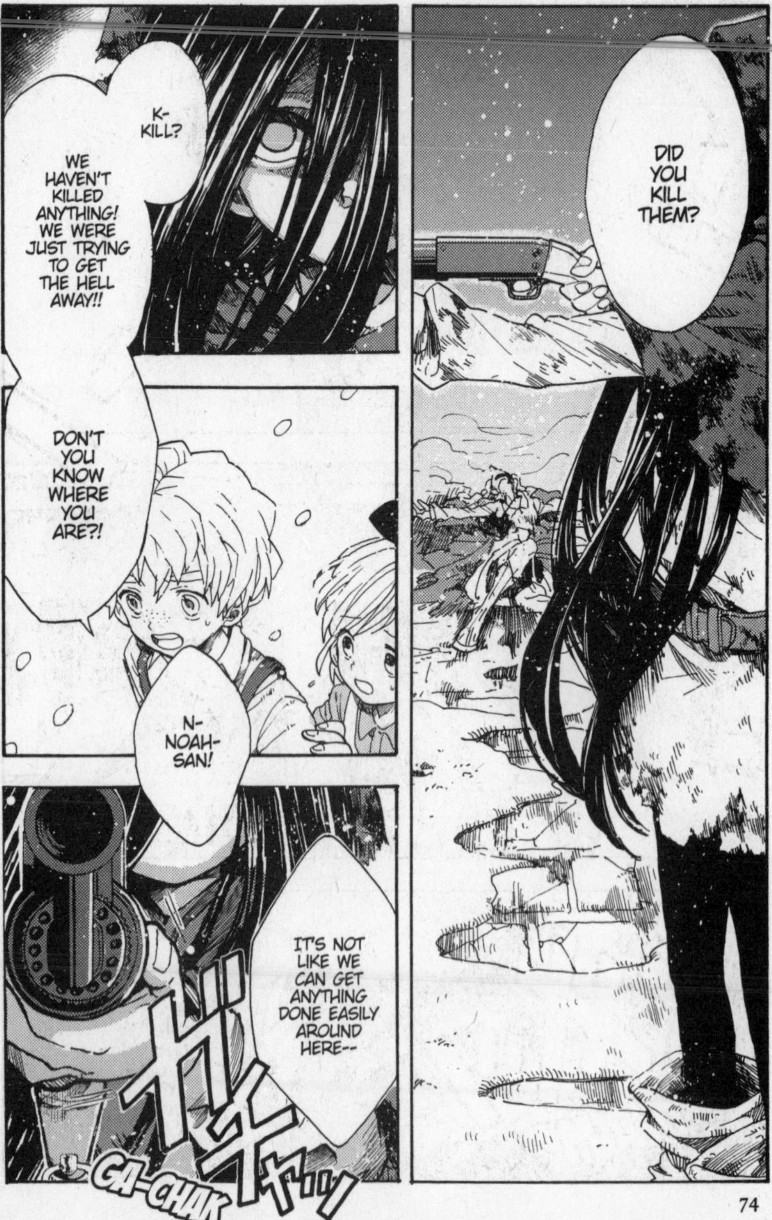
DID YOU KILL THEM?
K-KILL?
WE HAVEN'T KILLED ANYTHING! WE WERE JUST TRYING TO GET THE HELL AWAY!!
DON'T YOU KNOW WHERE YOU ARE?!
N-NOAH-SAN!
IT'S NOT LIKE WE CAN GET ANYTHING DONE EASILY AROUND HERE--
GA-CHAK

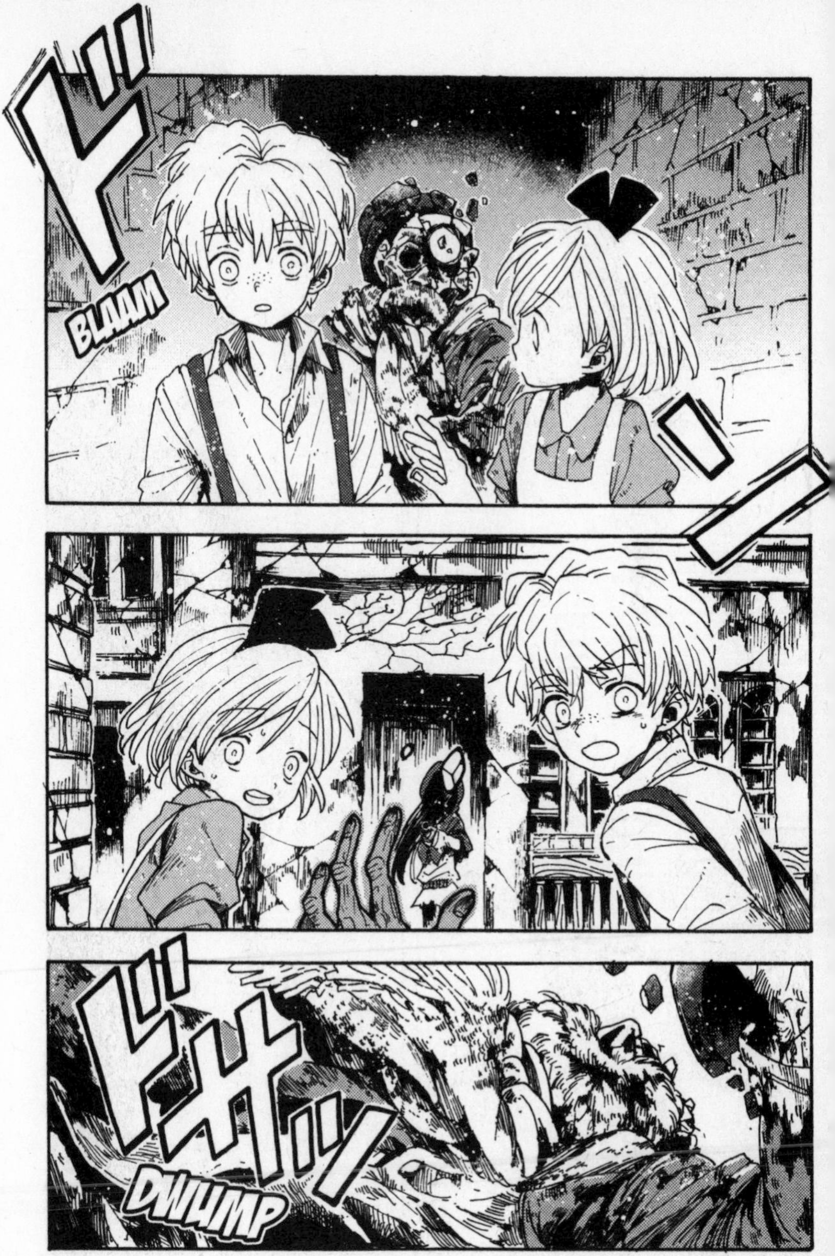
BLAAM
DWUMP

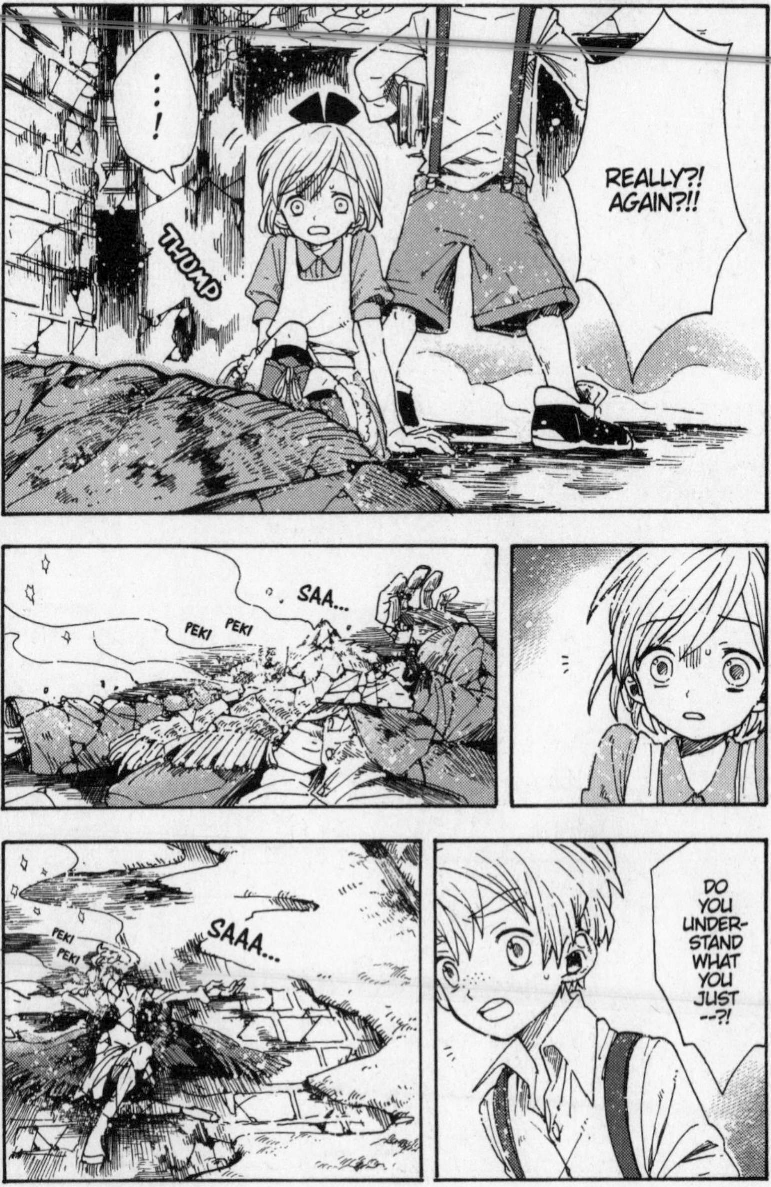
REALLY?! AGAIN?!!
...!
THUMP
SAA...
PEKI
PEKI
DO YOU UNDER-STAND WHAT YOU JUST --?!
SAAA...
PEKI
PEKI

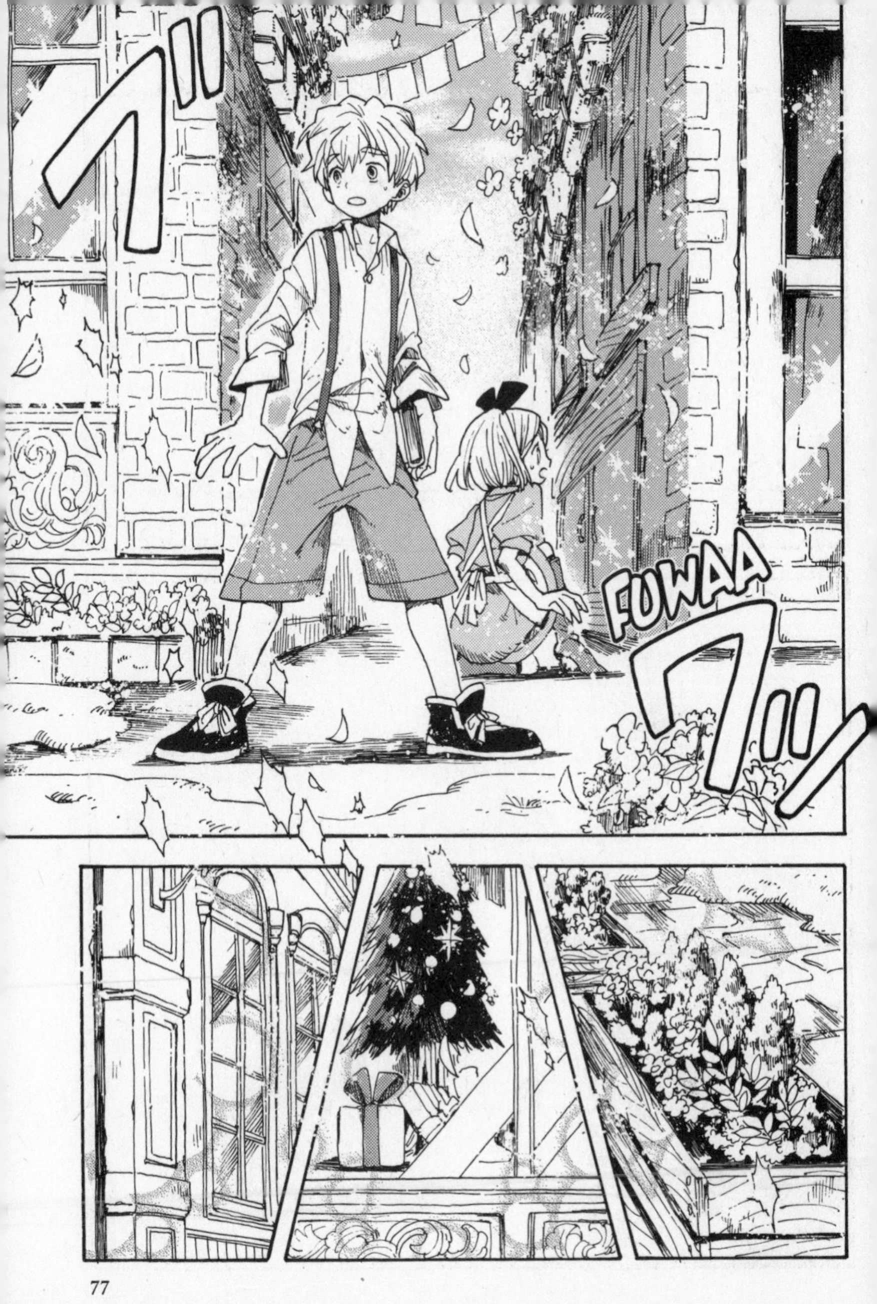
FUWAA

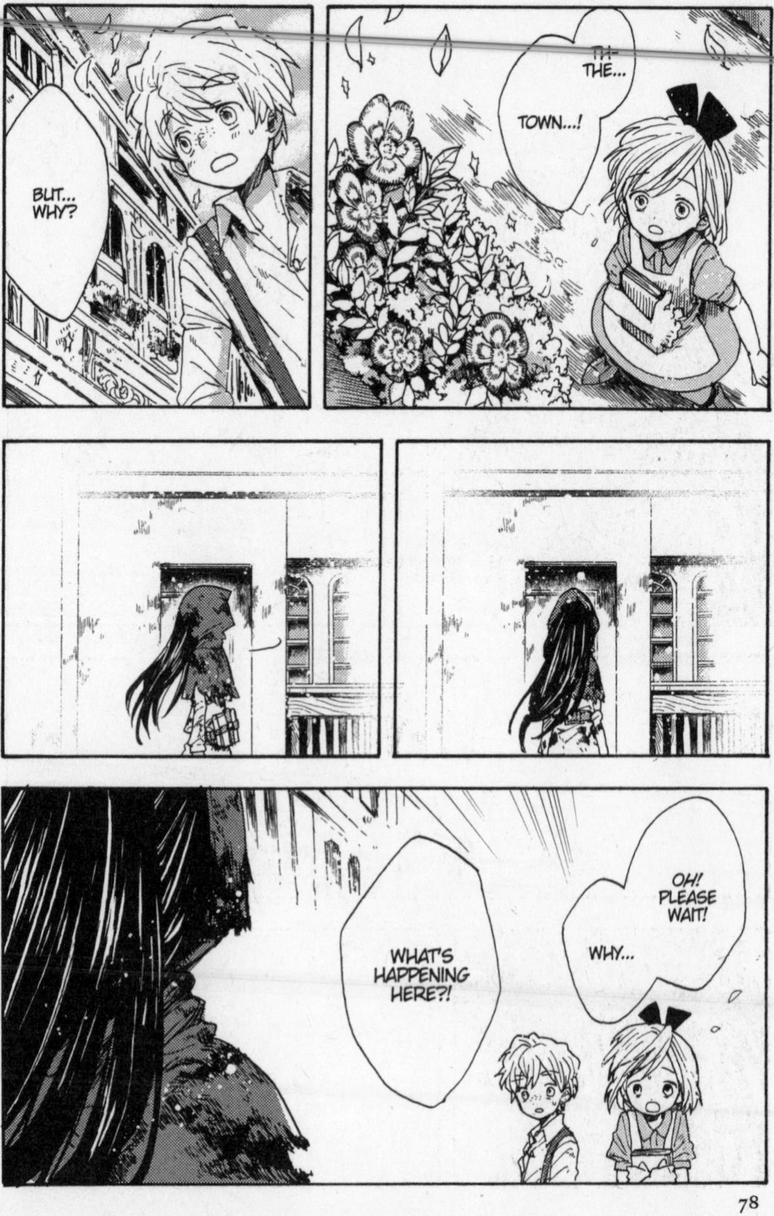
TH-THE...
TOWN...!
BUT... WHY?
OH! PLEASE WAIT!
WHY...
WHAT'S HAPPENING HERE?!

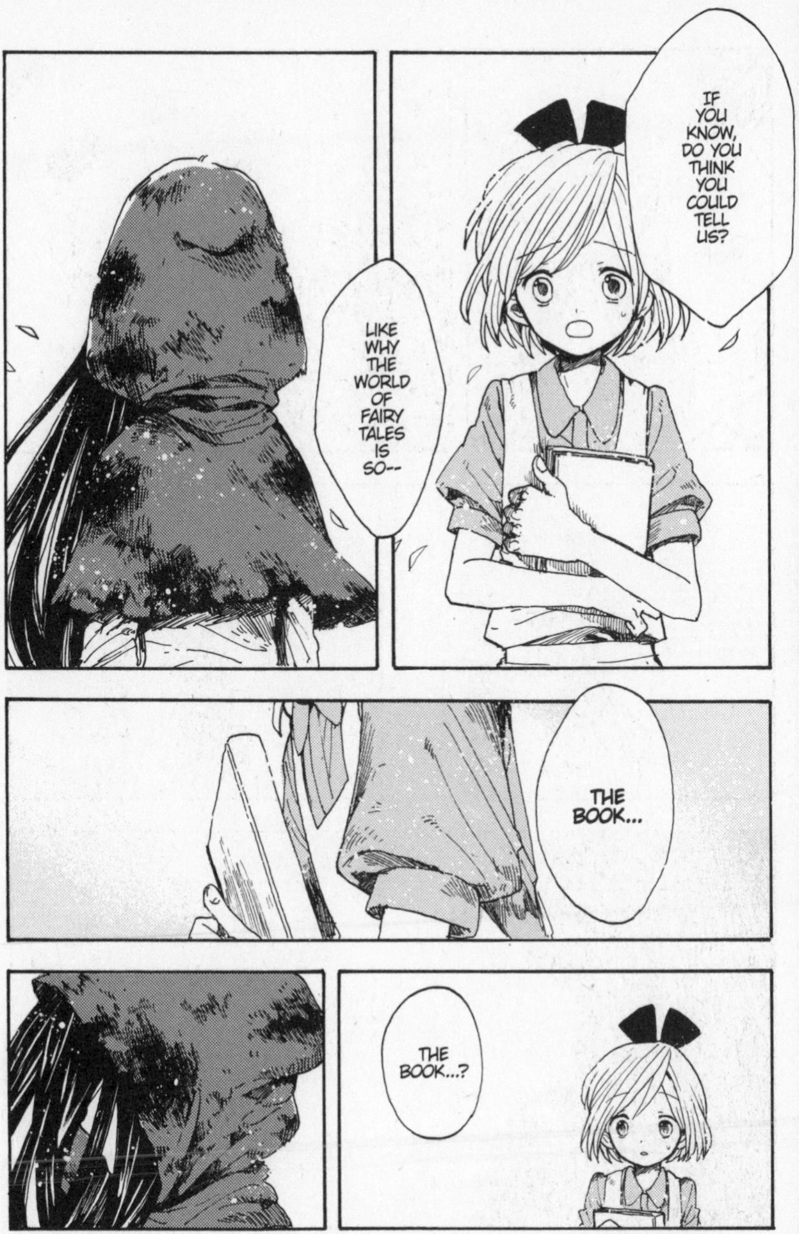
IF YOU KNOW, DO YOU THINK YOU COULD TELL US?
LIKE WHY THE WORLD OF FAIRY TALES IS SO--
THE BOOK...
THE BOOK...?

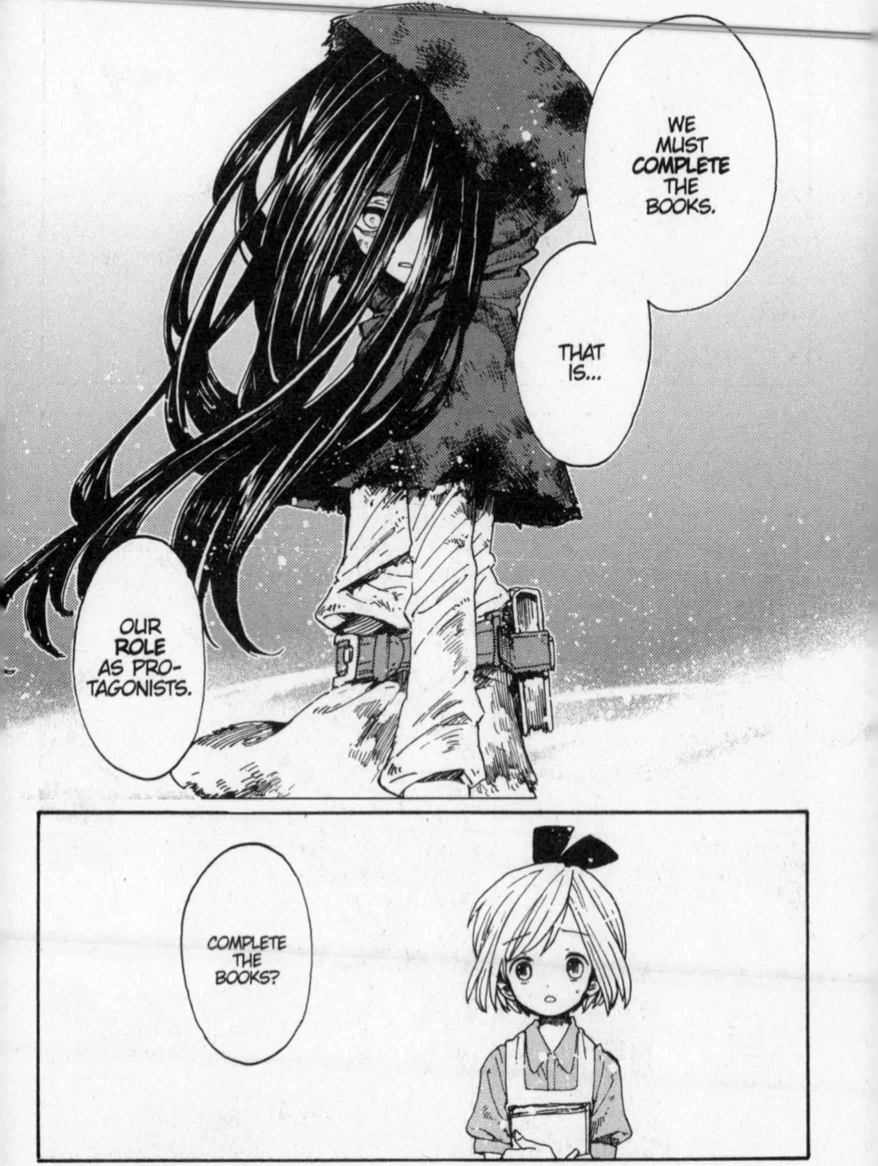
WE MUST COMPLETE THE BOOKS.
THAT IS...
OUR ROLE AS PRO-TAGONISTS.
COMPLETE THE BOOKS?

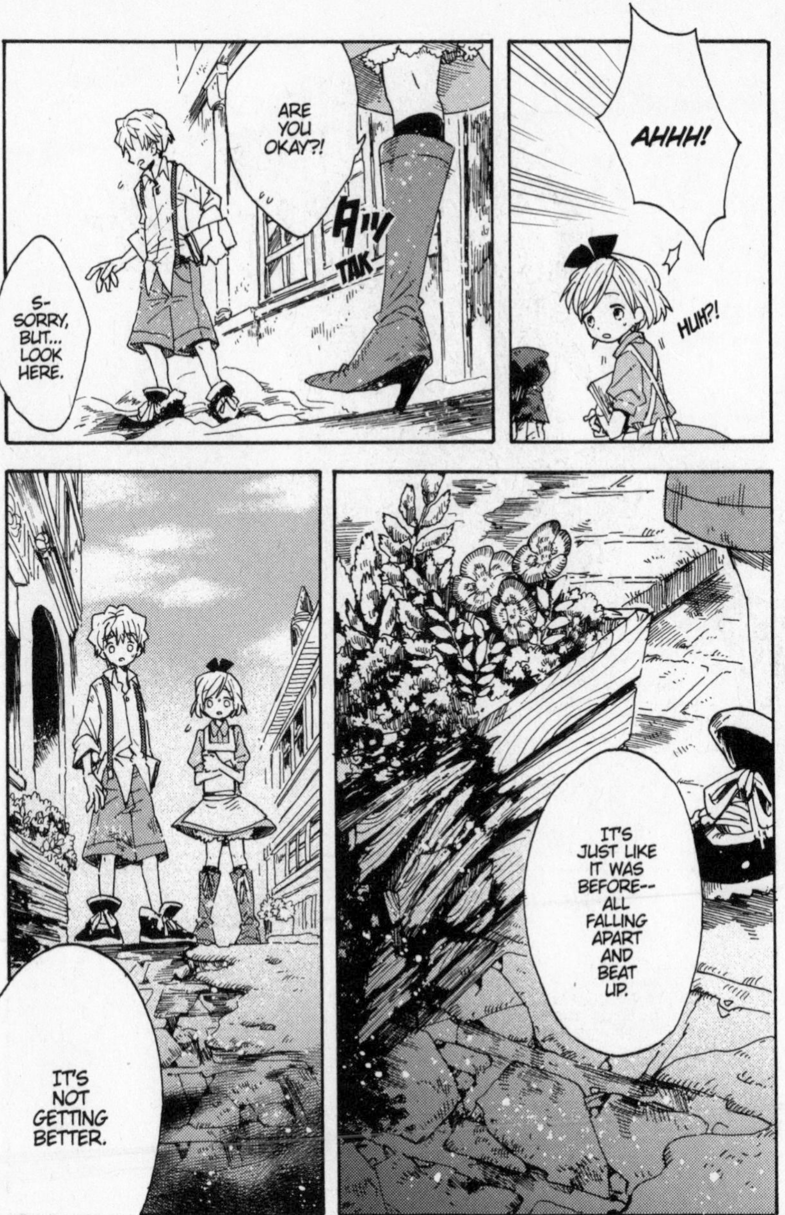
AHHH!
HUH?!
ARE YOU OKAY?!
タッ
TAK
S-SORRY, BUT... LOOK HERE.
IT'S JUST LIKE IT WAS BEFORE--ALL FALLING APART AND BEAT UP.
IT'S NOT GETTING BETTER.

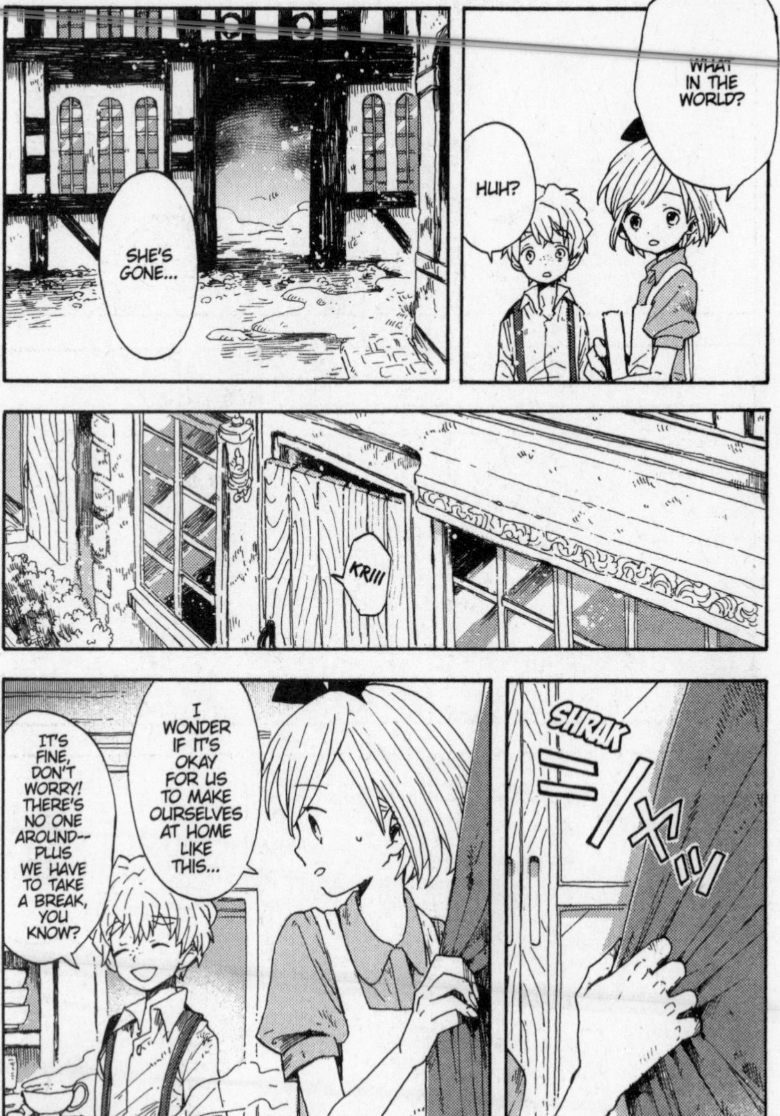
WHAT IN THE WORLD?
HUH?
SHE'S GONE...
KRIII
SHRAK
I WONDER IF IT'S OKAY FOR US TO MAKE OURSELVES AT HOME LIKE THIS...
IT'S FINE, DON'T WORRY! THERE'S NO ONE AROUND-- PLUS WE HAVE TO TAKE A BREAK, YOU KNOW?

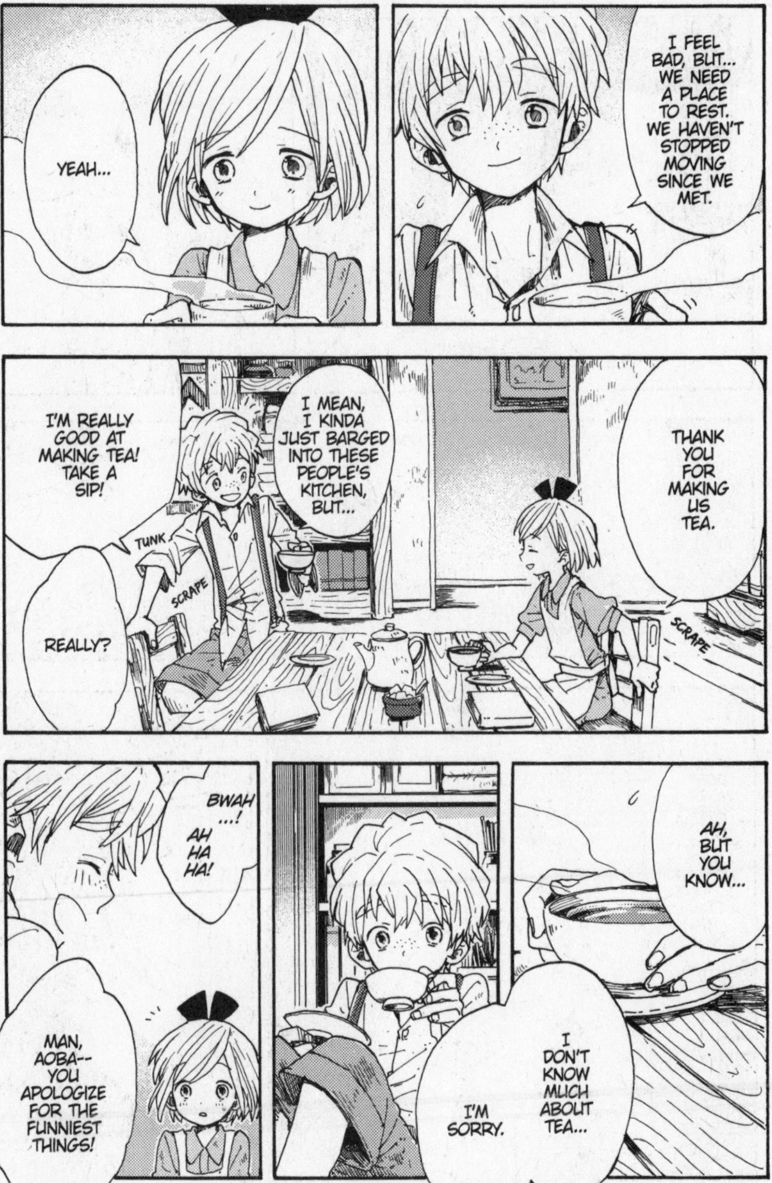
I FEEL BAD, BUT... WE NEED A PLACE TO REST. WE HAVEN'T STOPPED MOVING SINCE WE MET.
YEAH...
THANK YOU FOR MAKING US TEA.
SCRAPE
I MEAN, I KINDA JUST BARGED INTO THESE PEOPLE'S KITCHEN, BUT...
I'M REALLY GOOD AT MAKING TEA! TAKE A SIP!
TUNK
SCRAPE
REALLY?
AH, BUT YOU KNOW...
I DON'T KNOW MUCH ABOUT TEA...
I'M SORRY.
BWAH ...!
AH HA HA!
MAN, AOBA-- YOU APOLOGIZE FOR THE FUNNIEST THINGS!

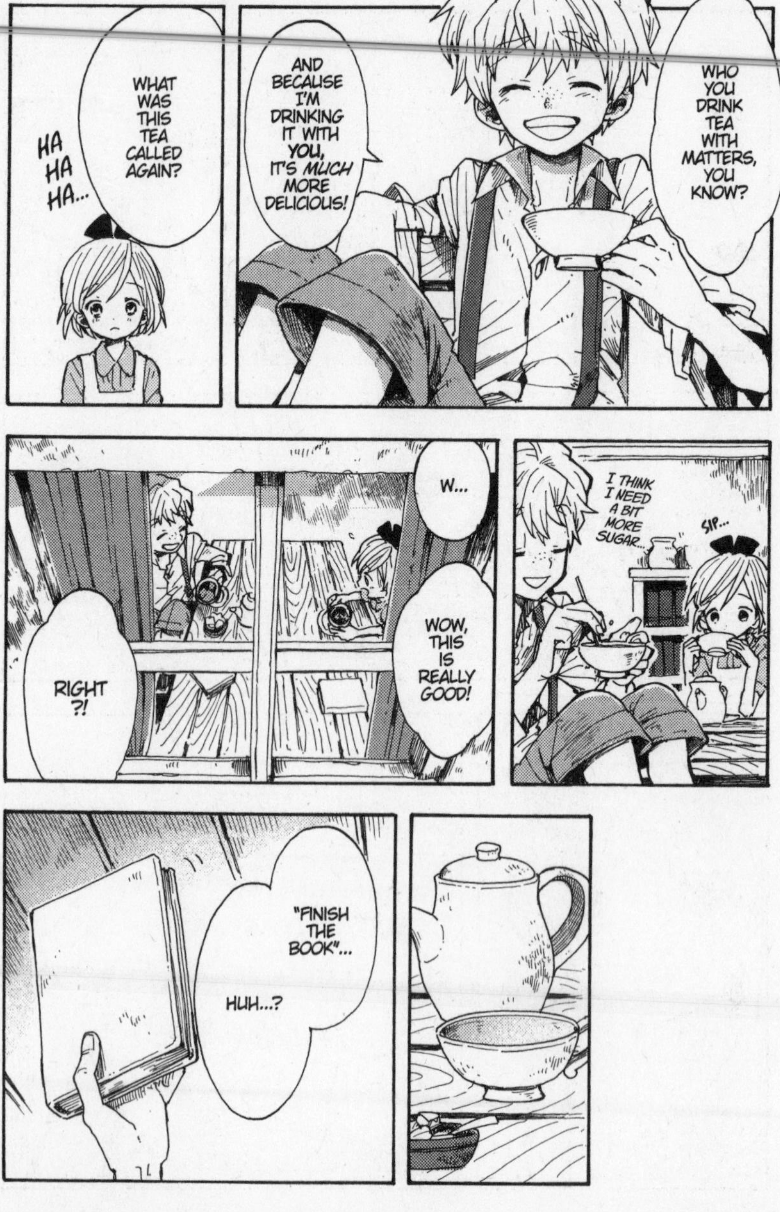
WHO YOU DRINK TEA WITH MATTERS, YOU KNOW?
AND BECAUSE I'M DRINKING IT WITH YOU, IT'S *MUCH* MORE DELICIOUS!
WHAT WAS THIS TEA CALLED AGAIN?
HA HA HA...
I THINK I NEED A BIT MORE SUGAR...
SIP...
W...
WOW, THIS IS REALLY GOOD!
RIGHT?!
"FINISH THE BOOK"...
HUH...?

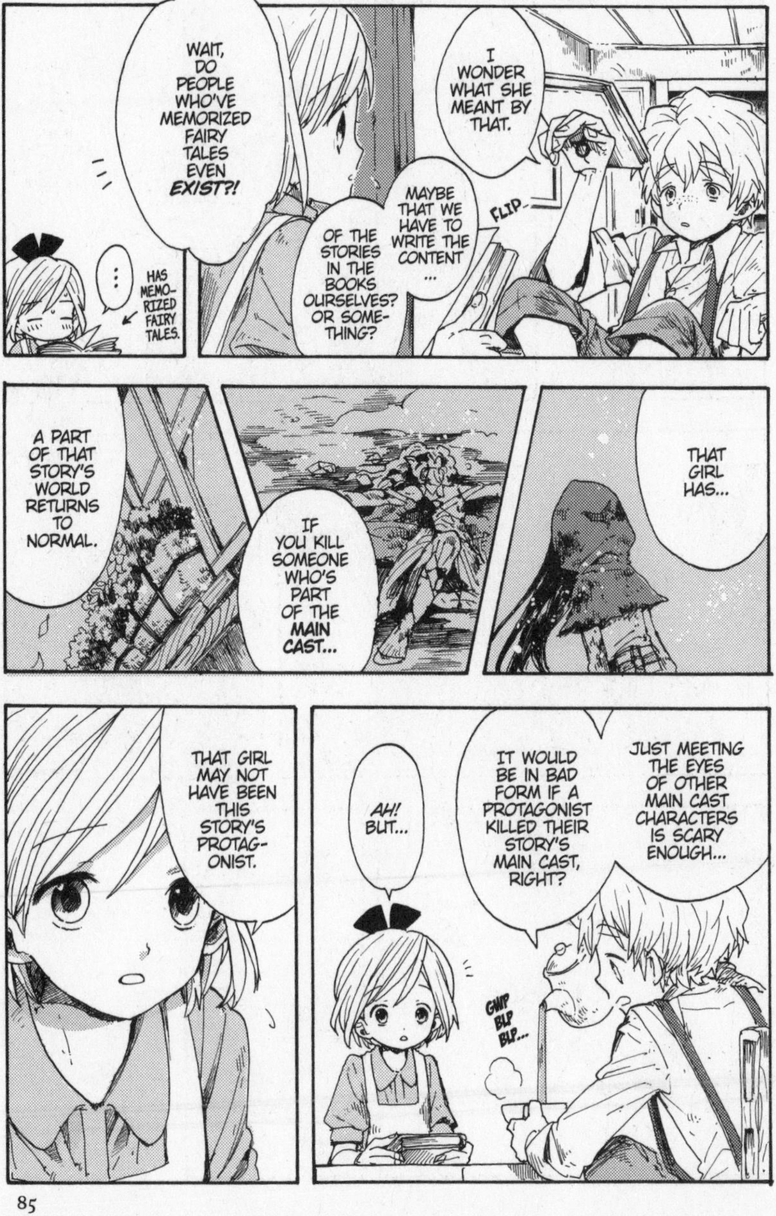
I WONDER WHAT SHE MEANT BY THAT.
FLIP
MAYBE THAT WE HAVE TO WRITE THE CONTENT ...
OF THE STORIES IN THE BOOKS OURSELVES? OR SOMETHING?
WAIT, DO PEOPLE WHO'VE MEMORIZED FAIRY TALES EVEN *EXIST?!*
...
HAS MEMORIZED FAIRY TALES.
THAT GIRL HAS...
IF YOU KILL SOMEONE WHO'S PART OF THE MAIN CAST...
A PART OF THAT STORY'S WORLD RETURNS TO NORMAL.
JUST MEETING THE EYES OF OTHER MAIN CAST CHARACTERS IS SCARY ENOUGH...
IT WOULD BE IN BAD FORM IF A PROTAGONIST KILLED THEIR STORY'S MAIN CAST, RIGHT?
GWIP BLP BLP...
AH! BUT...
THAT GIRL MAY NOT HAVE BEEN THIS STORY'S PROTAGONIST.

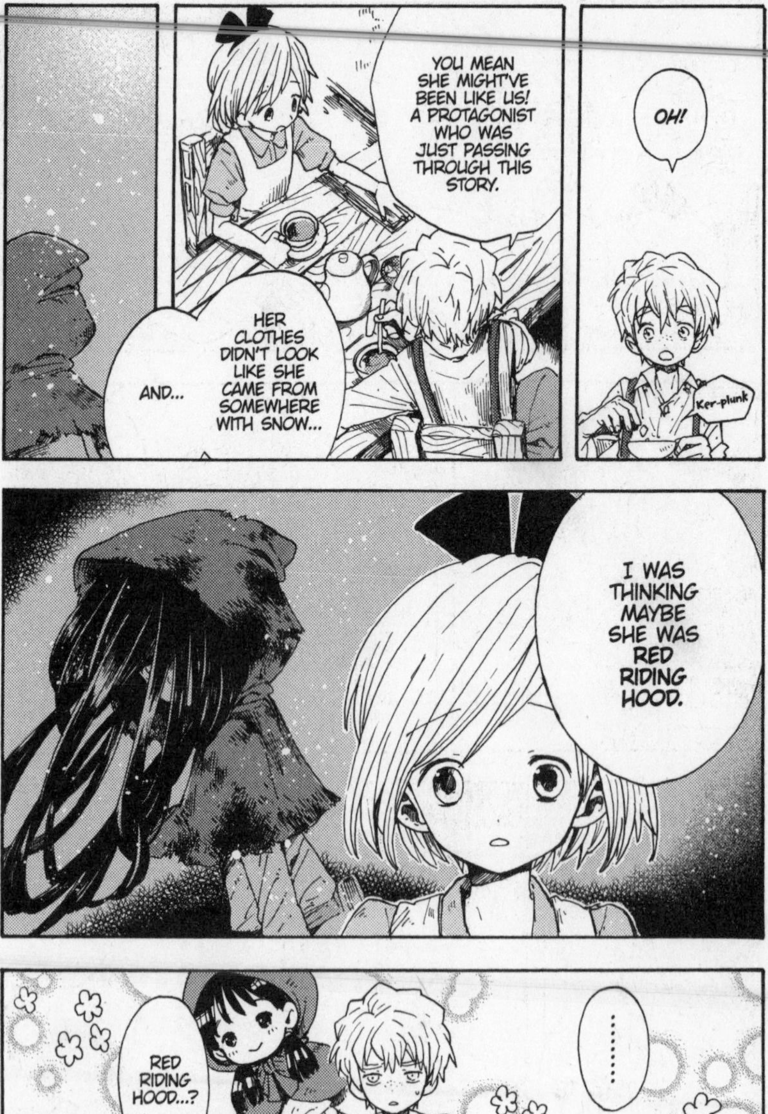
OH!
YOU MEAN SHE MIGHT'VE BEEN LIKE US! A PROTAGONIST WHO WAS JUST PASSING THROUGH THIS STORY.
Ker-plunk
HER CLOTHES DIDN'T LOOK LIKE SHE CAME FROM SOMEWHERE WITH SNOW...
AND...
I WAS THINKING MAYBE SHE WAS RED RIDING HOOD.
....
RED RIDING HOOD...?

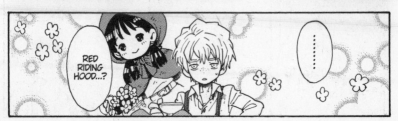

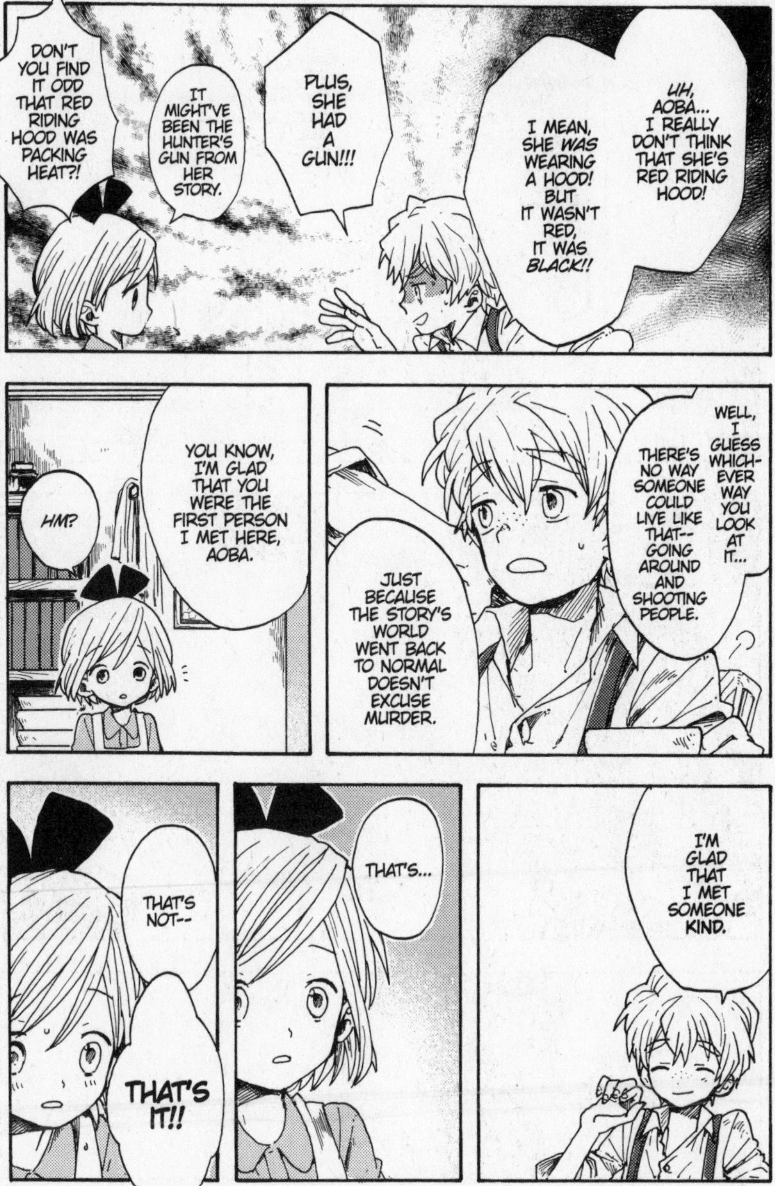
UH, AOBA... I REALLY DON'T THINK THAT SHE'S RED RIDING HOOD!
I MEAN, SHE *WAS* WEARING A HOOD! BUT IT WASN'T RED, IT WAS *BLACK!!*
PLUS, SHE HAD A GUN!!!
IT MIGHT'VE BEEN THE HUNTER'S GUN FROM HER STORY.
DON'T YOU FIND IT ODD THAT RED RIDING HOOD WAS PACKING HEAT?!
WELL, I GUESS WHICH-EVER WAY YOU LOOK AT IT...
THERE'S NO WAY SOMEONE COULD LIVE LIKE THAT-- GOING AROUND AND SHOOTING PEOPLE.
JUST BECAUSE THE STORY'S WORLD WENT BACK TO NORMAL DOESN'T EXCUSE MURDER.
YOU KNOW, I'M GLAD THAT YOU WERE THE FIRST PERSON I MET HERE, AOBA.
HM?
I'M GLAD THAT I MET SOMEONE KIND.
THAT'S...
THAT'S NOT--
THAT'S IT!!

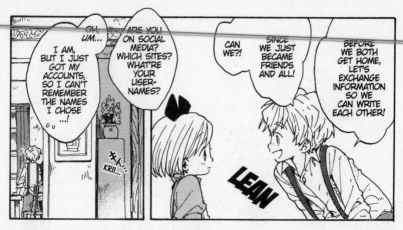

BEFORE WE BOTH GET HOME, LET'S EXCHANGE INFORMATION SO WE CAN WRITE EACH OTHER!
SINCE WE JUST BECAME FRIENDS AND ALL!
CAN WE?!
LEAN
ARE YOU ON SOCIAL MEDIA? WHICH SITES? WHAT'RE YOUR USER-NAMES?
OH, UM...
I AM, BUT I JUST GOT MY ACCOUNTS, SO I CAN'T REMEMBER THE NAMES I CHOSE ...!
KRII...
DON'T WORRY! I CAN HELP YOU LEARN THE ROPES! JUST PING ME!
I DON'T MIND! IT'S TOTALLY FINE!
AFTER ALL, WAITING FOR WOMEN IS WHAT MEN DO BEST, RIGHT?
I'M GONNA BORROW YOUR BOOK A SECOND, OKAY?
SWIPE
OH, OKAY!
SCRIBBLE SCRIBBLE SCRIBBLE~!
JOLT
!!

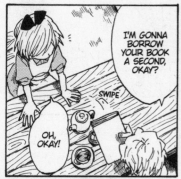

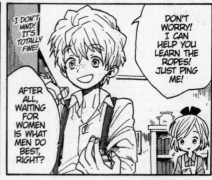

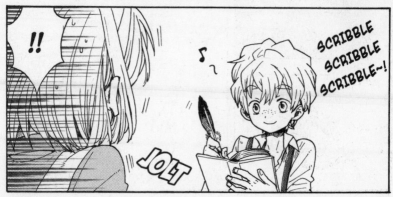

OKAY, HERE YOU GO!
TH-THANKS...
BUT... I WONDER IF IT'S OKAY TO WRITE IN HERE? I'M NOT REALLY SURE...
SHWFF
OH, I ONLY WROTE ON THE INSIDE OF THE COVER, SO IT SHOULD BE OKAY!
BUT MORE IMPORTANTLY...
THIS BOOK COMES WITH ITS OWN BOOKMARK.
Noah!!
YOU'RE RIGHT! I HADN'T EVEN NOTICED.
WHAT A LOVELY BOOKMARK...
WELL, MOST OF THIS BOOK IS TOTALLY BLANK, ANYWAY...
SO, THERE'S NOT MUCH TO MARK...
SHF

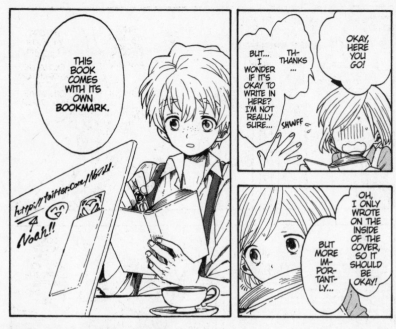

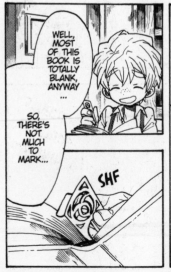

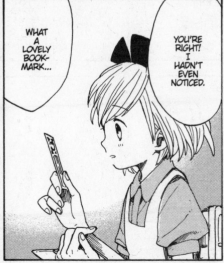

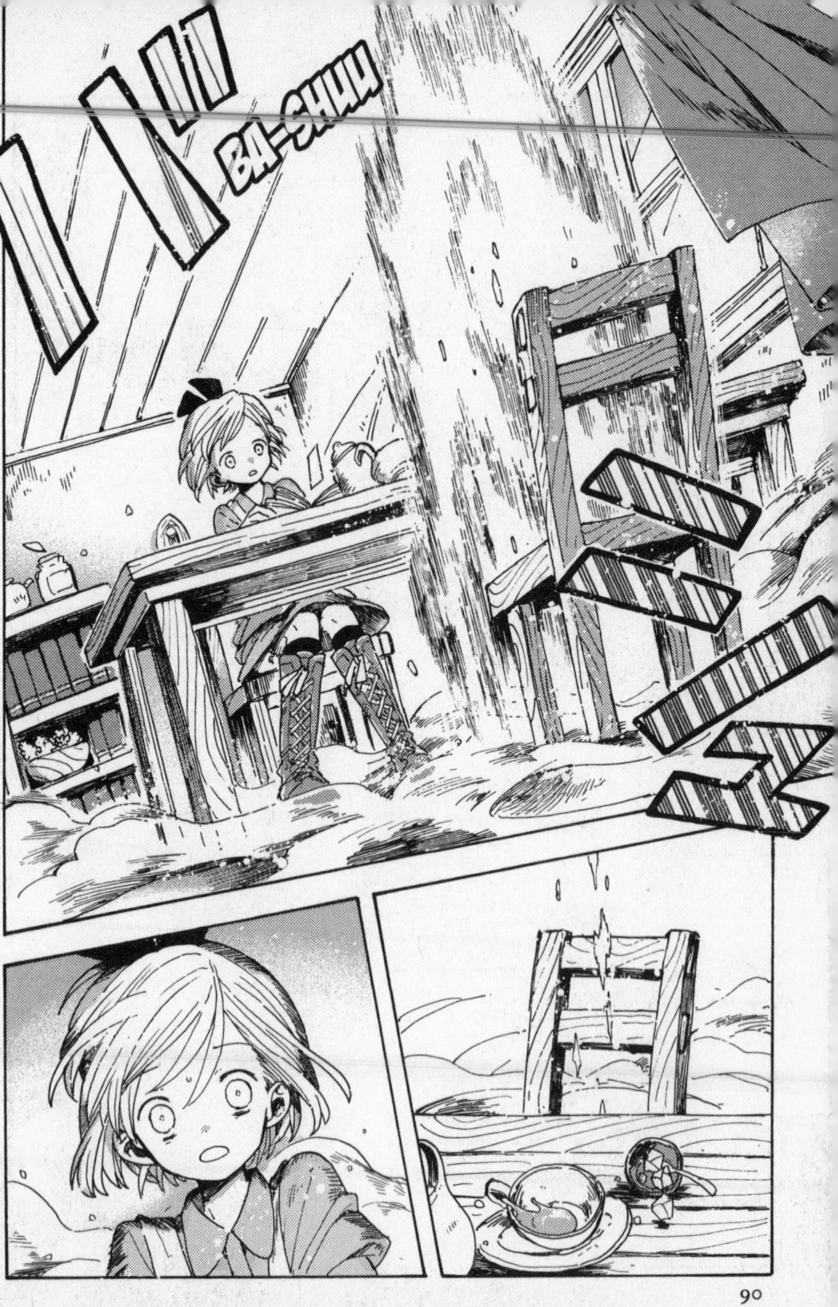
BA-SHUU

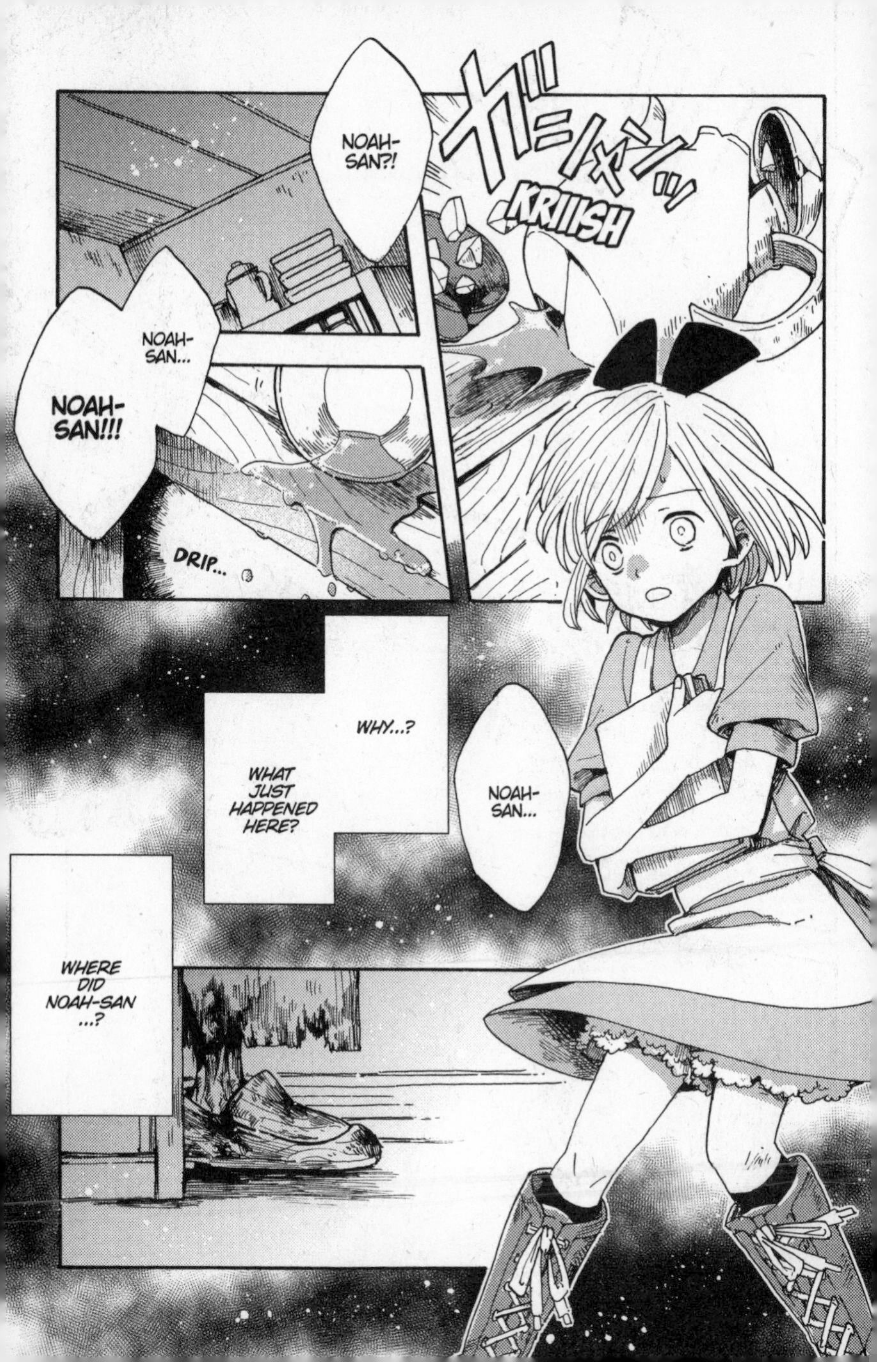

ガシャン
KRIIISH
NOAH-SAN?!
NOAH-SAN...
NOAH-SAN!!!
DRIP...
NOAH-SAN...
WHY...?
WHAT JUST HAPPENED HERE?
WHERE DID NOAH-SAN ...?

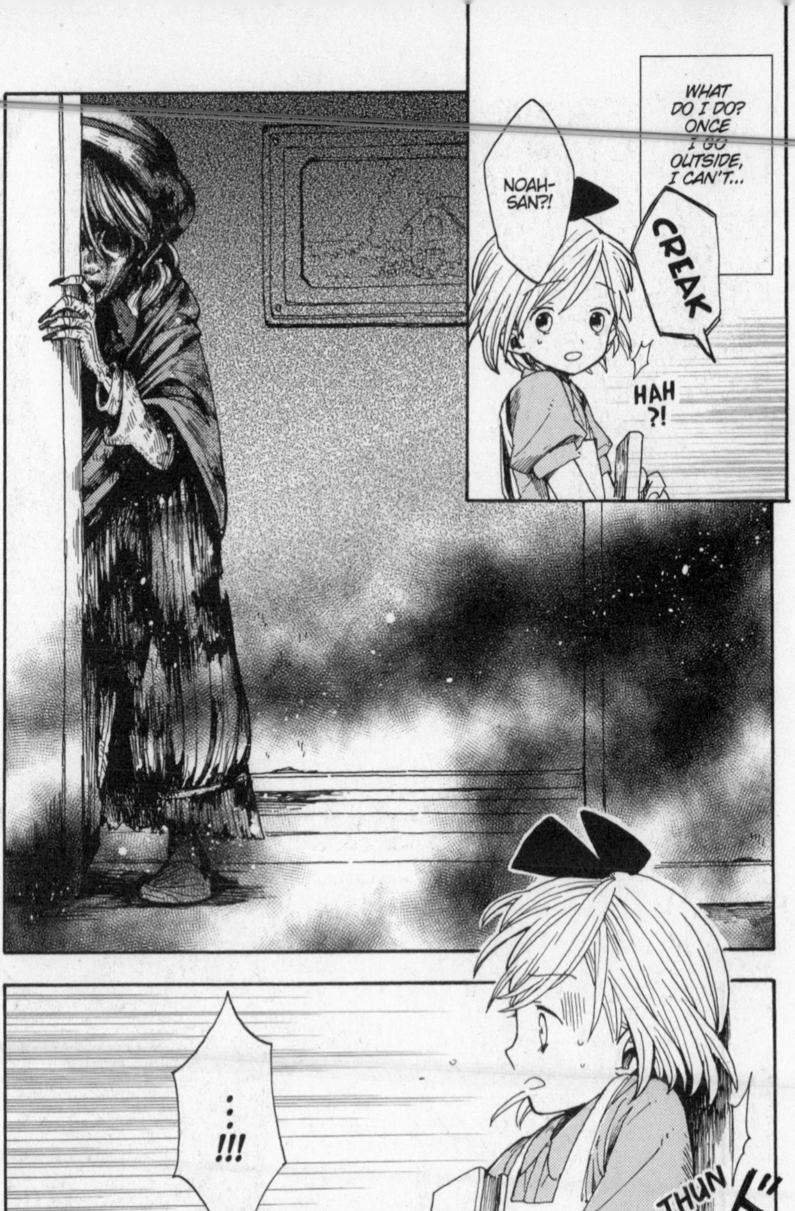
WHAT DO I DO? ONCE I GO OUTSIDE, I CAN'T...
NOAH-SAN?!
CREAK
HAH ?!
...!!!
THUN

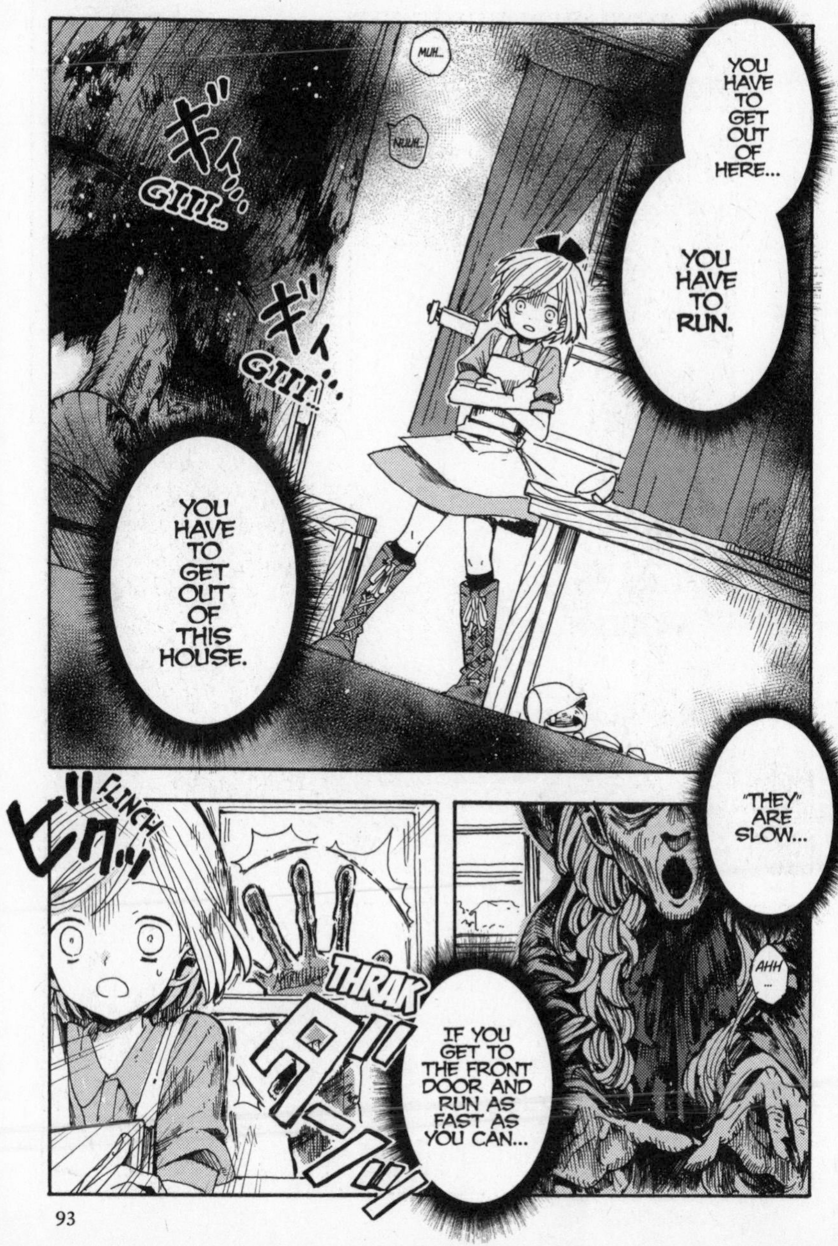
YOU HAVE TO GET OUT OF HERE...
YOU HAVE TO RUN.
MUH...
NUUH...
ギィ
GIII...
ギィ
GIII...
YOU HAVE TO GET OUT OF THIS HOUSE.
"THEY" ARE SLOW...
AHH ...
IF YOU GET TO THE FRONT DOOR AND RUN AS FAST AS YOU CAN...
THRAK
ダーン
FLINCH
ビクッ

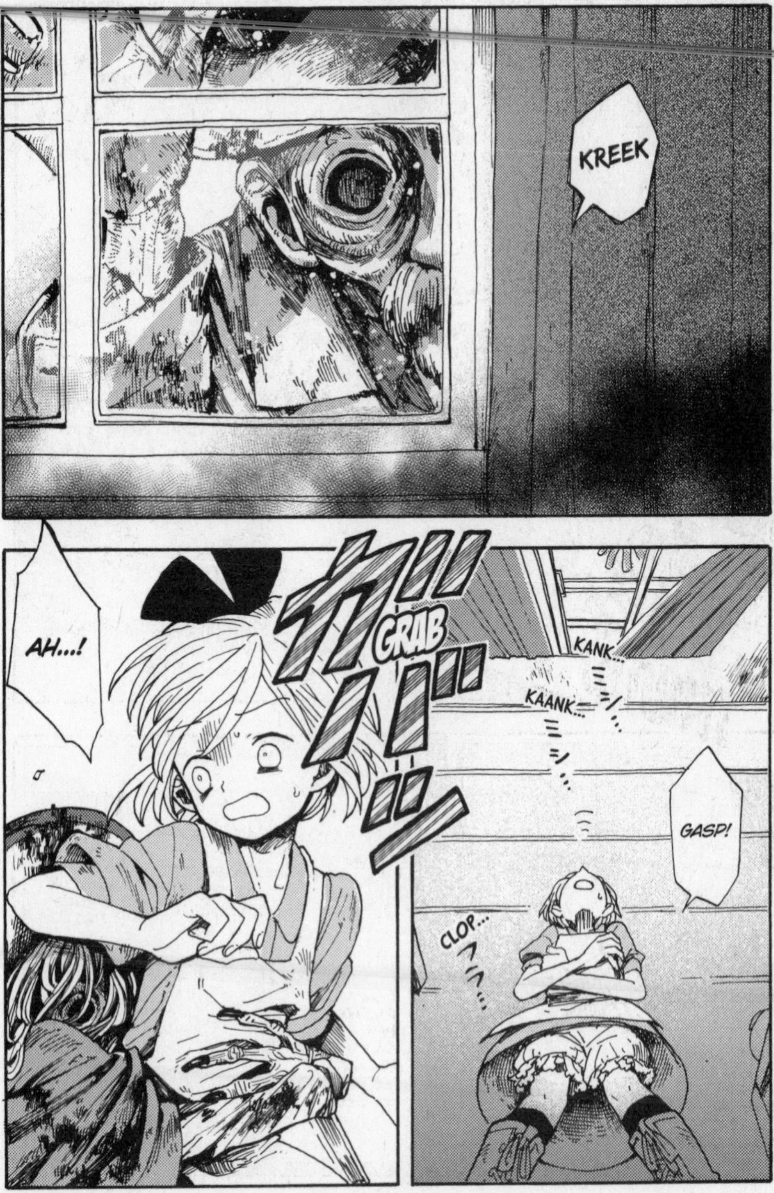
KREEK
GASP!
KANK...
KAANK...
CLOP...
GRAB
AH...!

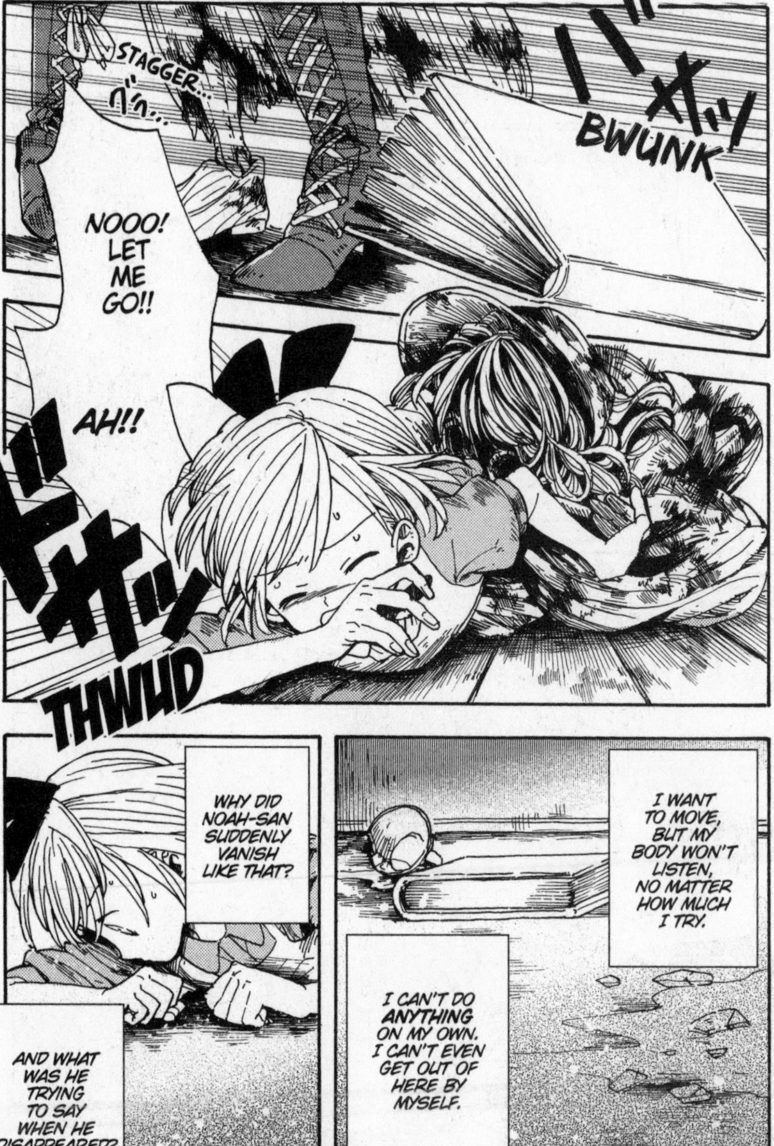
BWUNK
STAGGER...
NOOO! LET ME GO!!
AH!!
THWUD
I WANT TO MOVE, BUT MY BODY WON'T LISTEN, NO MATTER HOW MUCH I TRY.
I CAN'T DO ANYTHING ON MY OWN. I CAN'T EVEN GET OUT OF HERE BY MYSELF.
WHY DID NOAH-SAN SUDDENLY VANISH LIKE THAT?
AND WHAT WAS HE TRYING TO SAY WHEN HE DISAPPEARED?

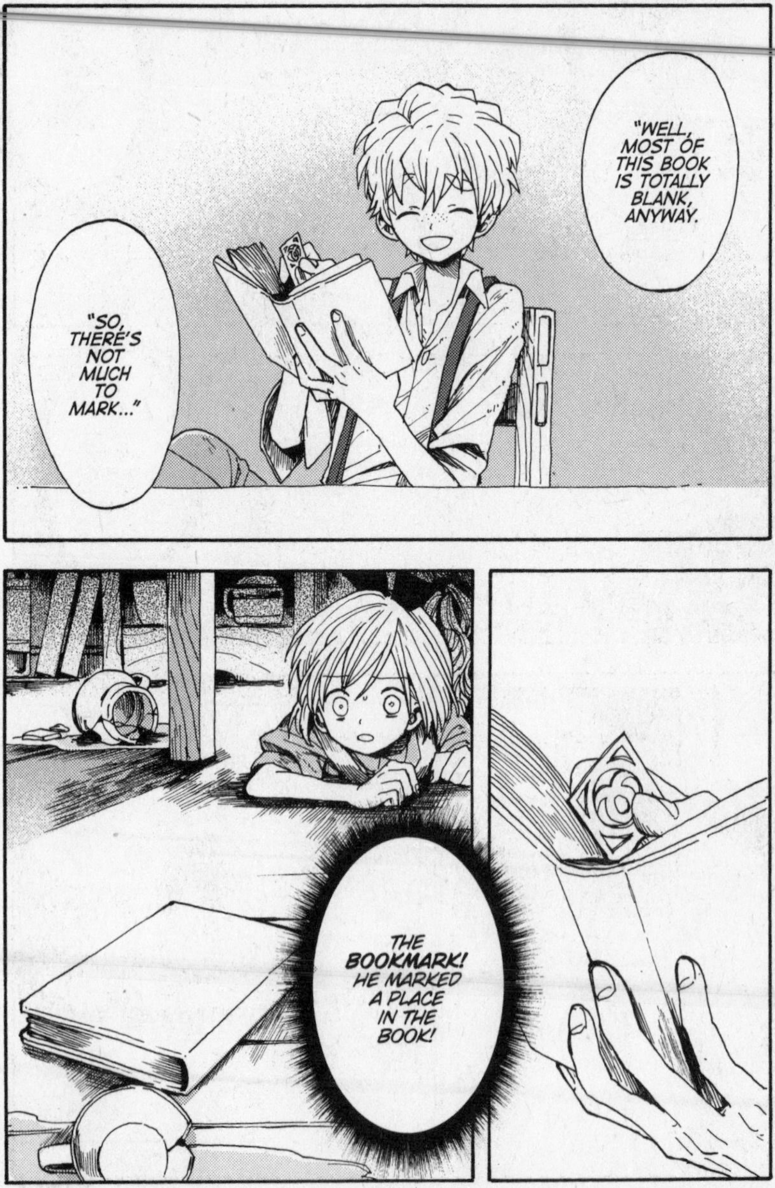
"WELL, MOST OF THIS BOOK IS TOTALLY BLANK, ANYWAY.
"SO, THERE'S NOT MUCH TO MARK..."
THE BOOKMARK! HE MARKED A PLACE IN THE BOOK!

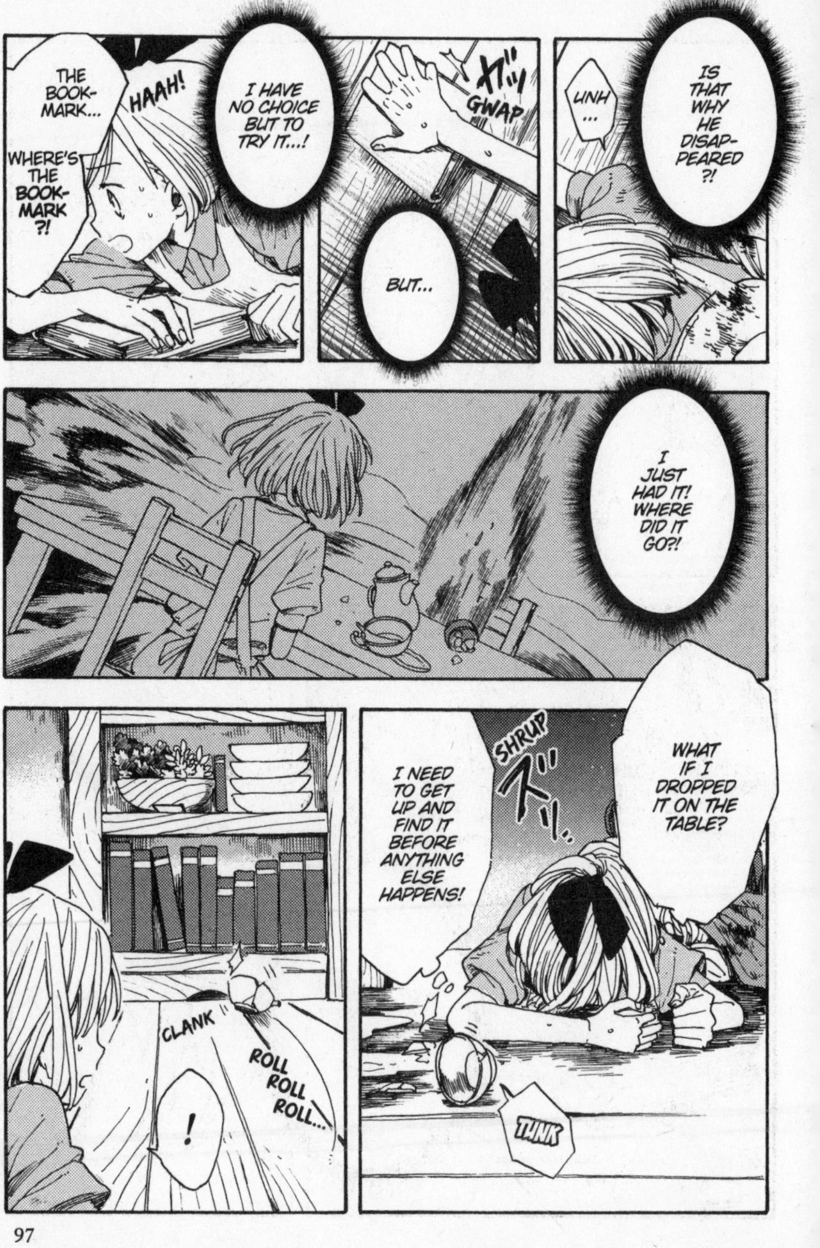
UNH...
IS THAT WHY HE DISAPPEARED?!
I HAVE NO CHOICE BUT TO TRY IT...!
GWAP
BUT...
THE BOOKMARK...
HAAH!
WHERE'S THE BOOKMARK?!
I JUST HAD IT! WHERE DID IT GO?!
WHAT IF I DROPPED IT ON THE TABLE?
SHRUP
I NEED TO GET UP AND FIND IT BEFORE ANYTHING ELSE HAPPENS!
THUNK
CLANK
ROLL ROLL ROLL...
!

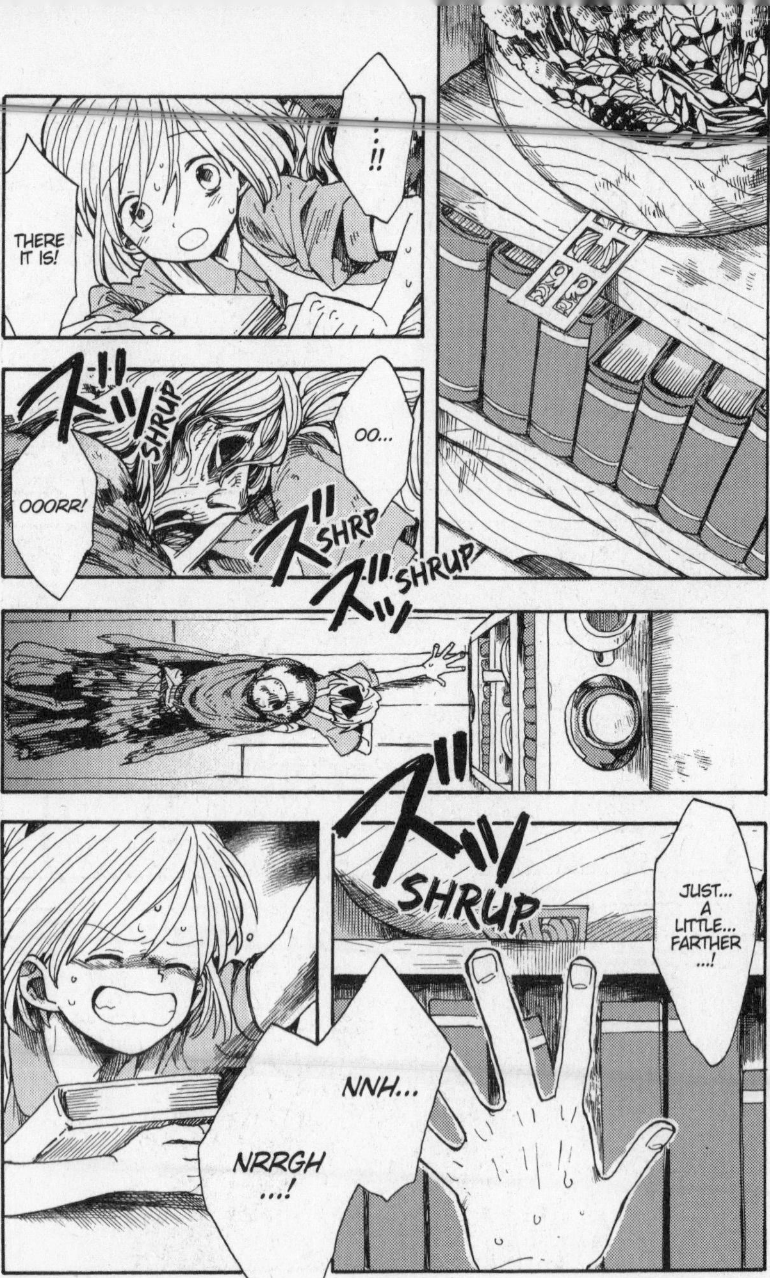

...!!
THERE IT IS!
OO...
OOORR!
SHRUP
SHRP
SHRUP
SHRUP
JUST... A LITTLE... FARTHER ...!
NNH...
NRRGH ...!

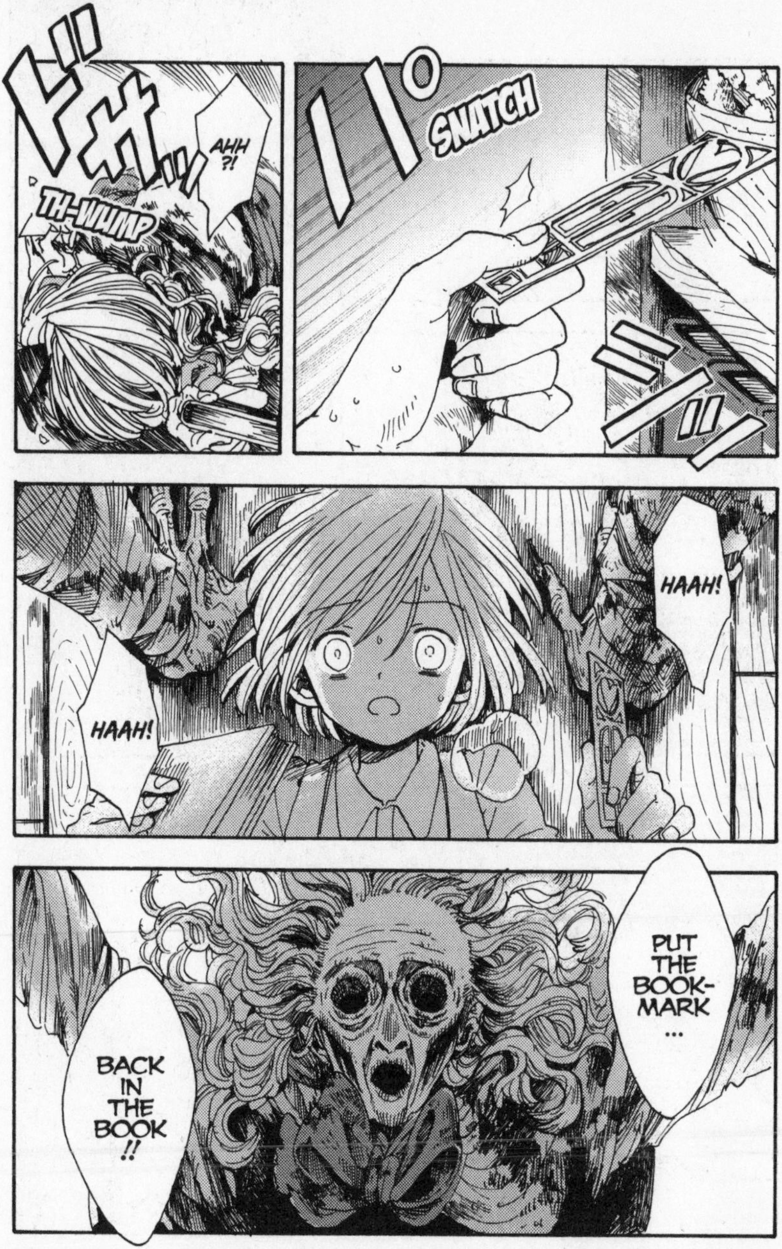
SNATCH
AHH ?!
TH-WUMP
HAAH!
HAAH!
PUT THE BOOK-MARK ...
BACK IN THE BOOK !!

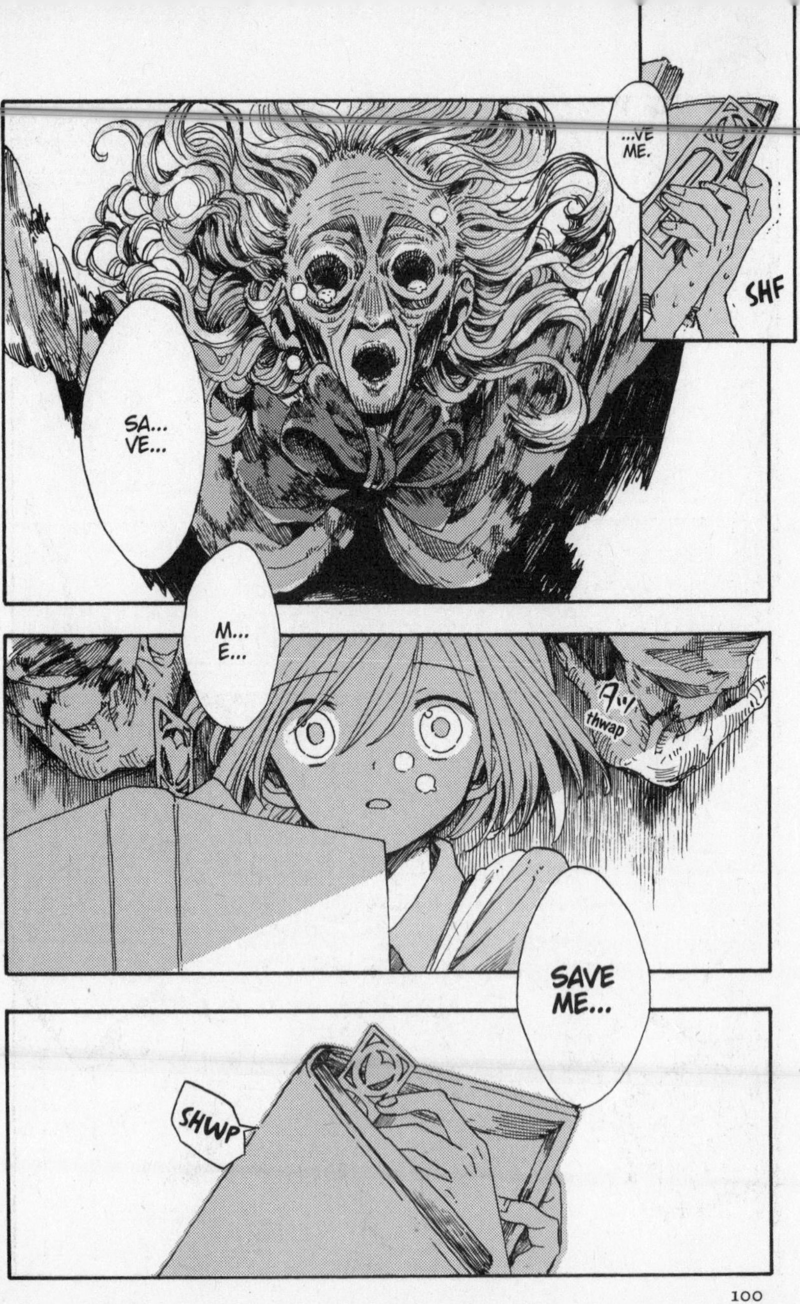
...VE
ME.
SHF
SA...
VE...
M...
E...
ﾀｯ
thwap
SAVE
ME...
SHWP

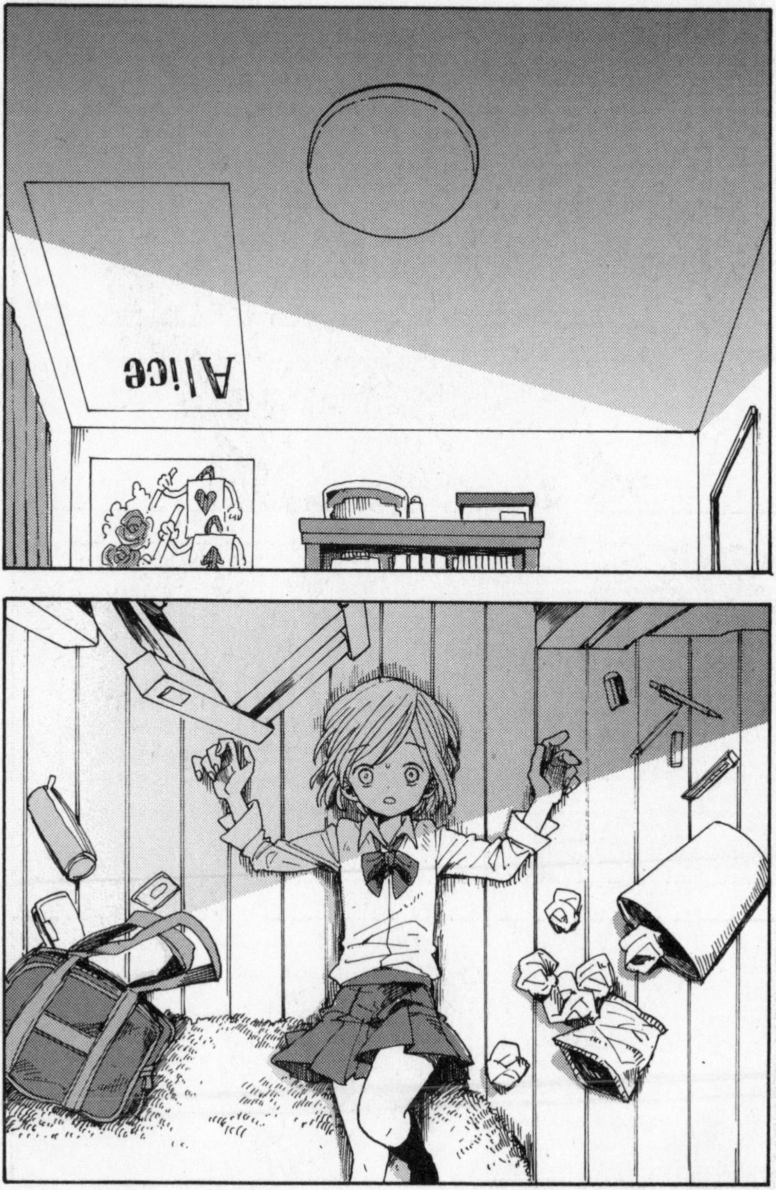
Alice

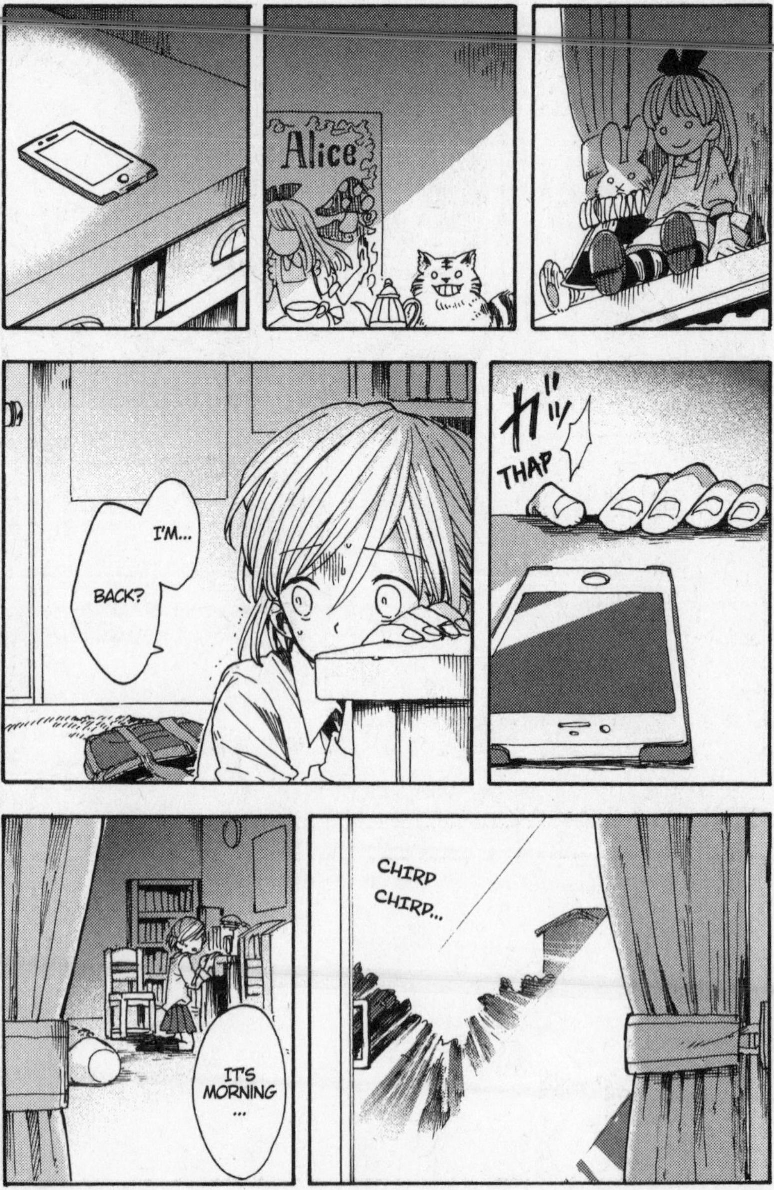
ガッ
THAP
I'M...
BACK?
CHIRP
CHIRP...
IT'S MORNING...

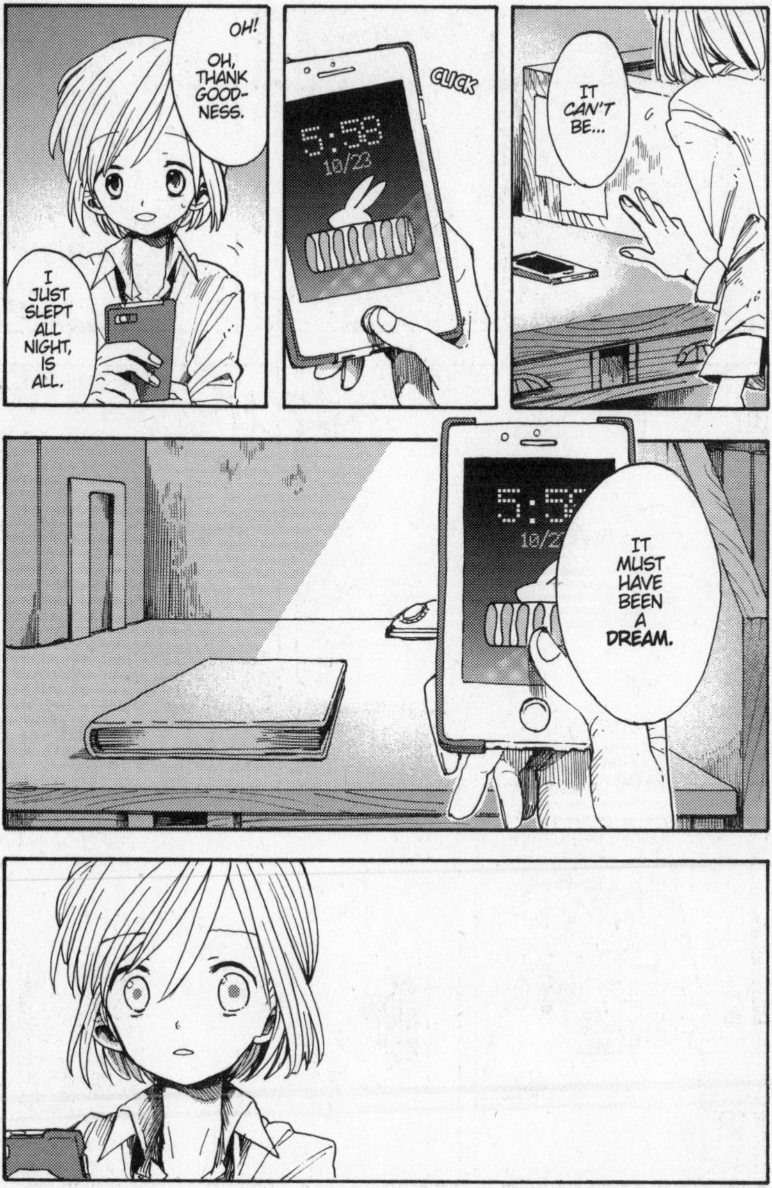
OH!
OH, THANK GOODNESS.
I JUST SLEPT ALL NIGHT, IS ALL.
CLICK
5:58
10/23
IT CAN'T BE...
IT MUST HAVE BEEN A DREAM.

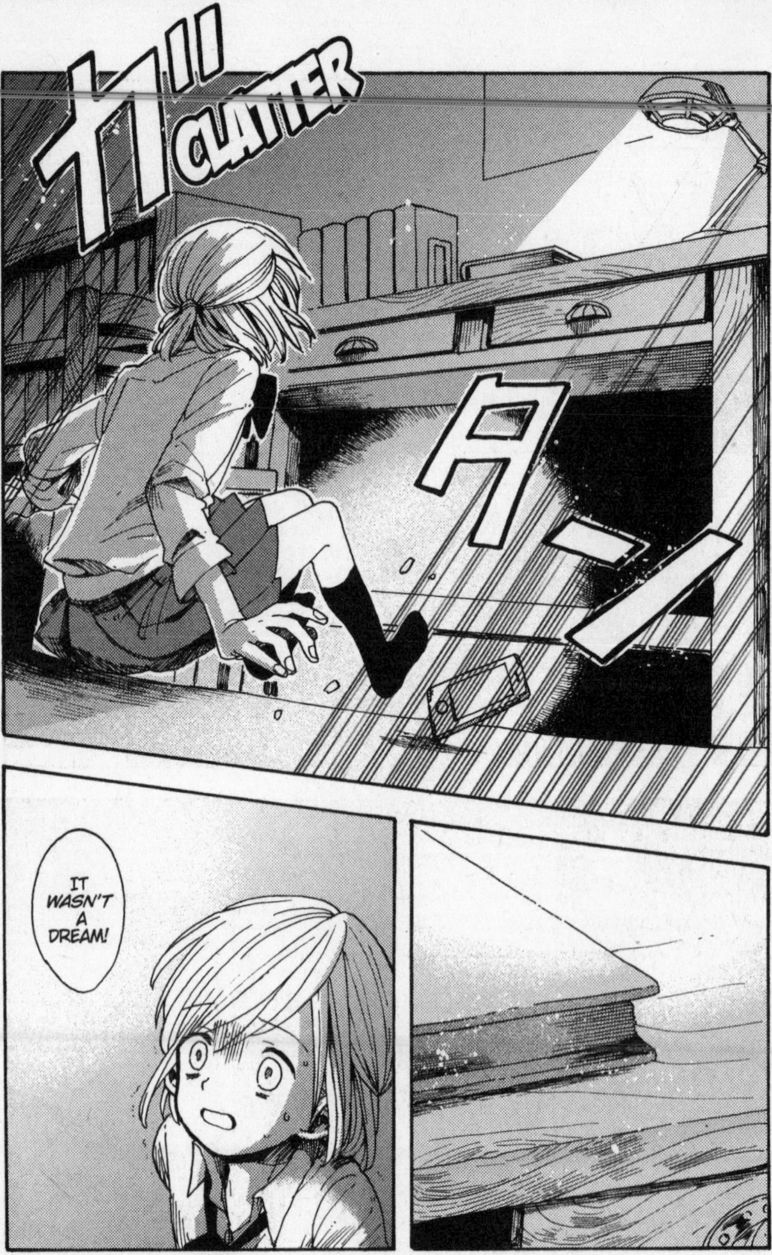
ガ
CLATTER
ター
IT WASN'T A DREAM!

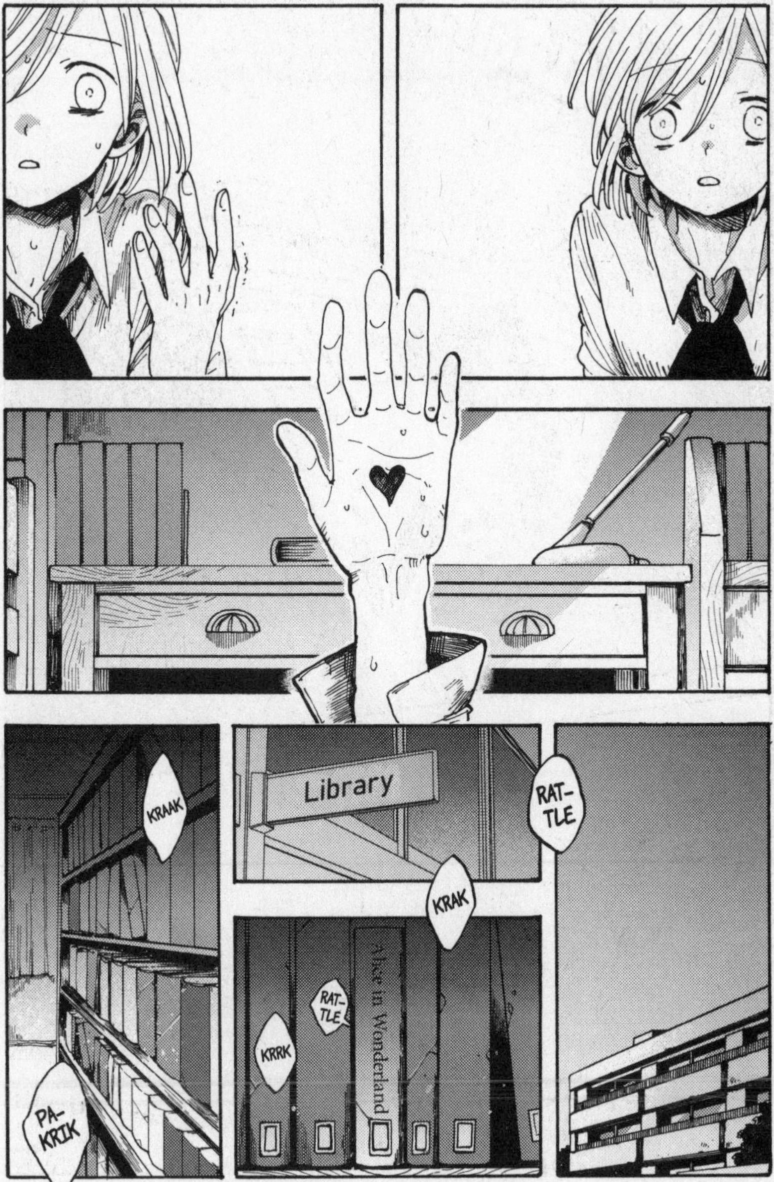
RAT-TLE
Library
KRAK
KRAAK
Alice in Wonderland
RAT-TLE
KRRK
PA-KRIK

FAIRY
TALE
BATTLE
ROYALE

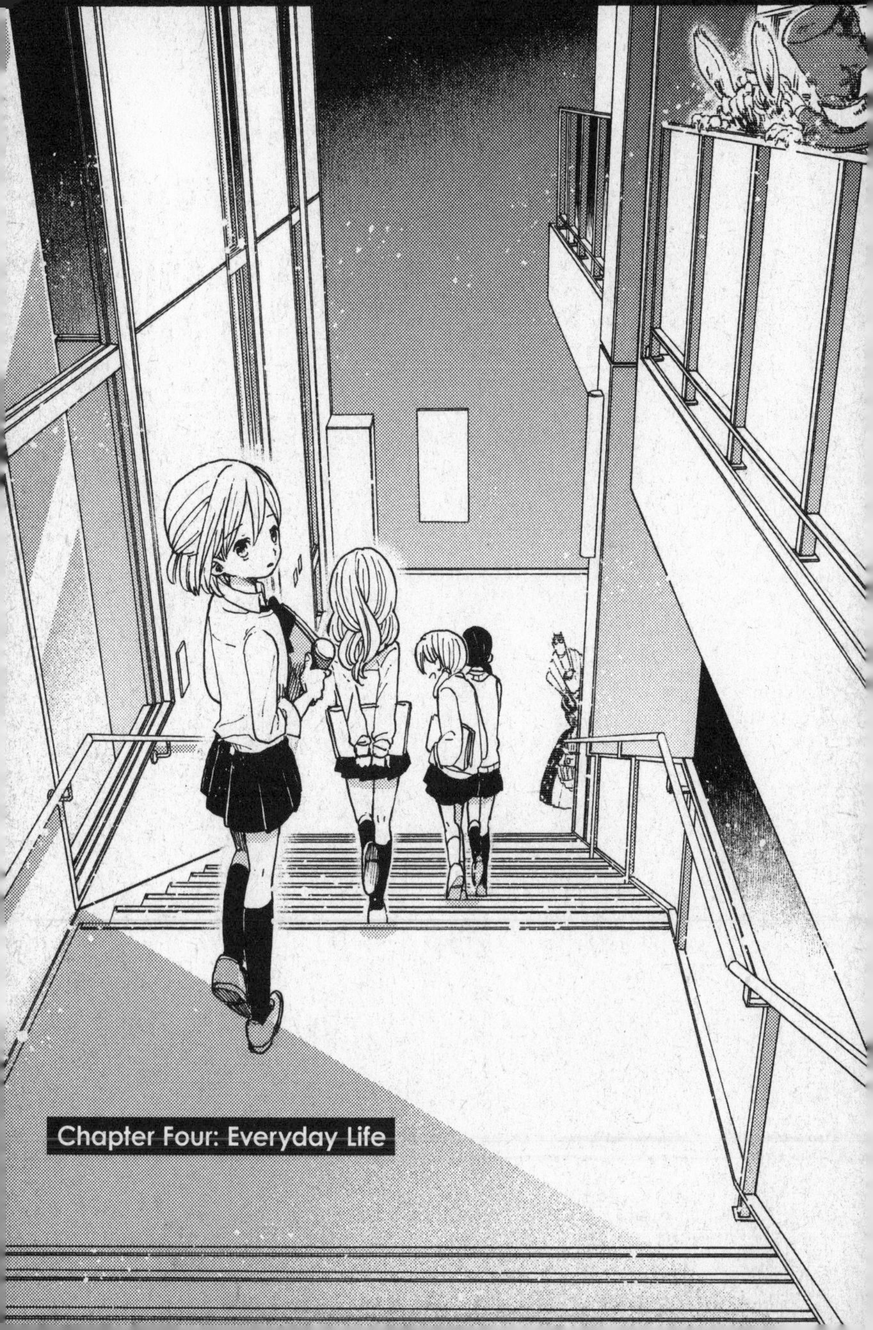
Chapter Four: Everyday Life

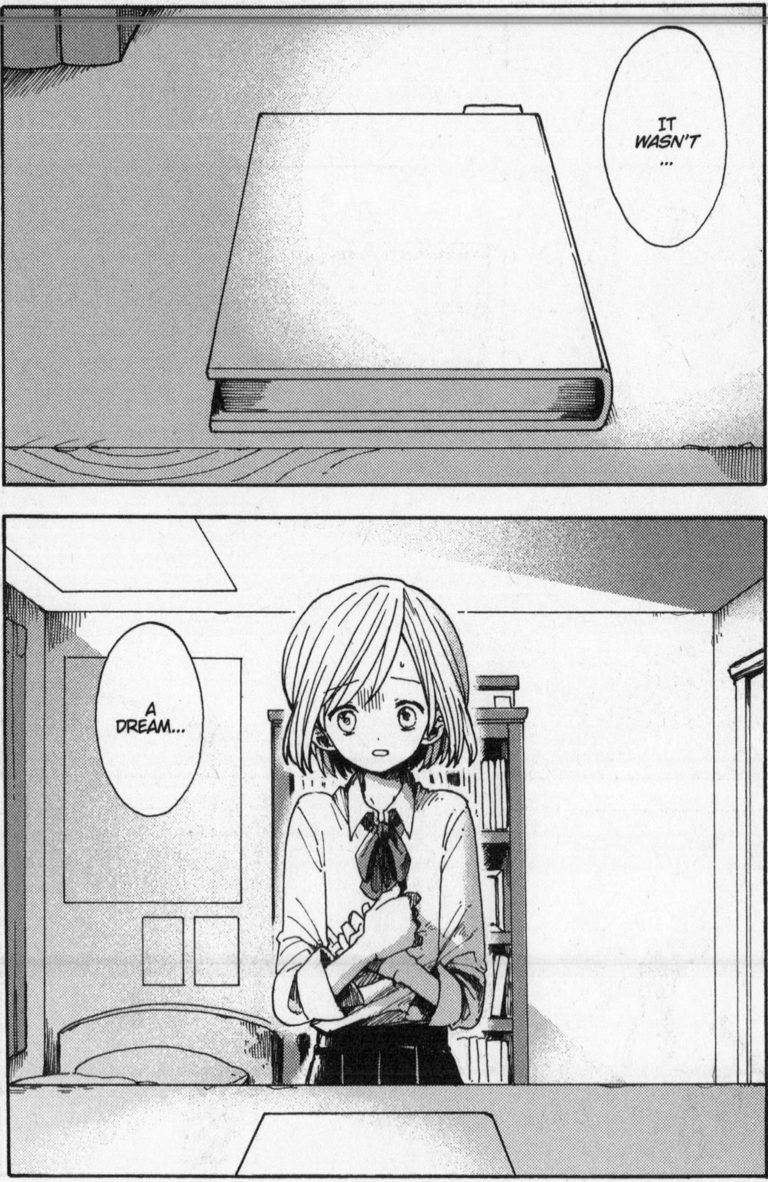
IT WASN'T ...
A DREAM...

AH!

M-MY CLOTHES ...!

THEY'RE ... BACK TO NORMAL?

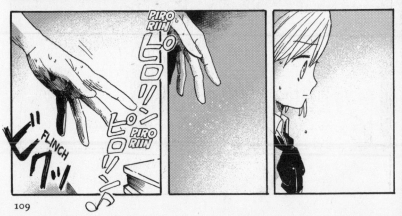

PIRO RIIN

PIRO RIIN

FLINCH

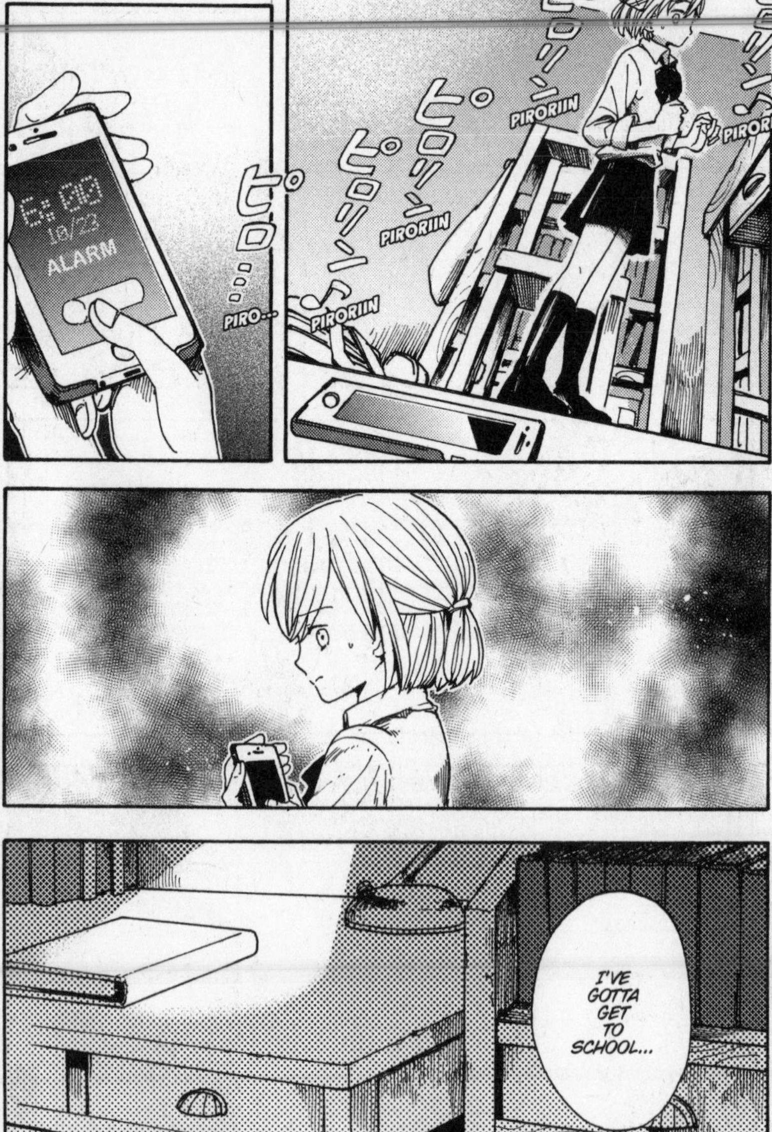
ピロリン♪
PIRORIIN
ピロリン
PIRORIIN
ピロリン
PIRORIIN
ピロリン♪
PIRORIIN
ピロ...
PIRO...
6:00
10/23
ALARM
I'VE GOTTA GET TO SCHOOL...

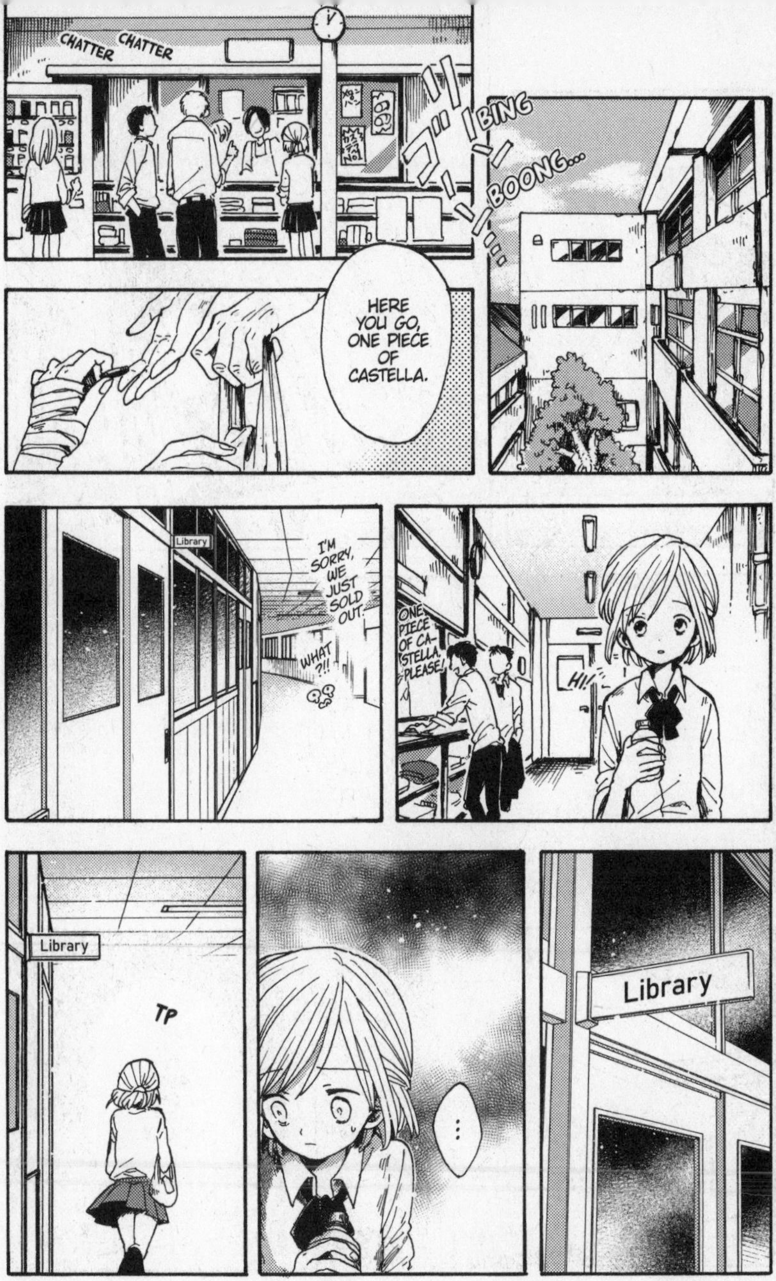
CHATTER CHATTER
BING
BOONG...
HERE YOU GO, ONE PIECE OF CASTELLA.
ONE PIECE OF CA-STELLA, PLEASE!
HI!
I'M SORRY, WE JUST SOLD OUT.
WHAT?!!
Library
Library
...
Library
TP

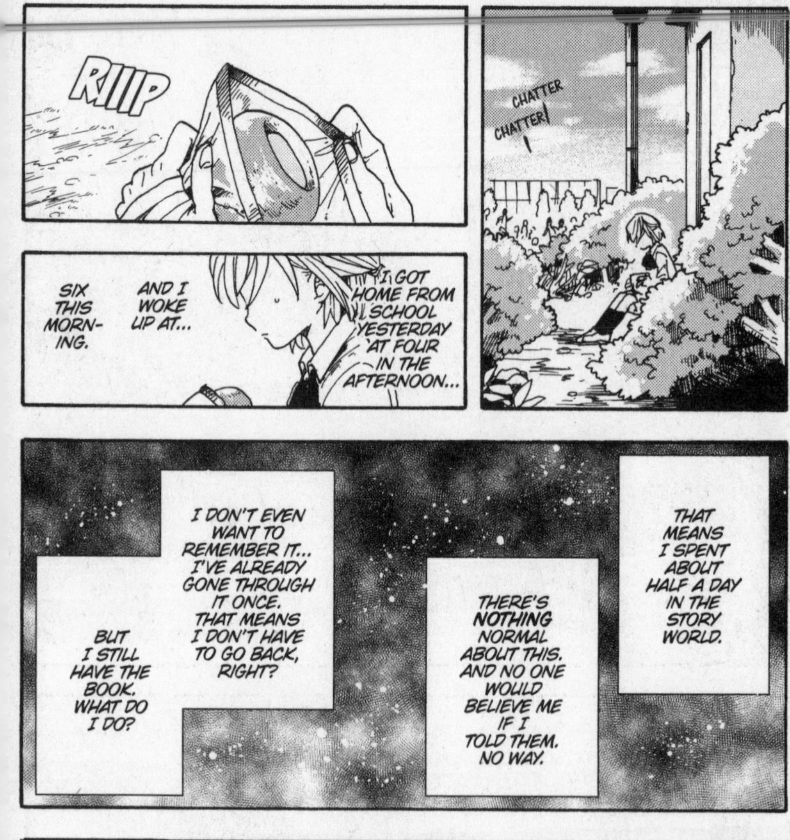
CHATTER CHATTER
RIIIP
I GOT HOME FROM SCHOOL YESTERDAY AT FOUR IN THE AFTERNOON...
AND I WOKE UP AT...
SIX THIS MORNING.
THAT MEANS I SPENT ABOUT HALF A DAY IN THE STORY WORLD.
THERE'S NOTHING NORMAL ABOUT THIS. AND NO ONE WOULD BELIEVE ME IF I TOLD THEM. NO WAY.
I DON'T EVEN WANT TO REMEMBER IT... I'VE ALREADY GONE THROUGH IT ONCE. THAT MEANS I DON'T HAVE TO GO BACK, RIGHT?
BUT I STILL HAVE THE BOOK. WHAT DO I DO?
NOAH AND I PARTED IN SUCH A TERRIBLE WAY.
IF I CAME BACK TO THIS WORLD IN ONE PIECE, THAT MEANS HE DID TOO, RIGHT? HE HAS TO BE OKAY.
I HOPE...
WAIT. I'M FORGETTING SOMETHING.
RSSH

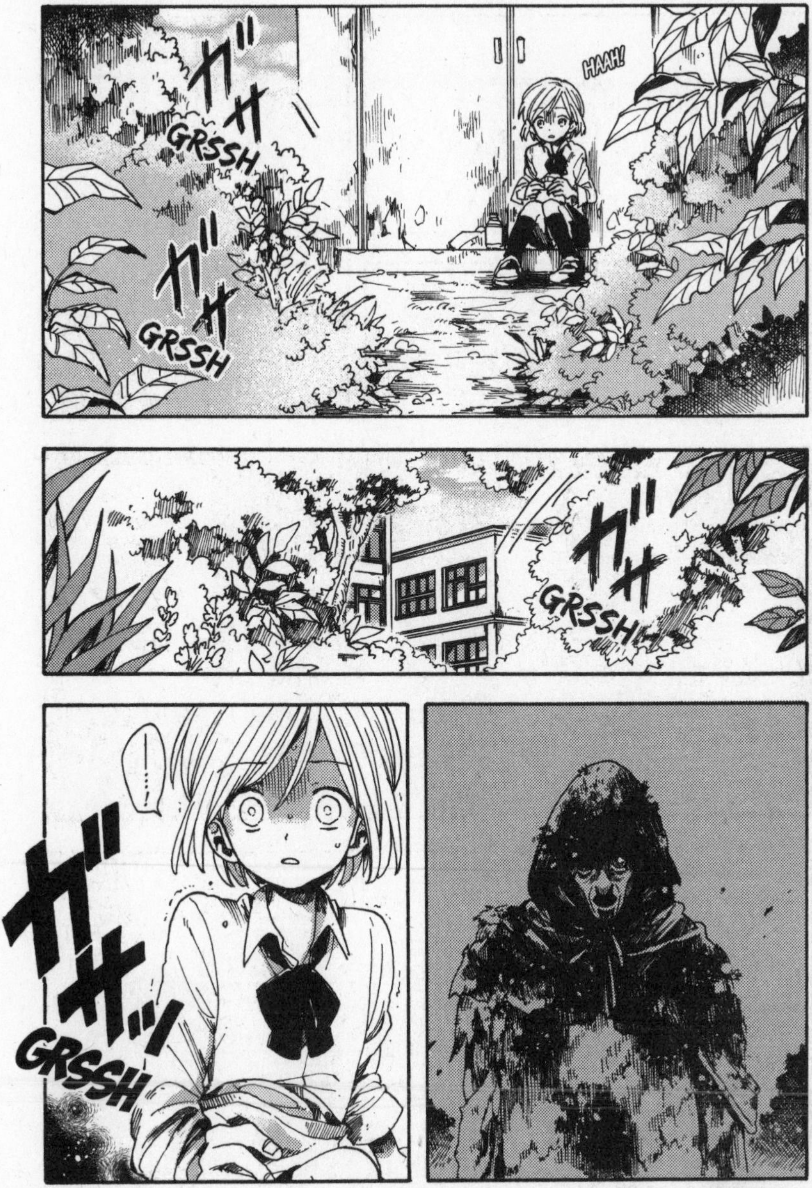
HAAH!
ガサ
GRSSH
ガサ
GRSSH
ガサ
GRSSH
…!
ガサッ!
GRSSH

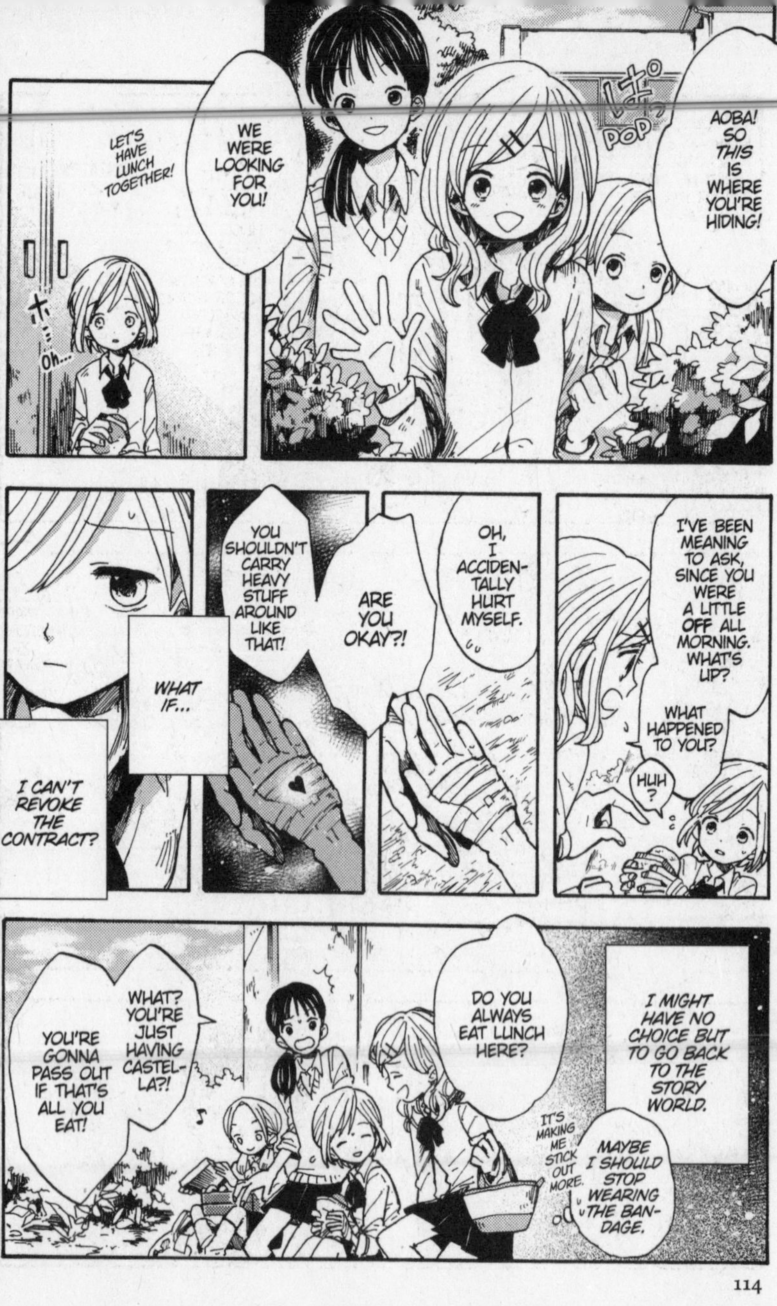
AOBA! SO THIS IS WHERE YOU'RE HIDING!
POP
WE WERE LOOKING FOR YOU!
LET'S HAVE LUNCH TOGETHER!
Oh...
I'VE BEEN MEANING TO ASK, SINCE YOU WERE A LITTLE OFF ALL MORNING. WHAT'S UP?
WHAT HAPPENED TO YOU?
HUH?
OH, I ACCIDENTALLY HURT MYSELF.
ARE YOU OKAY?!
YOU SHOULDN'T CARRY HEAVY STUFF AROUND LIKE THAT!
WHAT IF...
I CAN'T REVOKE THE CONTRACT?
I MIGHT HAVE NO CHOICE BUT TO GO BACK TO THE STORY WORLD.
MAYBE I SHOULD STOP WEARING THE BANDAGE.
IT'S MAKING ME STICK OUT MORE.
DO YOU ALWAYS EAT LUNCH HERE?
WHAT? YOU'RE JUST HAVING CASTELLA?!
YOU'RE GONNA PASS OUT IF THAT'S ALL YOU EAT!

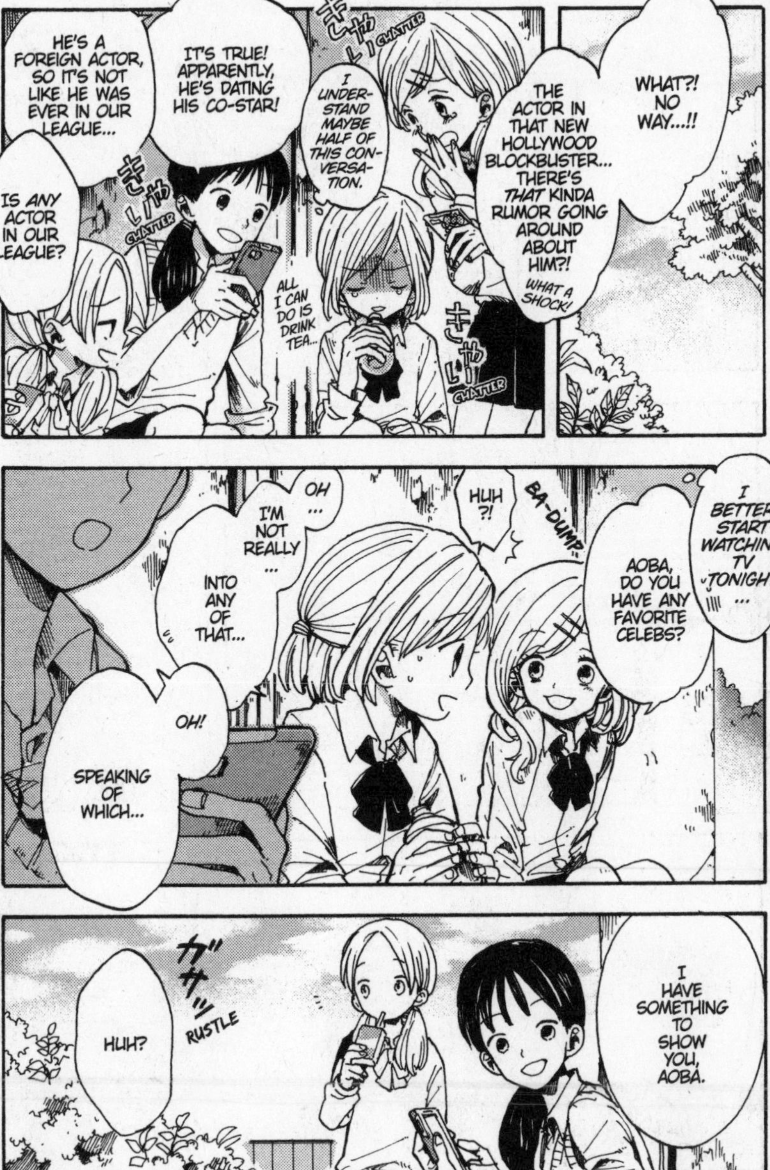
WHAT?! NO WAY...!!
THE ACTOR IN THAT NEW HOLLYWOOD BLOCKBUSTER... THERE'S THAT KINDA RUMOR GOING AROUND ABOUT HIM?!
WHAT A SHOCK!
CHATTER
CHATTER
IT'S TRUE! APPARENTLY, HE'S DATING HIS CO-STAR!
HE'S A FOREIGN ACTOR, SO IT'S NOT LIKE HE WAS EVER IN OUR LEAGUE...
I UNDERSTAND MAYBE HALF OF THIS CONVERSATION.
CHATTER
IS ANY ACTOR IN OUR LEAGUE?
ALL I CAN DO IS DRINK TEA...
CHATTER
I BETTER START WATCHING TV TONIGHT...
AOBA, DO YOU HAVE ANY FAVORITE CELEBS?
BA-DUMP
HUH?!
OH...
I'M NOT REALLY...
INTO ANY OF THAT...
OH!
SPEAKING OF WHICH...
I HAVE SOMETHING TO SHOW YOU, AOBA.
RUSTLE
HUH?

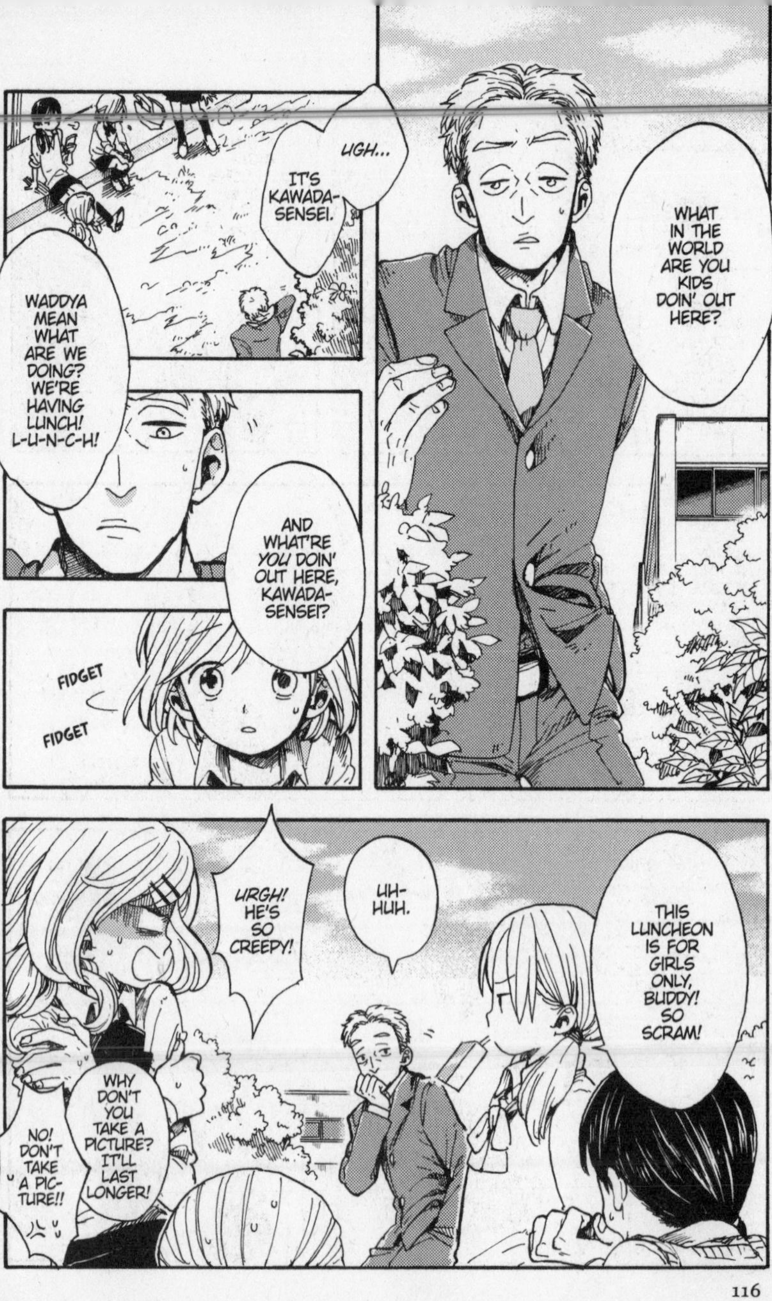

WHAT IN THE WORLD ARE YOU KIDS DOIN' OUT HERE?
UGH... IT'S KAWADA-SENSEI.
WADDYA MEAN WHAT ARE WE DOING? WE'RE HAVING LUNCH! L-U-N-C-H!
AND WHAT'RE *YOU* DOIN' OUT HERE, KAWADA-SENSEI?
FIDGET
FIDGET
THIS LUNCHEON IS FOR GIRLS ONLY, BUDDY! SO SCRAM!
UH-HUH.
URGH! HE'S SO CREEPY!
WHY DON'T YOU TAKE A PICTURE? IT'LL LAST LONGER!
NO! DON'T TAKE A PICTURE!!

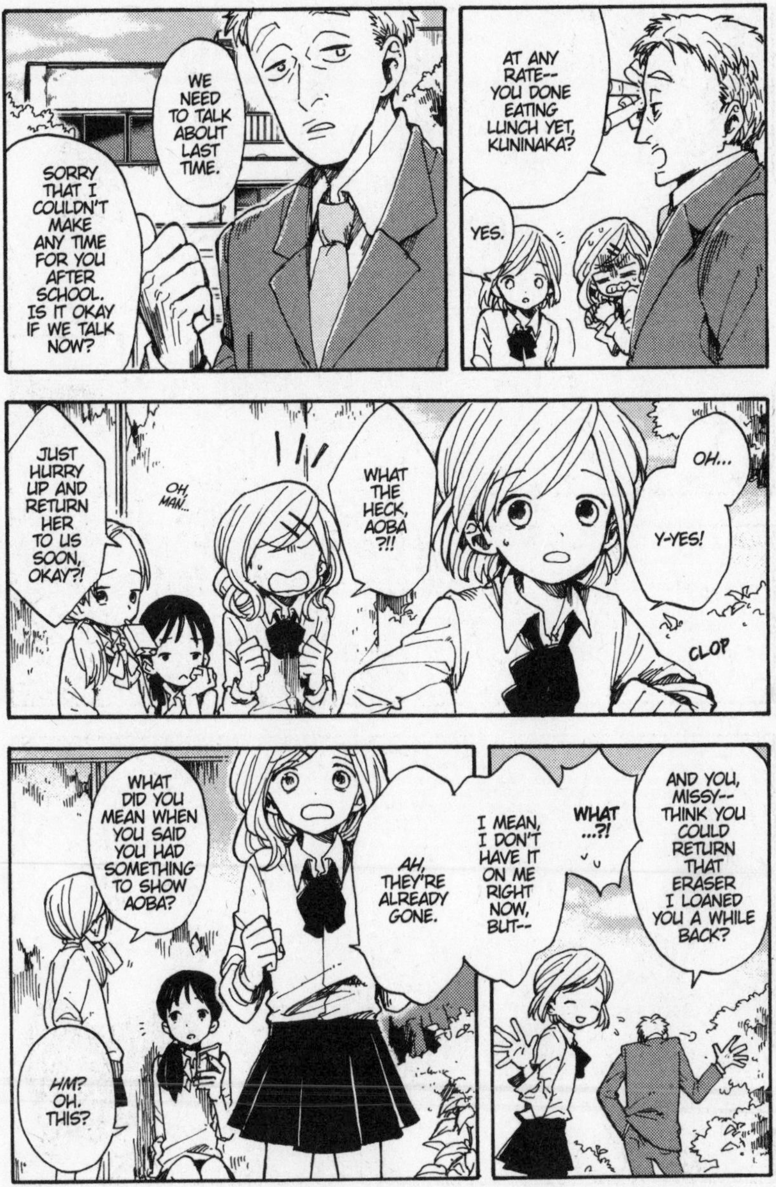
AT ANY RATE-- YOU DONE EATING LUNCH YET, KUNINAKA?
YES.
WE NEED TO TALK ABOUT LAST TIME.
SORRY THAT I COULDN'T MAKE ANY TIME FOR YOU AFTER SCHOOL. IS IT OKAY IF WE TALK NOW?
OH...
Y-YES!
CLOP
WHAT THE HECK, AOBA ?!!
OH, MAN...
JUST HURRY UP AND RETURN HER TO US SOON, OKAY?!
AND YOU, MISSY-- THINK YOU COULD RETURN THAT ERASER I LOANED YOU A WHILE BACK?
WHAT ...?!
I MEAN, I DON'T HAVE IT ON ME RIGHT NOW, BUT--
AH, THEY'RE ALREADY GONE.
WHAT DID YOU MEAN WHEN YOU SAID YOU HAD SOMETHING TO SHOW AOBA?
HM? OH. THIS?

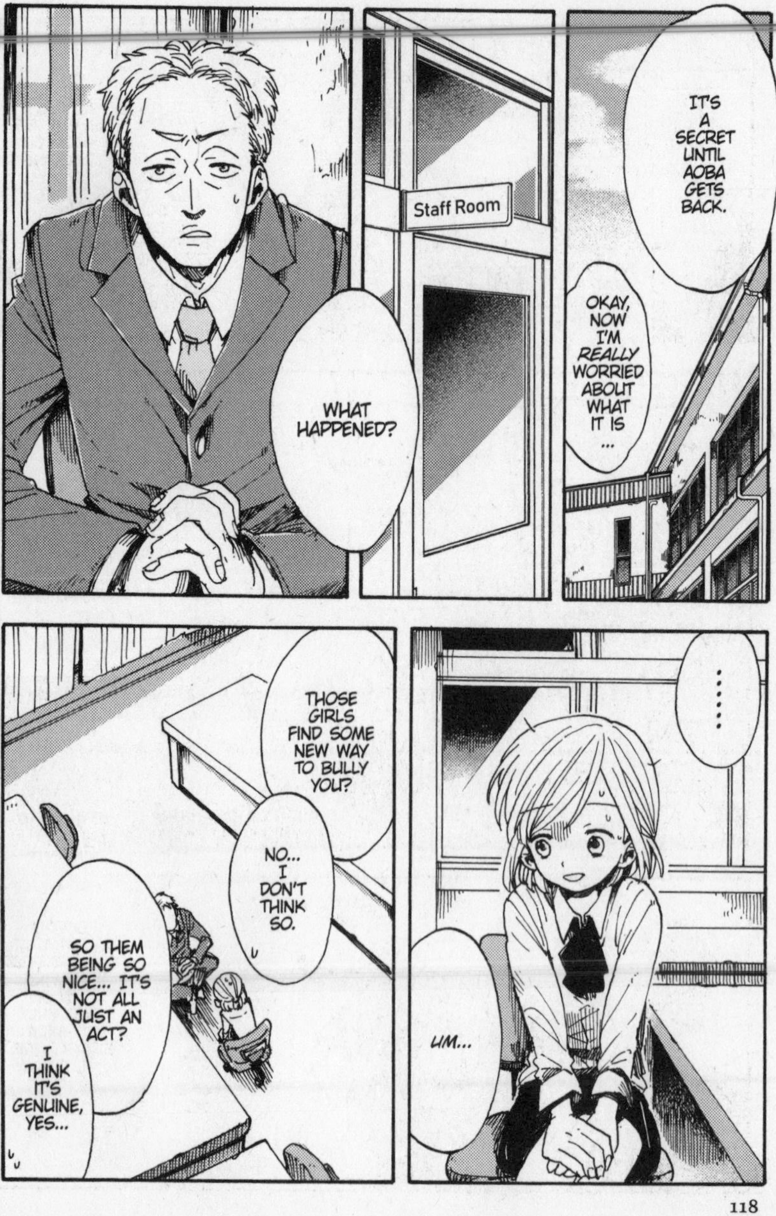
IT'S A SECRET UNTIL AOBA GETS BACK.
OKAY, NOW I'M *REALLY* WORRIED ABOUT WHAT IT IS ...
Staff Room
WHAT HAPPENED?
......
UM...
THOSE GIRLS FIND SOME NEW WAY TO BULLY YOU?
NO... I DON'T THINK SO.
SO THEM BEING SO NICE... IT'S NOT ALL JUST AN ACT?
I THINK IT'S GENUINE, YES...

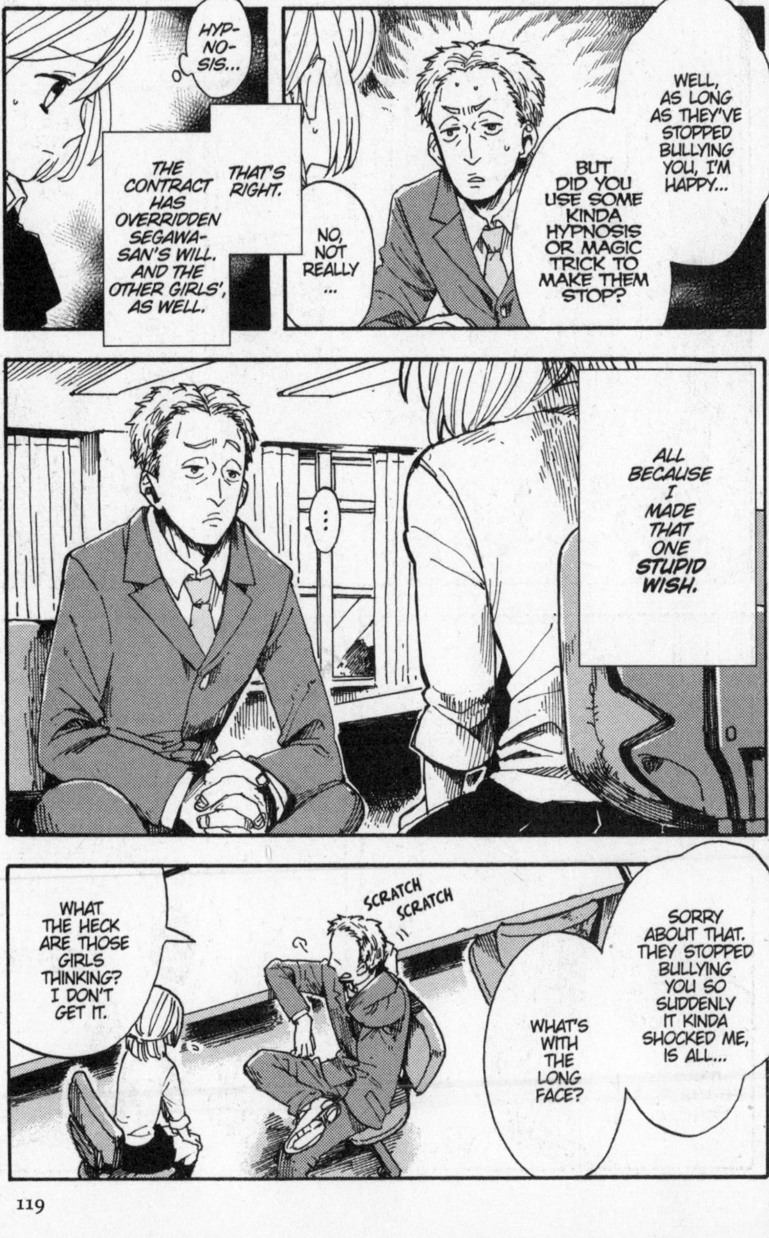
WELL, AS LONG AS THEY'VE STOPPED BULLYING YOU, I'M HAPPY...
BUT DID YOU USE SOME KINDA HYPNOSIS OR MAGIC TRICK TO MAKE THEM STOP?
NO, NOT REALLY ...
HYP-NO-SIS...
THAT'S RIGHT.
THE CONTRACT HAS OVERRIDDEN SEGAWA-SAN'S WILL. AND THE OTHER GIRLS', AS WELL.
ALL BECAUSE I MADE THAT ONE STUPID WISH.
...
SORRY ABOUT THAT. THEY STOPPED BULLYING YOU SO SUDDENLY IT KINDA SHOCKED ME, IS ALL...
WHAT'S WITH THE LONG FACE?
SCRATCH SCRATCH
WHAT THE HECK ARE THOSE GIRLS THINKING? I DON'T GET IT.

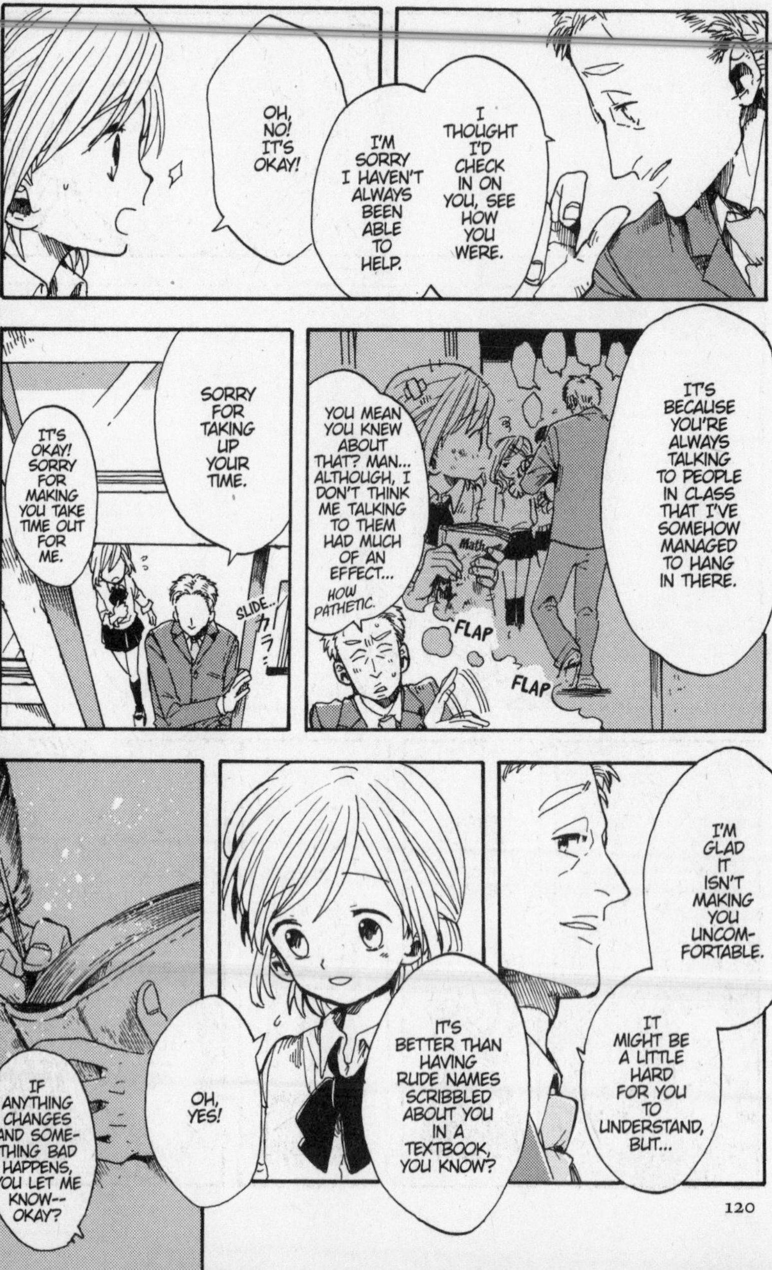
I THOUGHT I'D CHECK IN ON YOU, SEE HOW YOU WERE.
I'M SORRY I HAVEN'T ALWAYS BEEN ABLE TO HELP.
OH, NO! IT'S OKAY!
IT'S BECAUSE YOU'RE ALWAYS TALKING TO PEOPLE IN CLASS THAT I'VE SOMEHOW MANAGED TO HANG IN THERE.
Math
FLAP
FLAP
YOU MEAN YOU KNEW ABOUT THAT? MAN... ALTHOUGH, I DON'T THINK ME TALKING TO THEM HAD MUCH OF AN EFFECT...
HOW PATHETIC.
SORRY FOR TAKING UP YOUR TIME.
IT'S OKAY! SORRY FOR MAKING YOU TAKE TIME OUT FOR ME.
SLIDE...
カラ
I'M GLAD IT ISN'T MAKING YOU UNCOM-FORTABLE.
IT MIGHT BE A LITTLE HARD FOR YOU TO UNDERSTAND, BUT...
IT'S BETTER THAN HAVING RUDE NAMES SCRIBBLED ABOUT YOU IN A TEXTBOOK, YOU KNOW?
OH, YES!
IF ANYTHING CHANGES AND SOME-THING BAD HAPPENS, YOU LET ME KNOW--OKAY?

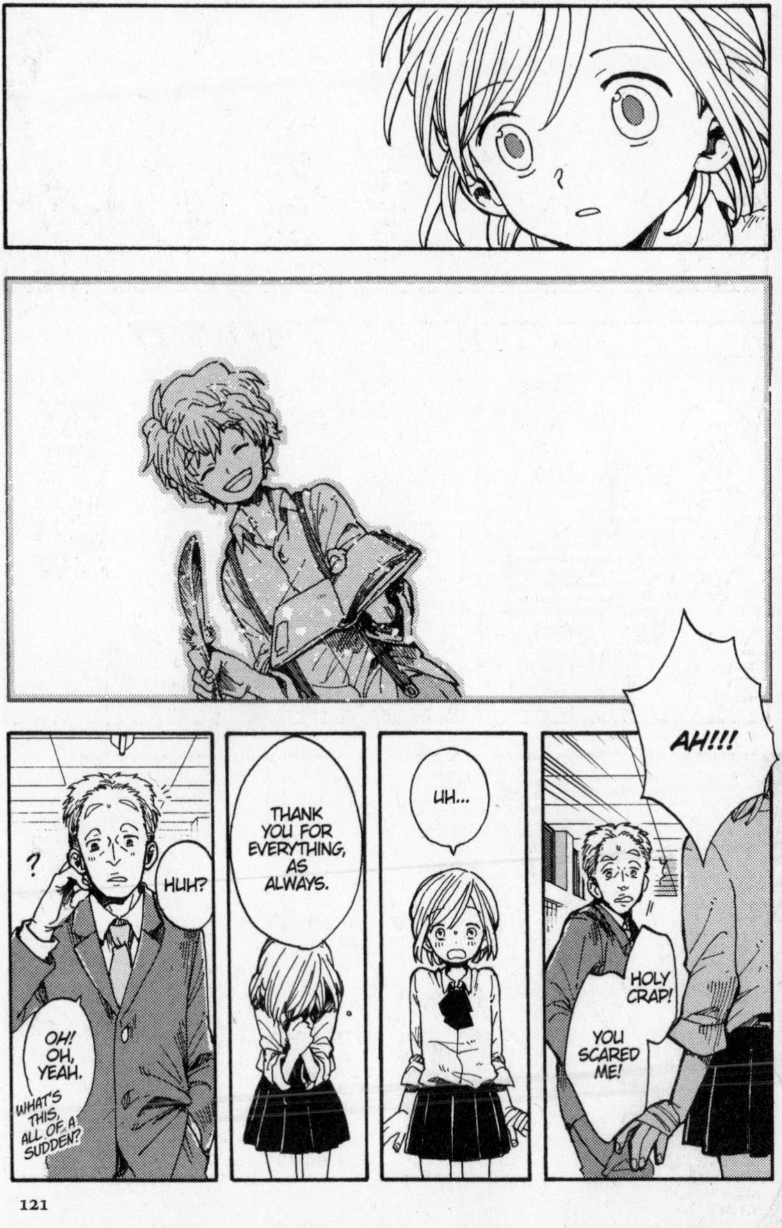
AH!!!
HOLY CRAP!
YOU SCARED ME!
UH...
THANK YOU FOR EVERYTHING, AS ALWAYS.
HUH?
OH! OH, YEAH.
WHAT'S THIS, ALL OF A SUDDEN?

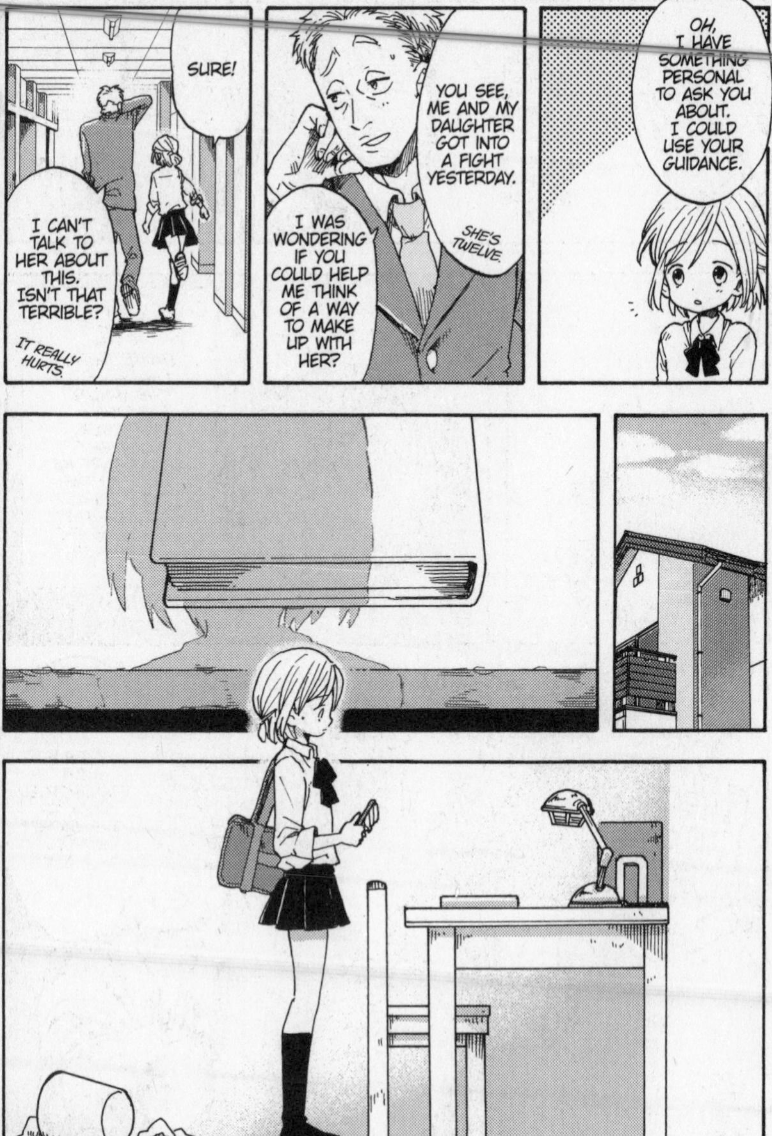
OH, I HAVE SOMETHING PERSONAL TO ASK YOU ABOUT. I COULD USE YOUR GUIDANCE.
YOU SEE, ME AND MY DAUGHTER GOT INTO A FIGHT YESTERDAY.
SHE'S TWELVE.
I WAS WONDERING IF YOU COULD HELP ME THINK OF A WAY TO MAKE UP WITH HER?
SURE!
I CAN'T TALK TO HER ABOUT THIS. ISN'T THAT TERRIBLE?
IT REALLY HURTS.

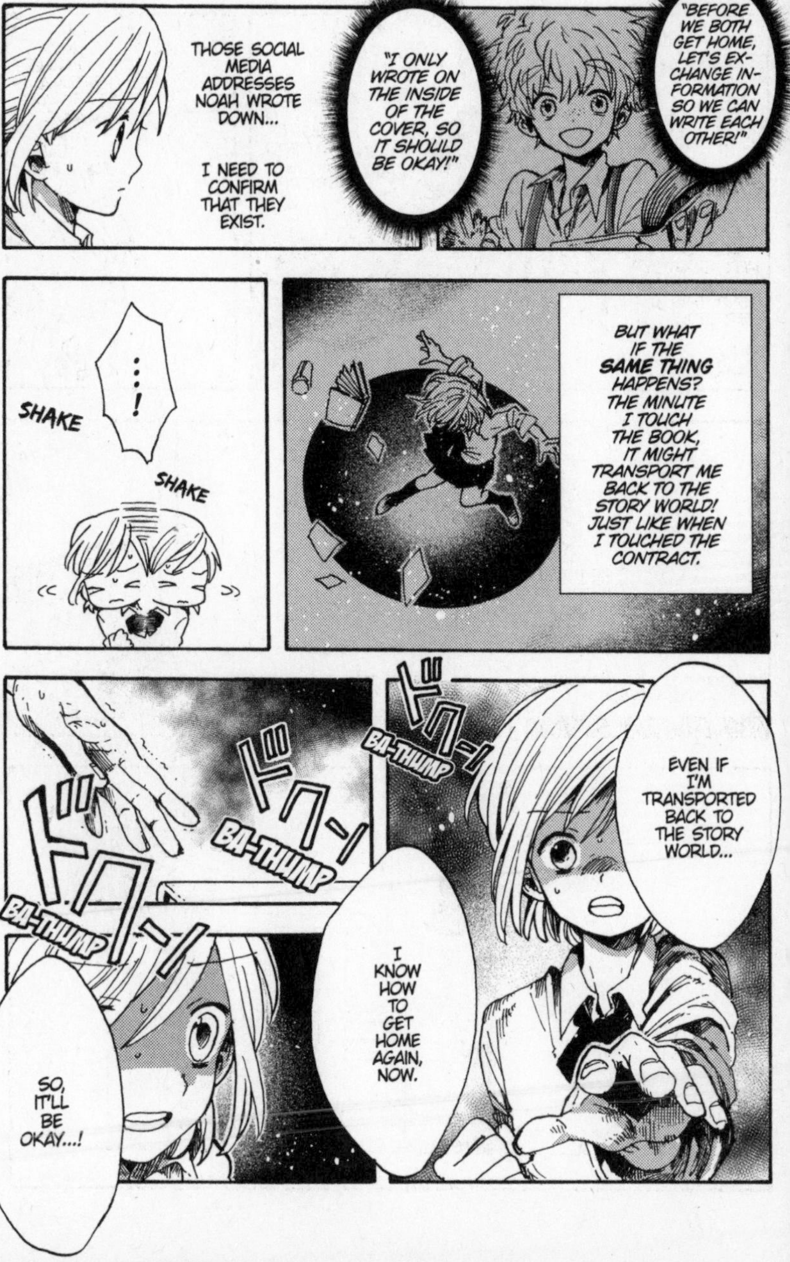
"BEFORE WE BOTH GET HOME, LET'S EX-CHANGE IN-FORMATION SO WE CAN WRITE EACH OTHER!"
"I ONLY WROTE ON THE INSIDE OF THE COVER, SO IT SHOULD BE OKAY!"
THOSE SOCIAL MEDIA ADDRESSES NOAH WROTE DOWN...
I NEED TO CONFIRM THAT THEY EXIST.
BUT WHAT IF THE **SAME THING** HAPPENS? THE MINUTE I TOUCH THE BOOK, IT MIGHT TRANSPORT ME BACK TO THE STORY WORLD! JUST LIKE WHEN I TOUCHED THE CONTRACT.
...!
SHAKE
SHAKE
ドクン
BA-THUMP
EVEN IF I'M TRANSPORTED BACK TO THE STORY WORLD...
I KNOW HOW TO GET HOME AGAIN, NOW.
ドクン
BA-THUMP
ドクン
BA-THUMP
SO, IT'LL BE OKAY...!

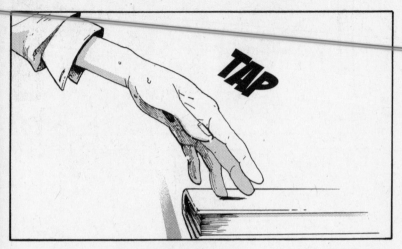

TAP

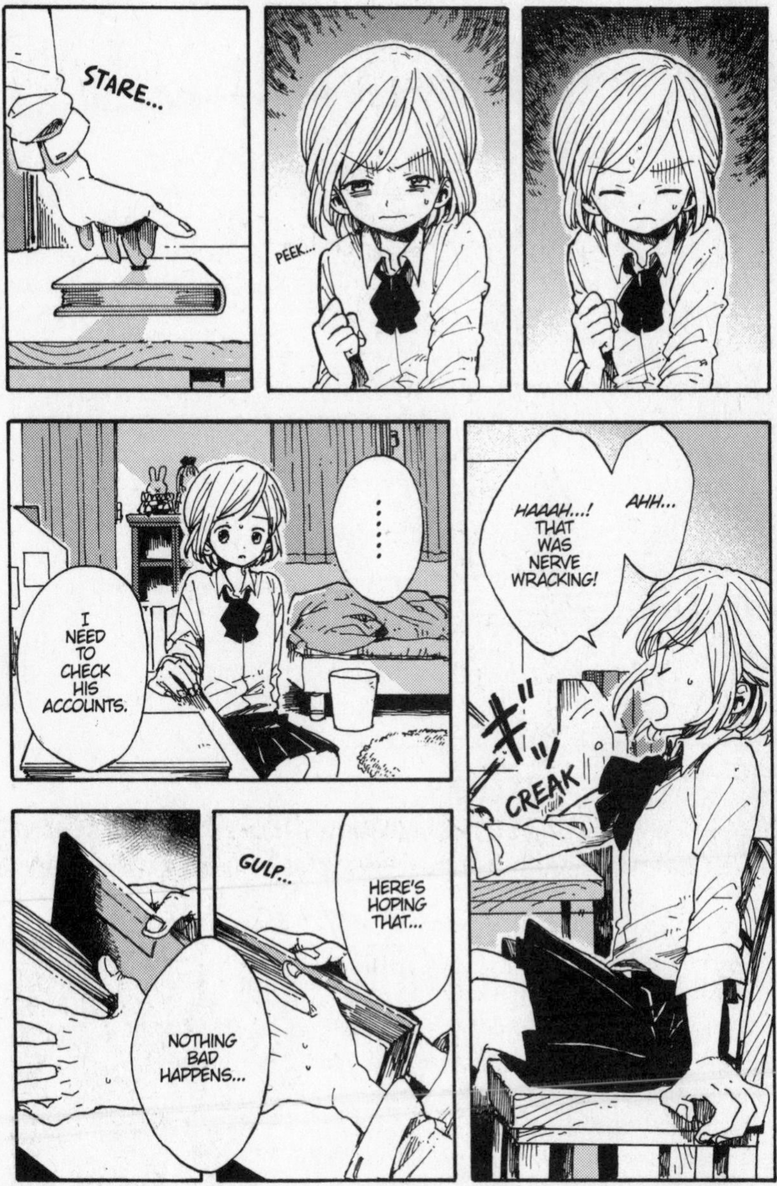
PEEK...
STARE...
AHH...
HAAAH...! THAT WAS NERVE WRACKING!
CREAK
......
I NEED TO CHECK HIS ACCOUNTS.
GULP...
HERE'S HOPING THAT...
NOTHING BAD HAPPENS...

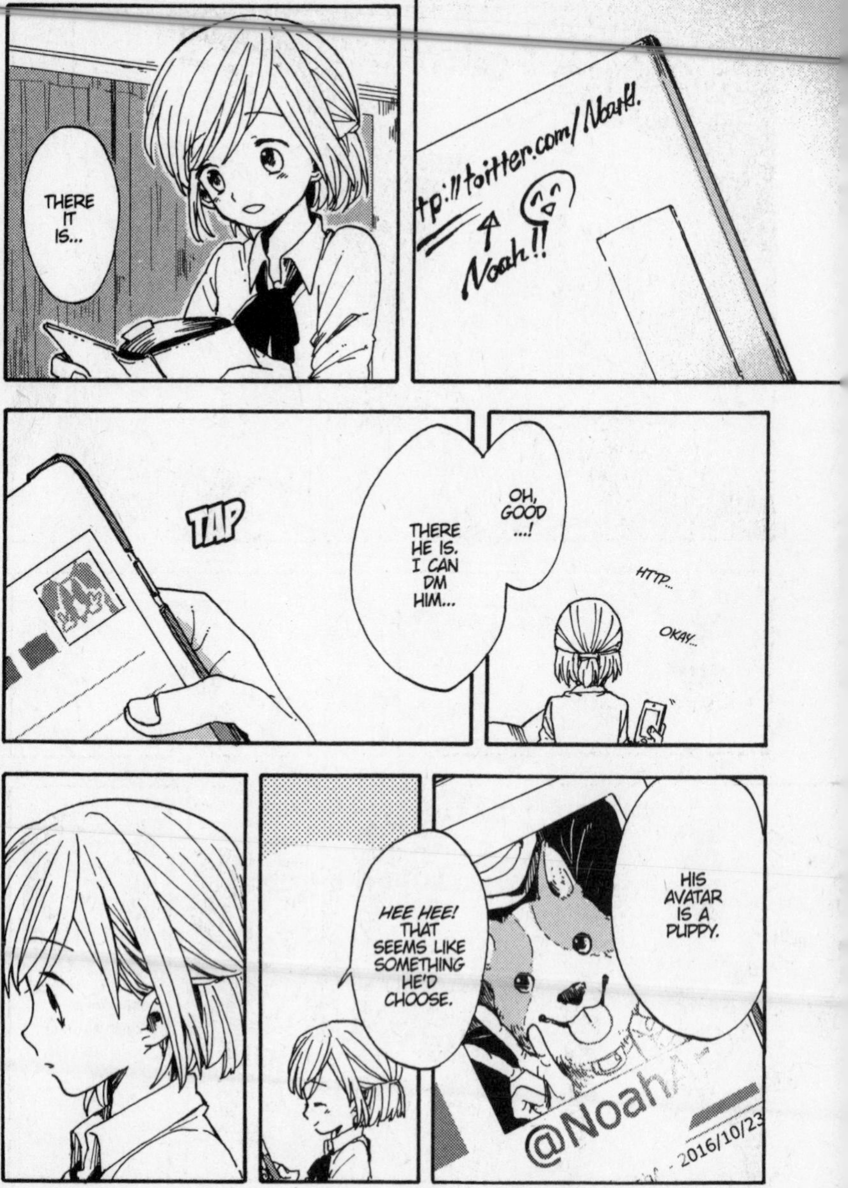
tp://toitter.com/Noah1.
Noah!!
THERE IT IS...
OH, GOOD ...!
THERE HE IS. I CAN DM HIM...
HTTP...
OKAY...
TAP
HIS AVATAR IS A PUPPY.
@Noah
2016/10/23
HEE HEE! THAT SEEMS LIKE SOMETHING HE'D CHOOSE.

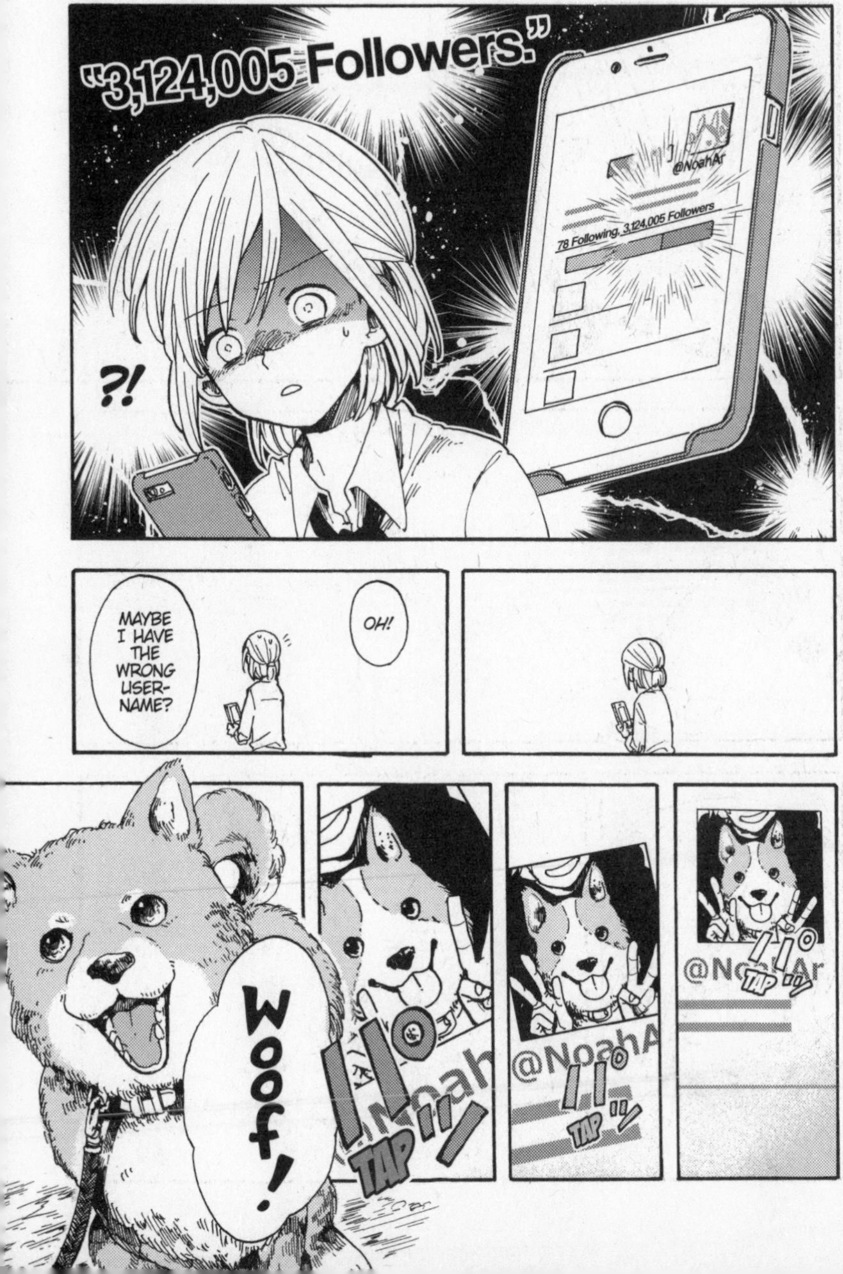
"3,124,005 Followers."
@NoahAr
78 Following, 3,124,005 Followers
?!
OH!
MAYBE I HAVE THE WRONG USER-NAME?
@NoahAr
TAP
@NoahA
TAP
@Noah
TAP
Woof!

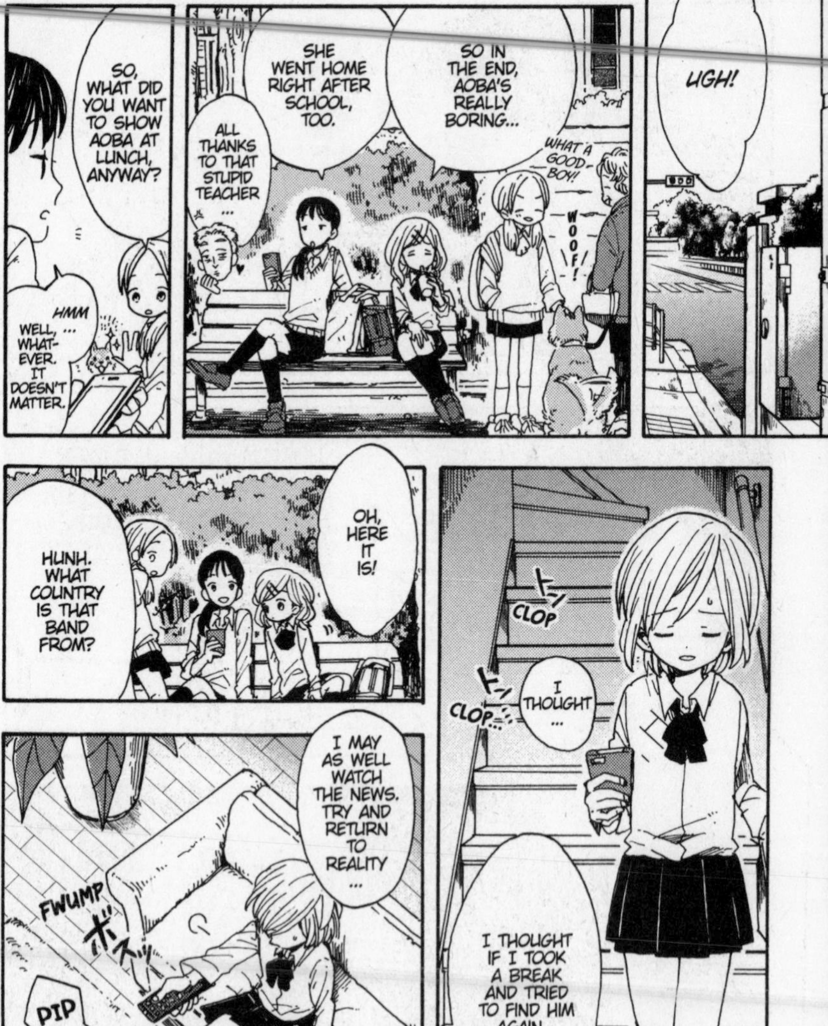
UGH!
SO IN THE END, AOBA'S REALLY BORING...
SHE WENT HOME RIGHT AFTER SCHOOL, TOO.
ALL THANKS TO THAT STUPID TEACHER ...
WHAT A GOOD BOY!
WOOF!
SO, WHAT DID YOU WANT TO SHOW AOBA AT LUNCH, ANYWAY?
HMM
WELL, ... WHATEVER. IT DOESN'T MATTER.
CLOP
CLOP...
I THOUGHT ...
I THOUGHT IF I TOOK A BREAK AND TRIED TO FIND HIM AGAIN...
MUTTER
I GUESS IT WOULDN'T BE THAT EASY, HUH?
MUTTER
OH, HERE IT IS!
HUNH. WHAT COUNTRY IS THAT BAND FROM?
I MAY AS WELL WATCH THE NEWS. TRY AND RETURN TO REALITY ...
FWUMP
ボスッ
PIP

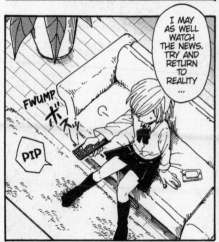

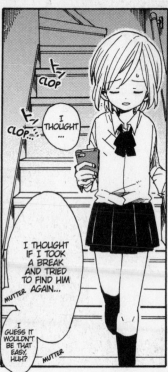

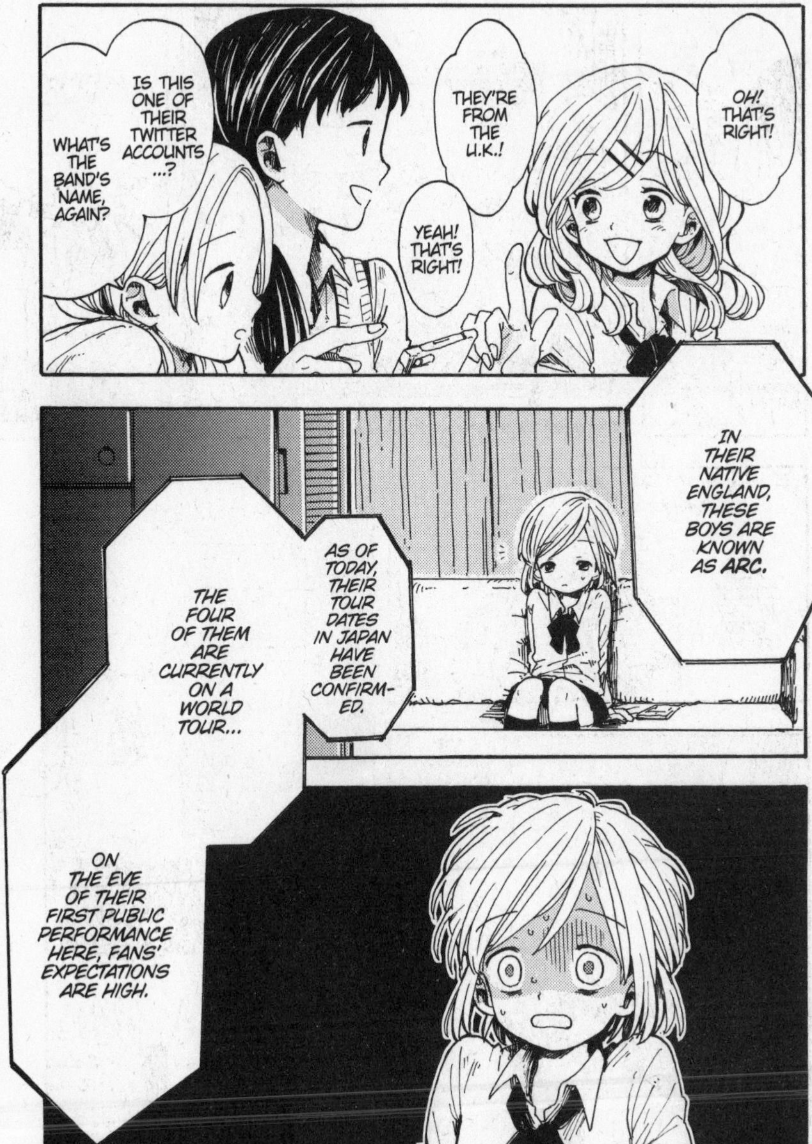
OH! THAT'S RIGHT!
THEY'RE FROM THE U.K.!
YEAH! THAT'S RIGHT!
IS THIS ONE OF THEIR TWITTER ACCOUNTS ...?
WHAT'S THE BAND'S NAME, AGAIN?
IN THEIR NATIVE ENGLAND, THESE BOYS ARE KNOWN AS ARC.
AS OF TODAY, THEIR TOUR DATES IN JAPAN HAVE BEEN CONFIRM-ED.
THE FOUR OF THEM ARE CURRENTLY ON A WORLD TOUR...
ON THE EVE OF THEIR FIRST PUBLIC PERFORMANCE HERE, FANS' EXPECTATIONS ARE HIGH.

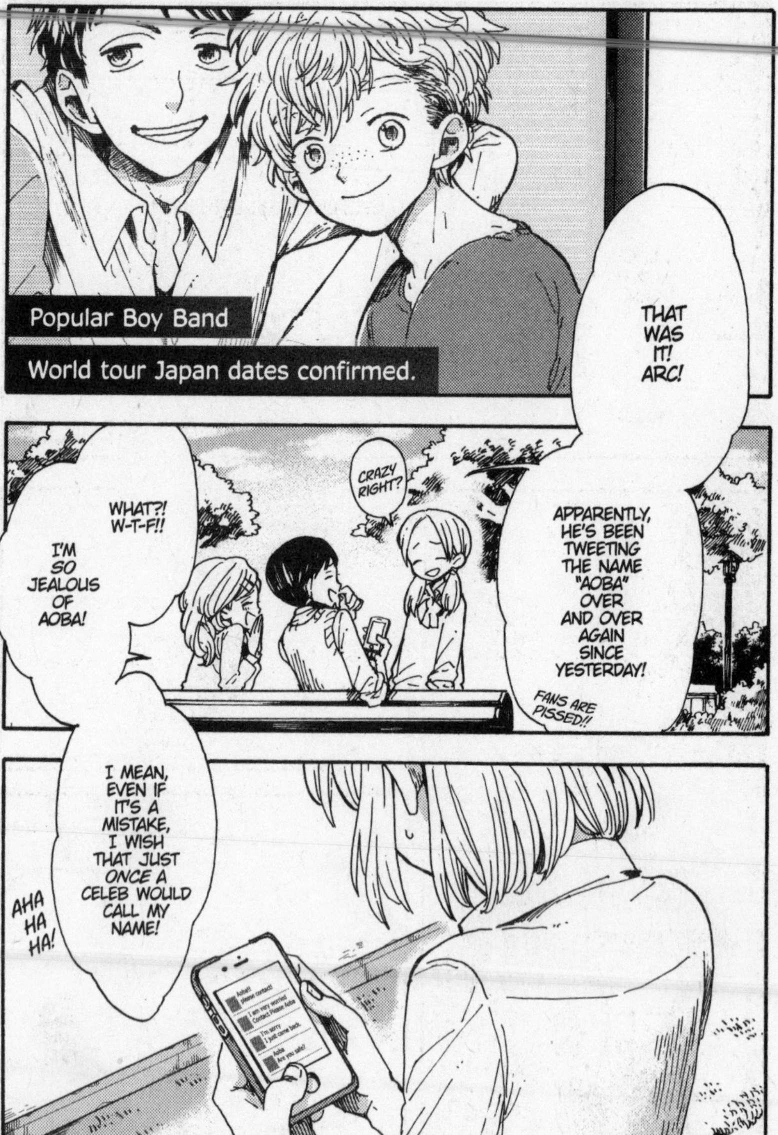
Popular Boy Band
World tour Japan dates confirmed.
THAT WAS IT! ARC!
APPARENTLY, HE'S BEEN TWEETING THE NAME "AOBA" OVER AND OVER AGAIN SINCE YESTERDAY!
FANS ARE PISSED!!
CRAZY RIGHT?
WHAT?! W-T-F!!
I'M SO JEALOUS OF AOBA!
I MEAN, EVEN IF IT'S A MISTAKE, I WISH THAT JUST ONCE A CELEB WOULD CALL MY NAME!
AHA HA HA!
Aoba!! please contact!
I am very worried Contact Please Aoba
I'm sorry I just came back.
Aoba Are you safe?

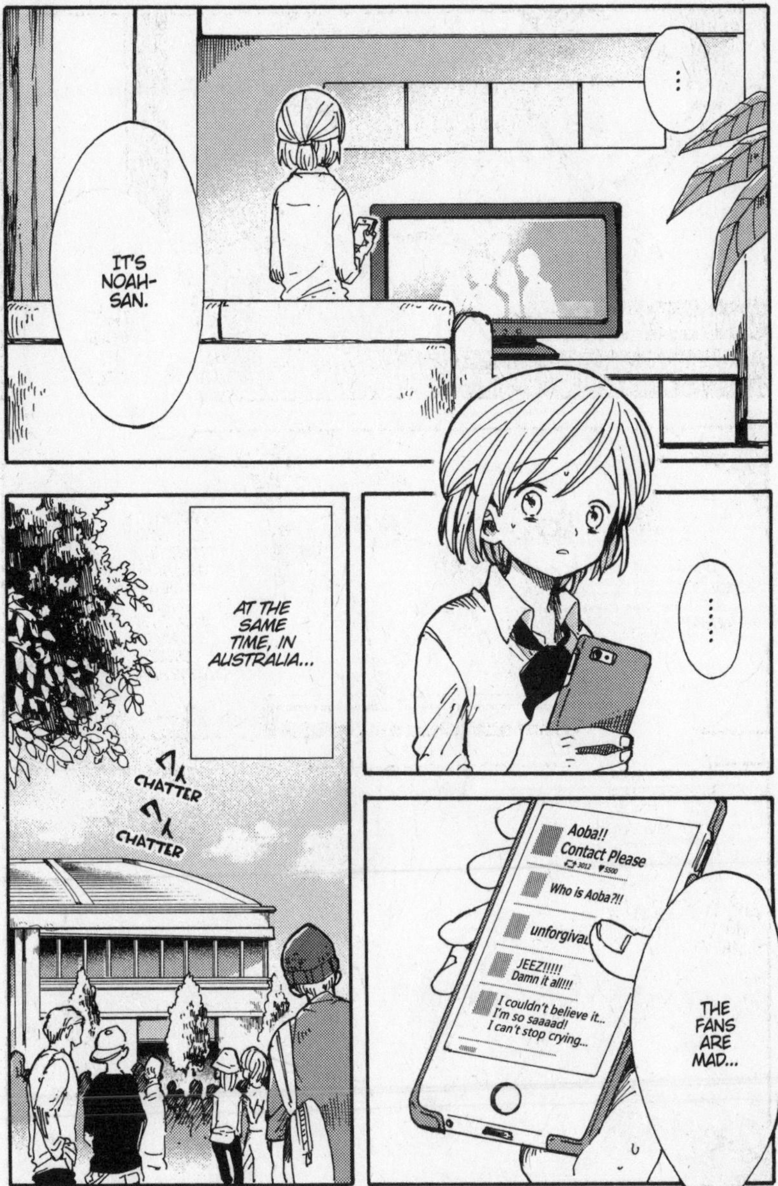

…
IT'S NOAH-SAN.
……
Aoba!! Contact Please
3012
5500
Who is Aoba?!!
unforgiva
JEEZ!!!!! Damn it all!!!
I couldn't believe it.. I'm so saaaad! I can't stop crying...
THE FANS ARE MAD...
AT THE SAME TIME, IN AUSTRALIA...
CHATTER
CHATTER

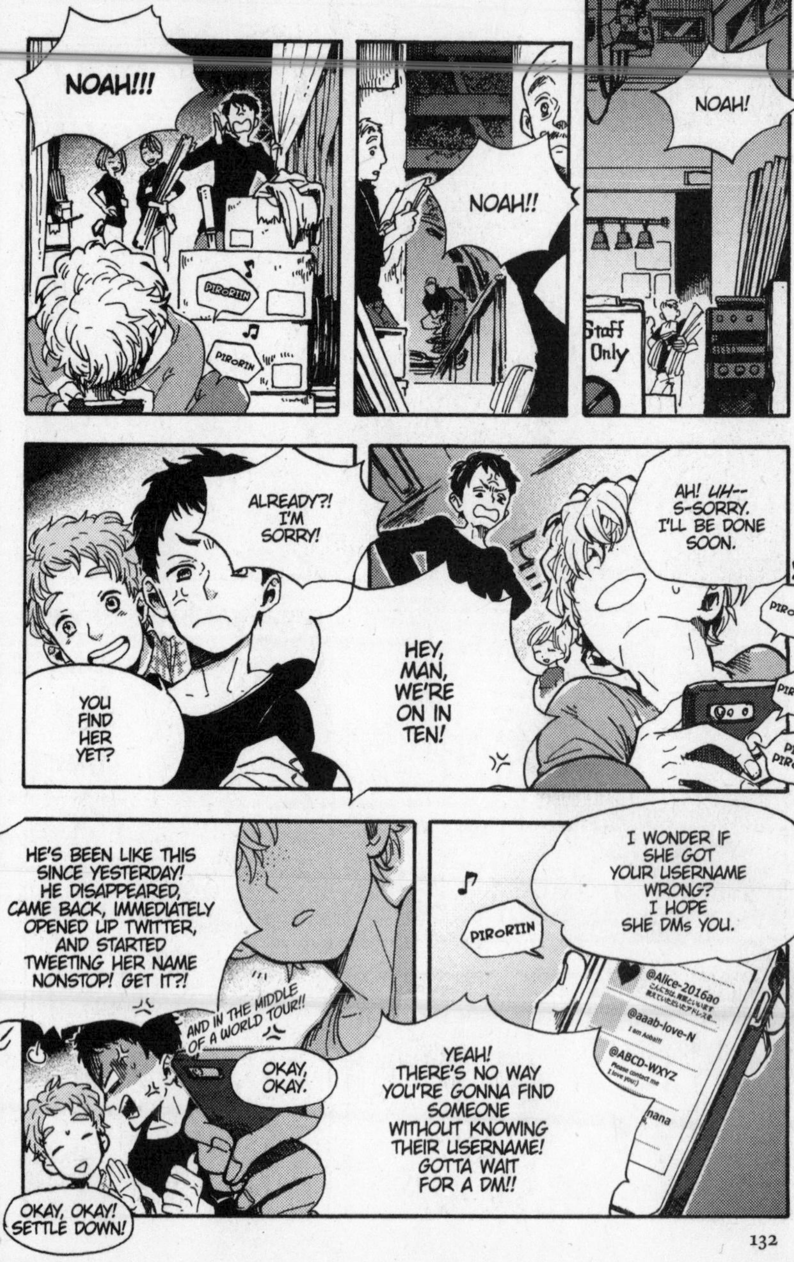
NOAH!!!
PIRORIIN
PIRORIN
NOAH!!
NOAH!
Staff Only
ALREADY?! I'M SORRY!
YOU FIND HER YET?
HEY, MAN, WE'RE ON IN TEN!
AH! UH-- S-SORRY. I'LL BE DONE SOON.
PIRORIIN
PIRORIIIN
PIPIPI PIRORIIN
HE'S BEEN LIKE THIS SINCE YESTERDAY! HE DISAPPEARED, CAME BACK, IMMEDIATELY OPENED UP TWITTER, AND STARTED TWEETING HER NAME NONSTOP! GET IT?!
AND IN THE MIDDLE OF A WORLD TOUR!!
OKAY, OKAY.
OKAY, OKAY! SETTLE DOWN!
PIRORIIN
I WONDER IF SHE GOT YOUR USERNAME WRONG? I HOPE SHE DMs YOU.
@Alice-2016ao
@aaab-love-N
@ABCD-WXYZ
nana
YEAH! THERE'S NO WAY YOU'RE GONNA FIND SOMEONE WITHOUT KNOWING THEIR USERNAME! GOTTA WAIT FOR A DM!!

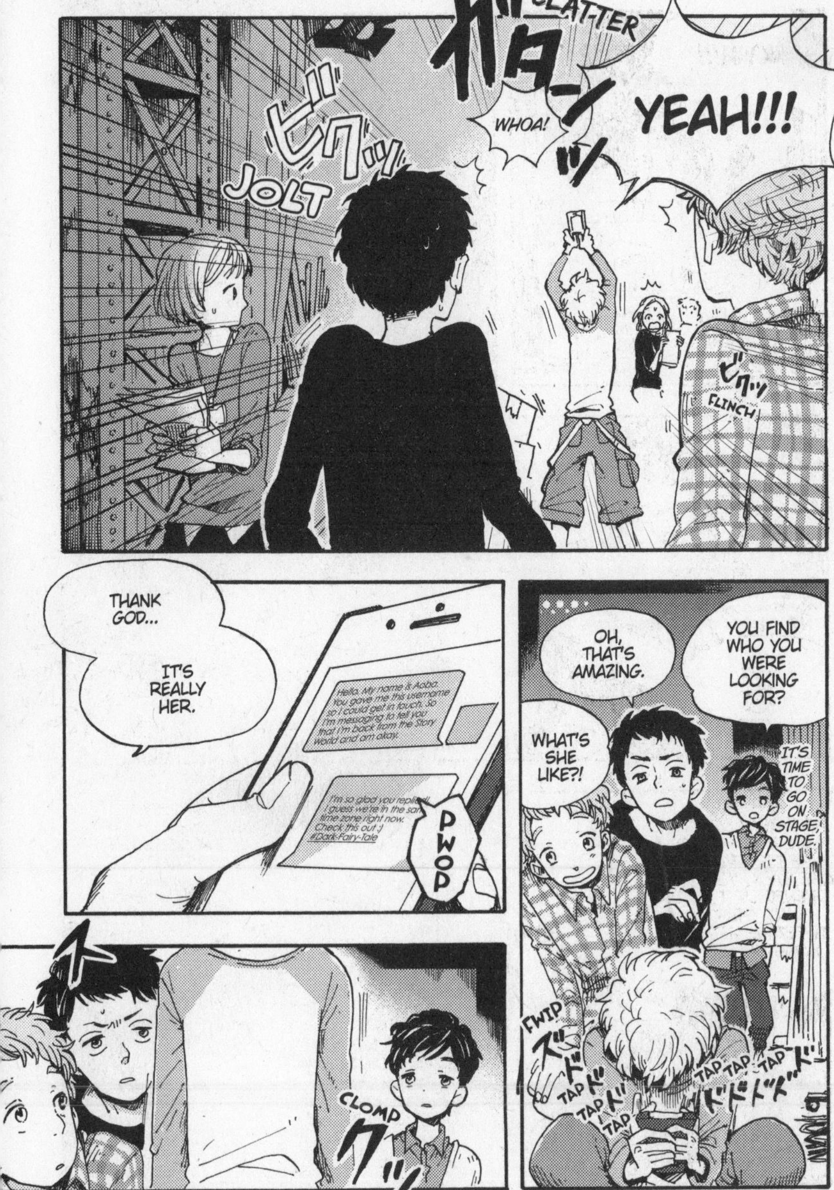
CLATTER
WHOA!
YEAH!!!
JOLT
FLINCH
YOU FIND WHO YOU WERE LOOKING FOR?
OH, THAT'S AMAZING.
WHAT'S SHE LIKE?!
IT'S TIME TO GO ON STAGE, DUDE.
FWIP
TAP TAP TAP TAP TAP TAP
THANK GOD...
IT'S REALLY HER.
Hello. My name is Aoba. You gave me this username so I could get in touch. So I'm messaging to tell you that I'm back from the Story World and am okay.
I'm so glad you repli
I guess we're in the sa
time zone right now.
Check this out :)
#Dark-Fairy-Tale
PWOP
CLOMP

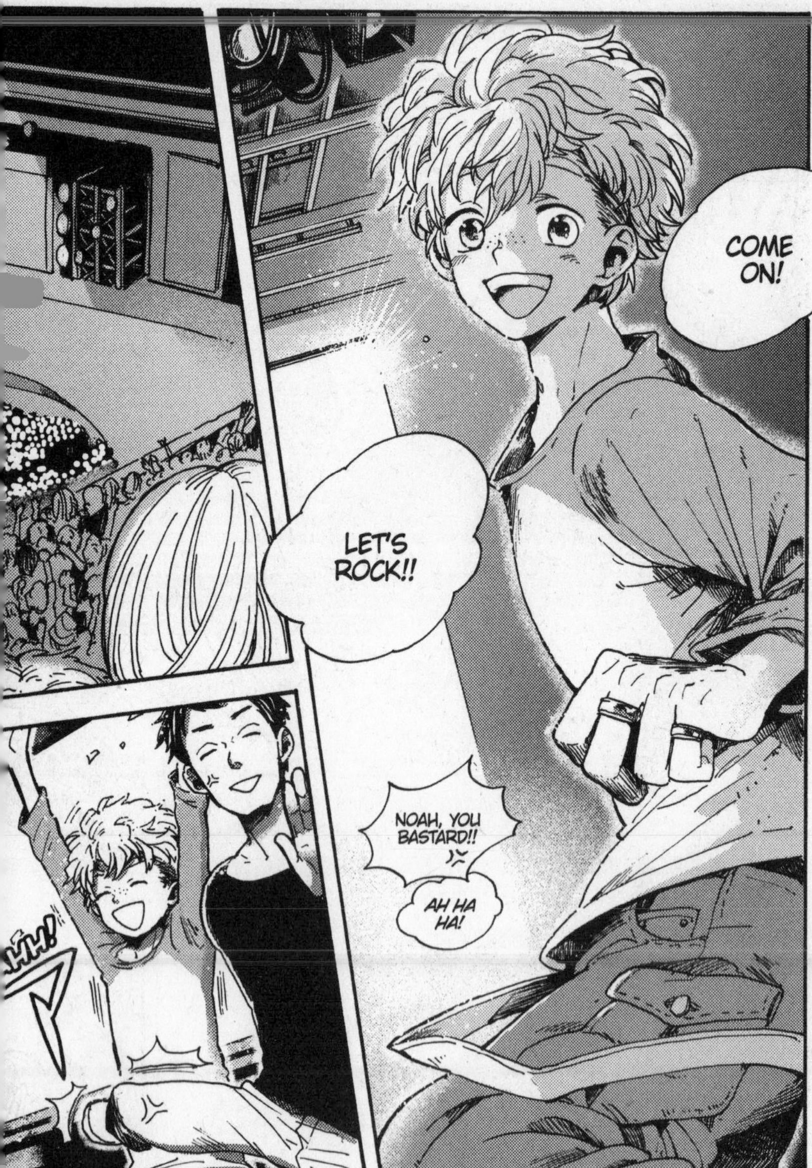
COME ON!
LET'S ROCK!!
NOAH, YOU BASTARD!!
AH HA HA!

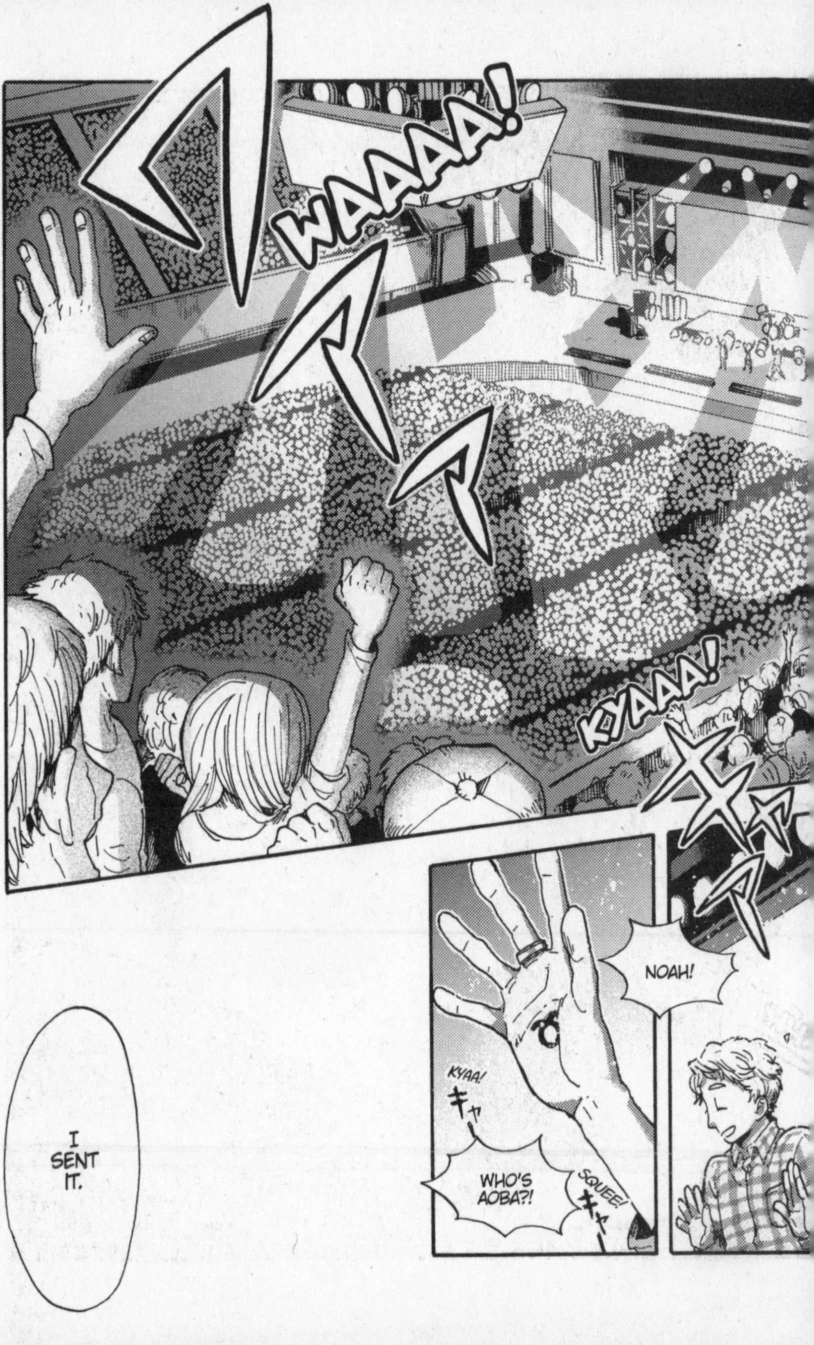
WAAAA!
KYAAA!
NOAH!
KYAA!
キャ
WHO'S AOBA?!
SQUEE!
キャ
I SENT IT.

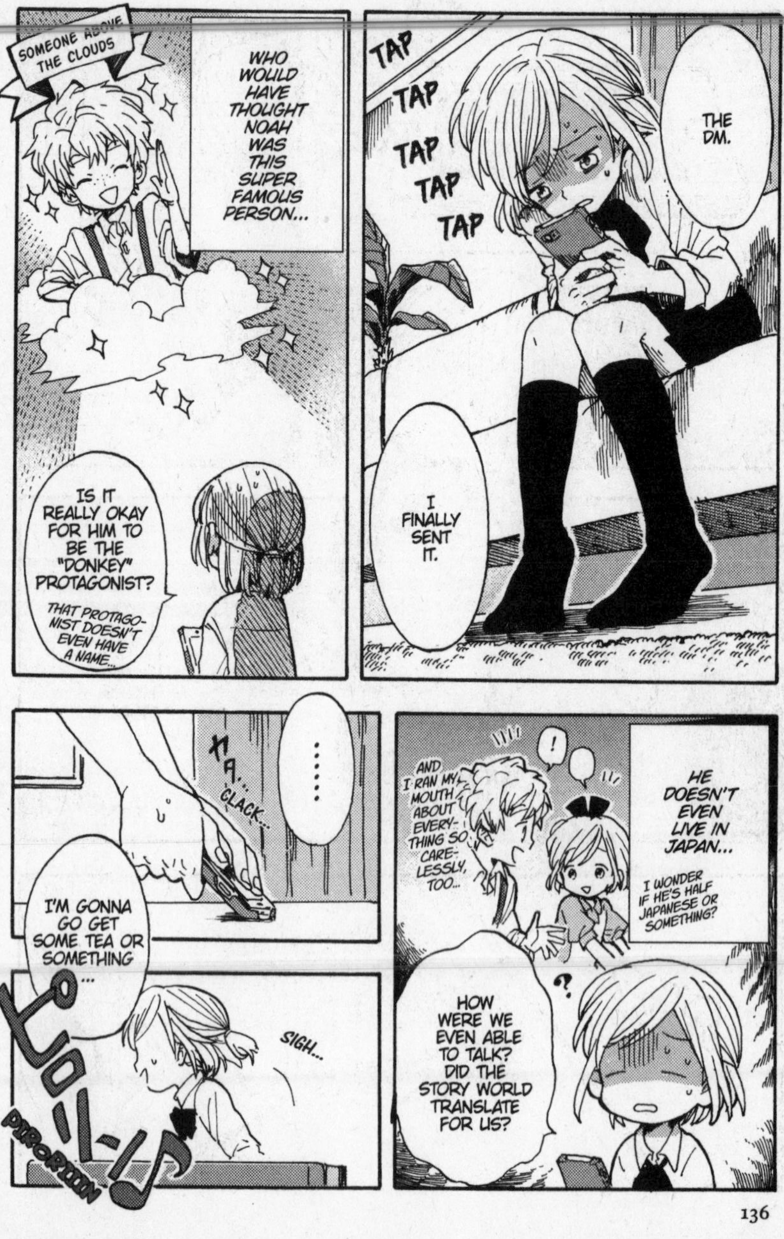
TAP TAP TAP TAP TAP
THE DM.
I FINALLY SENT IT.
SOMEONE ABOVE THE CLOUDS
WHO WOULD HAVE THOUGHT NOAH WAS THIS SUPER FAMOUS PERSON...
IS IT REALLY OKAY FOR HIM TO BE THE "DONKEY" PROTAGONIST?
THAT PROTAGONIST DOESN'T EVEN HAVE A NAME...
HE DOESN'T EVEN LIVE IN JAPAN...
I WONDER IF HE'S HALF JAPANESE OR SOMETHING?
!
AND I RAN MY MOUTH ABOUT EVERYTHING SO CARELESSLY, TOO...
?
HOW WERE WE EVEN ABLE TO TALK? DID THE STORY WORLD TRANSLATE FOR US?
......
CLACK...
I'M GONNA GO GET SOME TEA OR SOMETHING...
SIGH...
PIROPIIIN

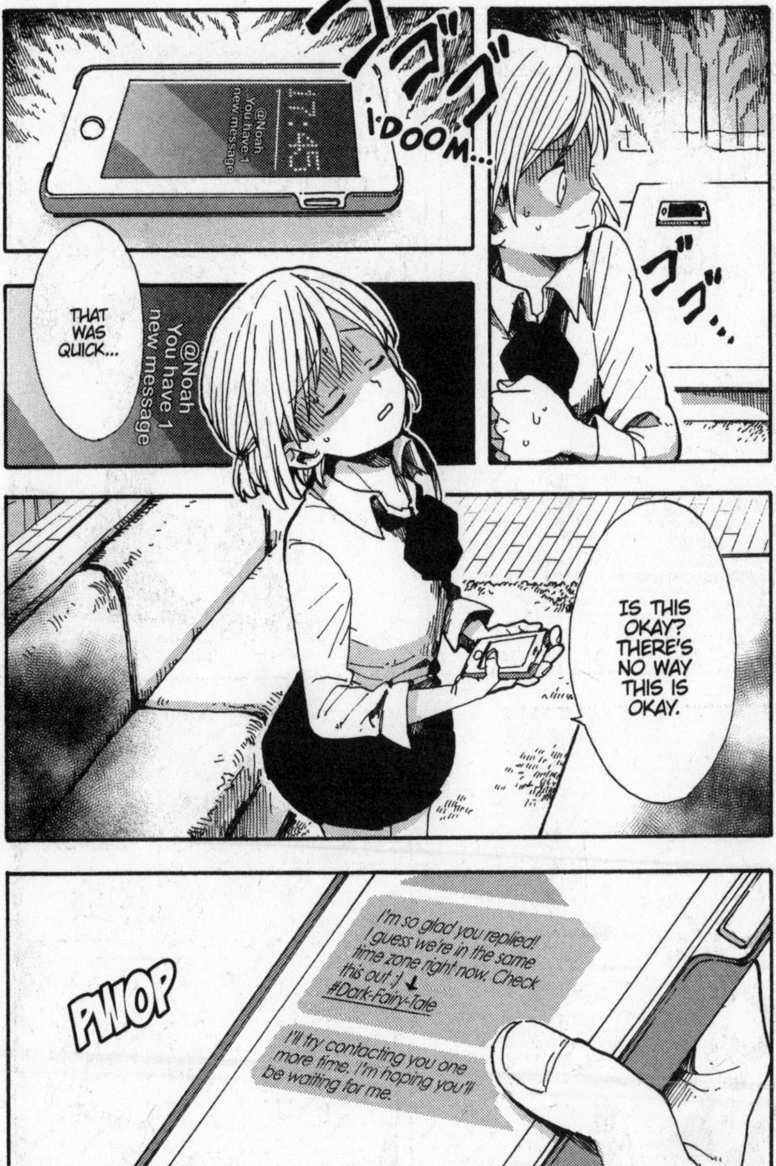
ゴゴゴ
DOOM...
17:45
@Noah
You have 1
new message
ゴゴ...
THAT WAS QUICK...
@Noah
You have 1
new message
IS THIS OKAY? THERE'S NO WAY THIS IS OKAY.
I'm so glad you replied! I guess we're in the same time zone right now. Check this out ♪
#Dark-Fairy-Tale
I'll try contacting you one more time, I'm hoping you'll be waiting for me.
PWOP

OH!

HE WROTE BACK IN JAPANESE!

MAYBE IT WOULD'VE BEEN BETTER IF I'D WRITTEN IN ENGLISH...

I WAS BEING TOO CAREFUL, I GUESS...

...?

A HASH-TAG?

...so glad you [...] I guess we're [in] the same time zone right now. Check this out :) ↓ #Dark-Fairy-Tale

I'm so glad that you replied I guess we're in th[e] same ti[me zone] right [now] Chec[k] #Da[rk]

TAP

PWOP

@Taaa0_ppp
I'll never go back there a[ga]in... It's c[r]eepy.
#Dark-Fairy-Tale

@mmoops-010
我很高兴回来。
口是怎么回事？口勿触摸口惊…
#Dark-Fairy-Tale

@Oniku-daisuki
Other people are in this same situation.
What a relief...
#Dark-Fairy-Tale

@p-p-p-777

138

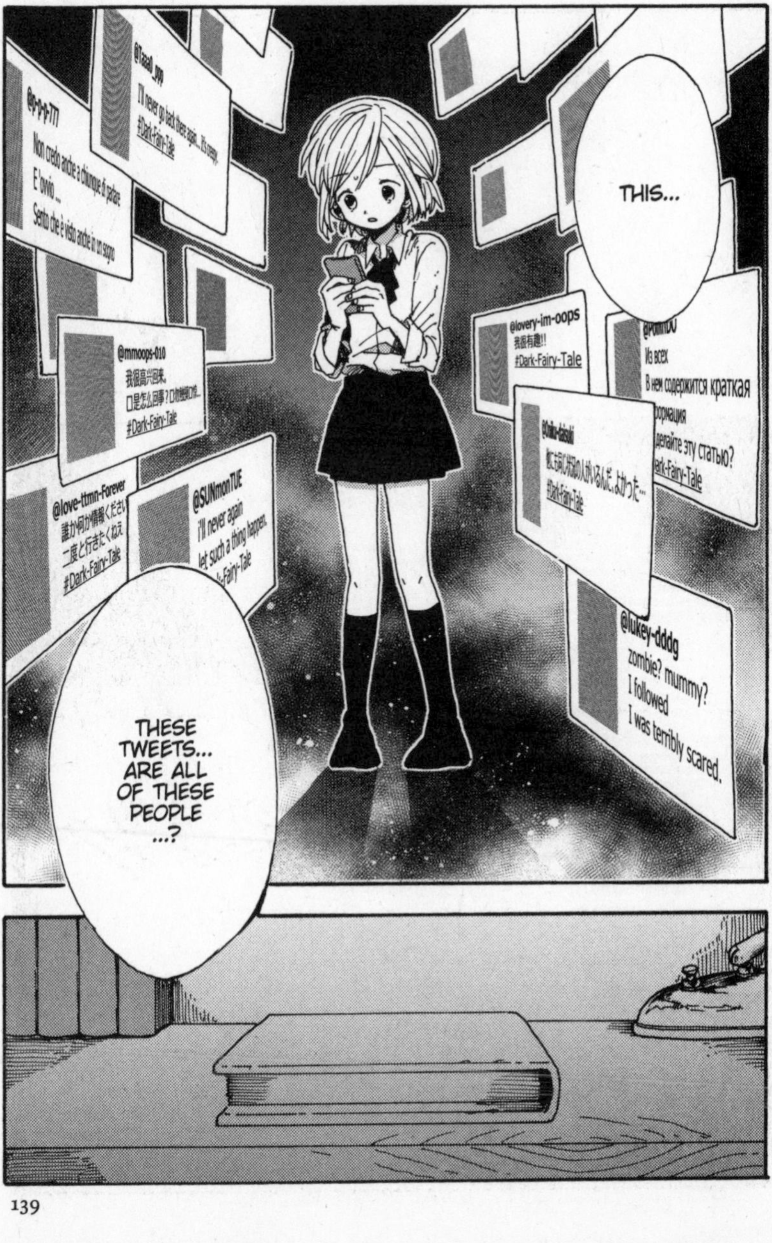
THIS...
THESE TWEETS... ARE ALL OF THESE PEOPLE ...?
@Taaa0_ppp
I'll never go back there again... it's creepy.
#Dark-Fairy-Tale
Non credo anche a chiunque di parlare
E' ovvio ...
Sento che è visto anche in un sogno
@mmoops-010
#Dark-Fairy-Tale
@love-ttmn-Forever
#Dark-Fairy-Tale
@SUNmonTUE
I'll never again
let such a thing happen.
@lovery-im-oops
我很有趣!!
#Dark-Fairy-Tale
Из всех
В нем содержится краткая
#Dark-Fairy-Tale
zombie? mummy?
I followed
I was terribly scared.

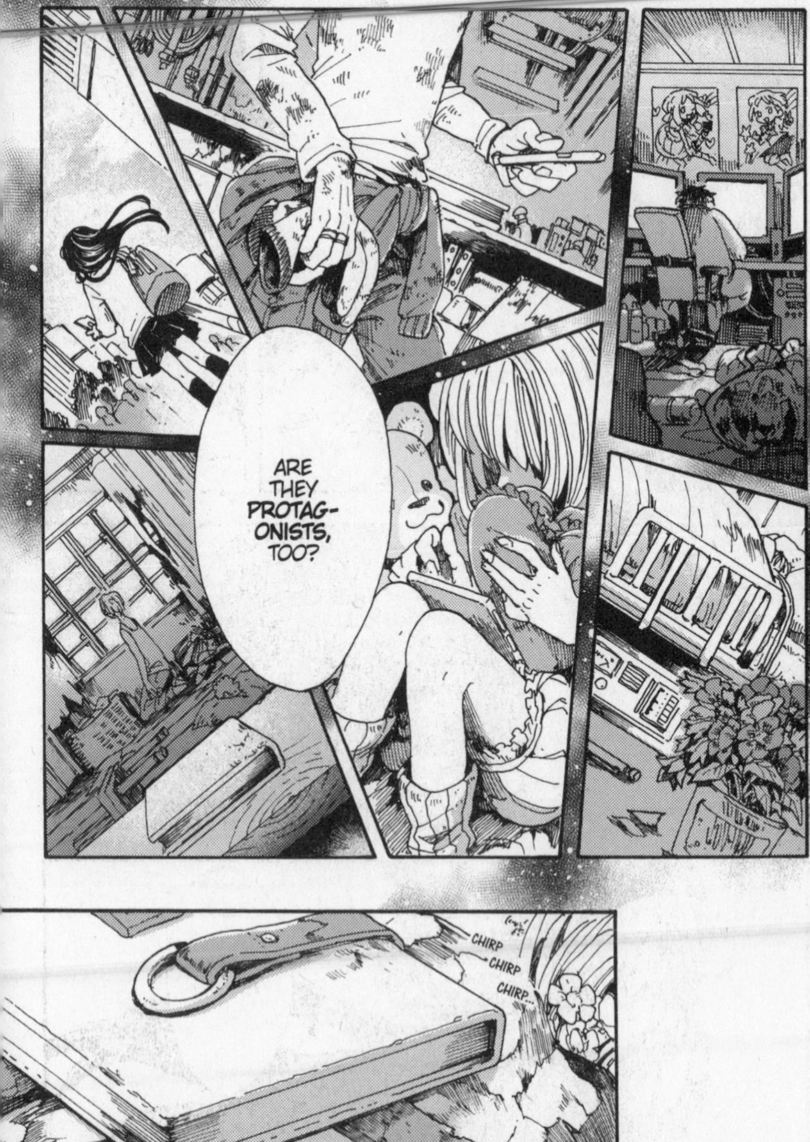
ARE THEY PROTAG-ONISTS, TOO?
CHIRP
CHIRP
CHIRP...

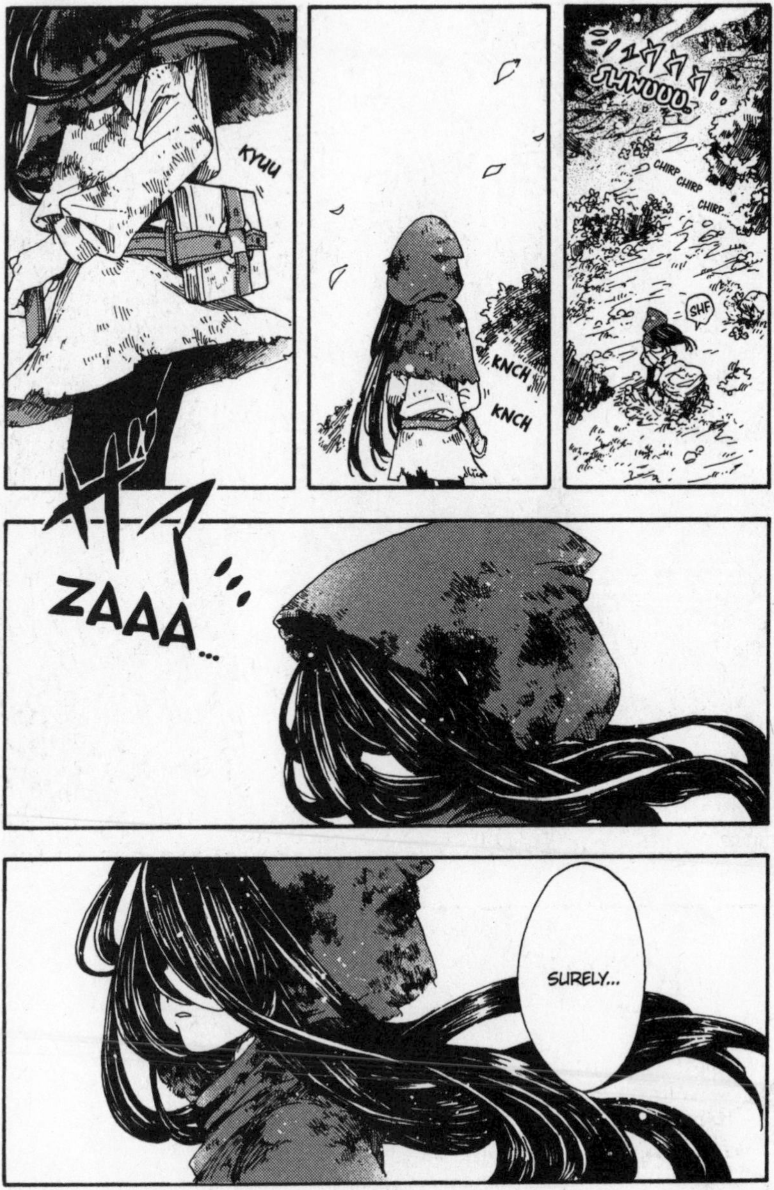
SHWUUU...
CHIRP CHIRP
CHIRP...
SHF
KNCH
KNCH
KYUU
ZAAA...
SURELY...

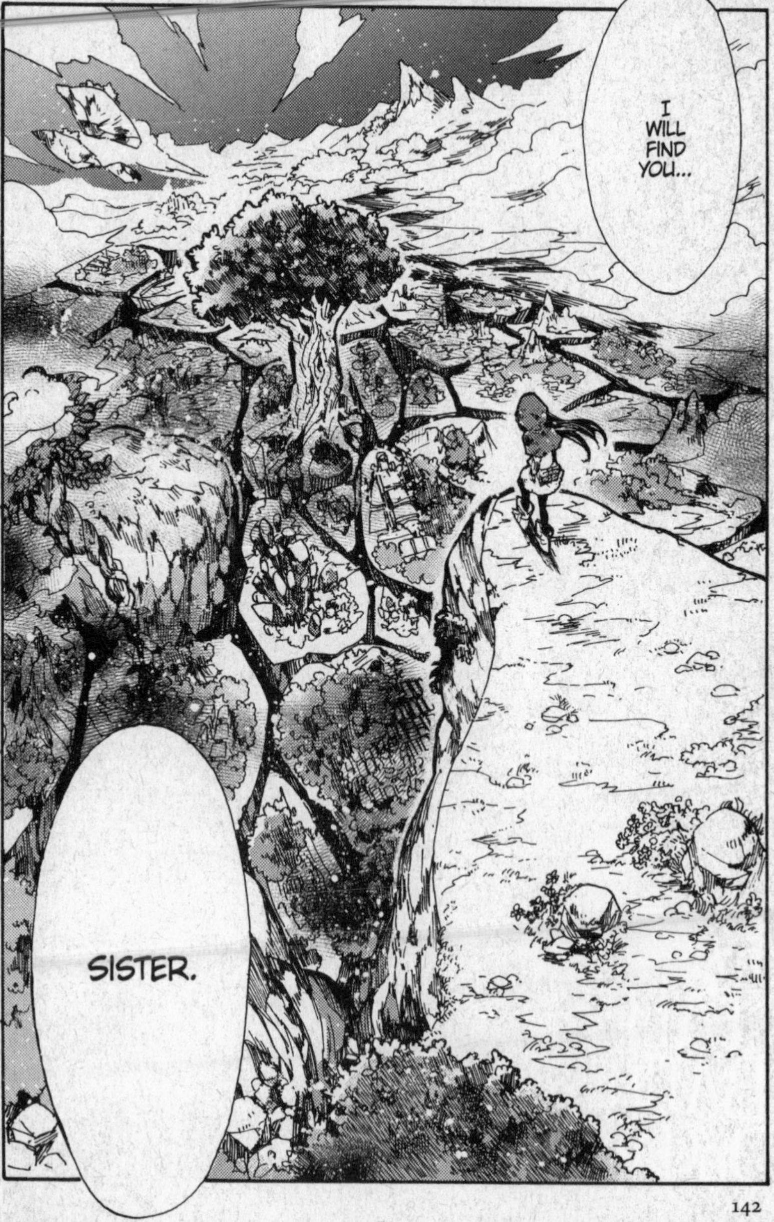
I WILL FIND YOU...
SISTER.

FAIRY
TALE
BATTLE
ROYALE

FAIRY
TALE
BATTLE
ROYALE

Extras

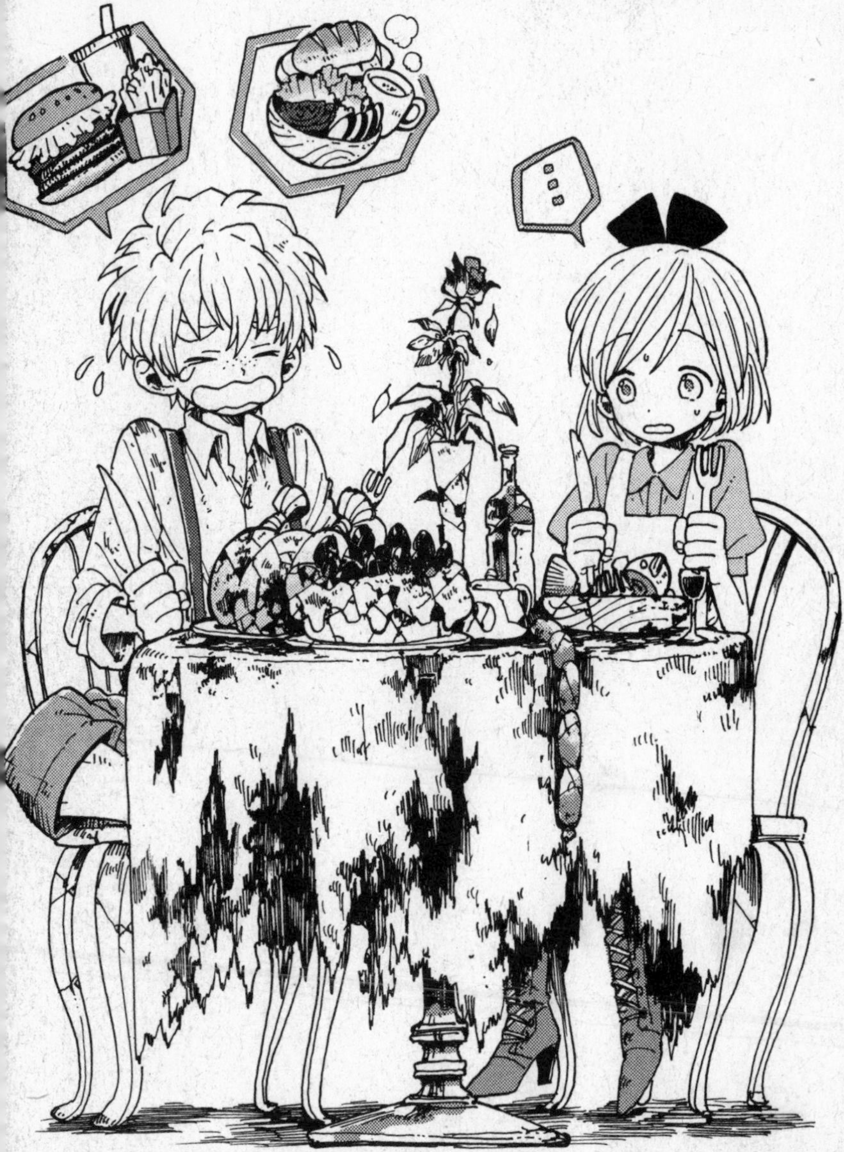
...

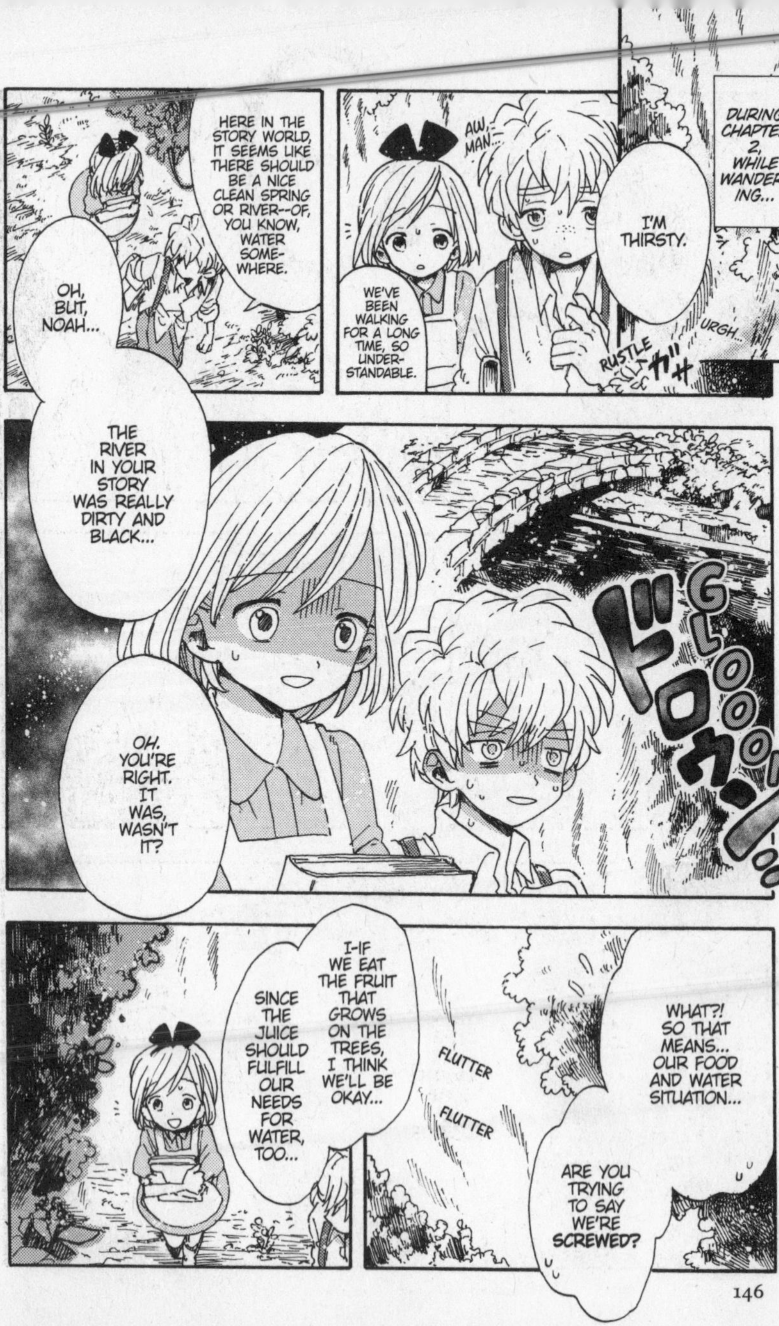
DURING CHAPTER 2, WHILE WANDERING...
I'M THIRSTY.
URGH...
RUSTLE
AW, MAN...
WE'VE BEEN WALKING FOR A LONG TIME, SO UNDERSTANDABLE.
HERE IN THE STORY WORLD, IT SEEMS LIKE THERE SHOULD BE A NICE CLEAN SPRING OR RIVER--OF, YOU KNOW, WATER SOMEWHERE.
OH, BUT, NOAH...
THE RIVER IN YOUR STORY WAS REALLY DIRTY AND BLACK...
GLOOOOOM...
OH. YOU'RE RIGHT. IT WAS, WASN'T IT?
WHAT?! SO THAT MEANS... OUR FOOD AND WATER SITUATION...
ARE YOU TRYING TO SAY WE'RE SCREWED?
FLUTTER
FLUTTER
I-IF WE EAT THE FRUIT THAT GROWS ON THE TREES, I THINK WE'LL BE OKAY...
SINCE THE JUICE SHOULD FULFILL OUR NEEDS FOR WATER, TOO...

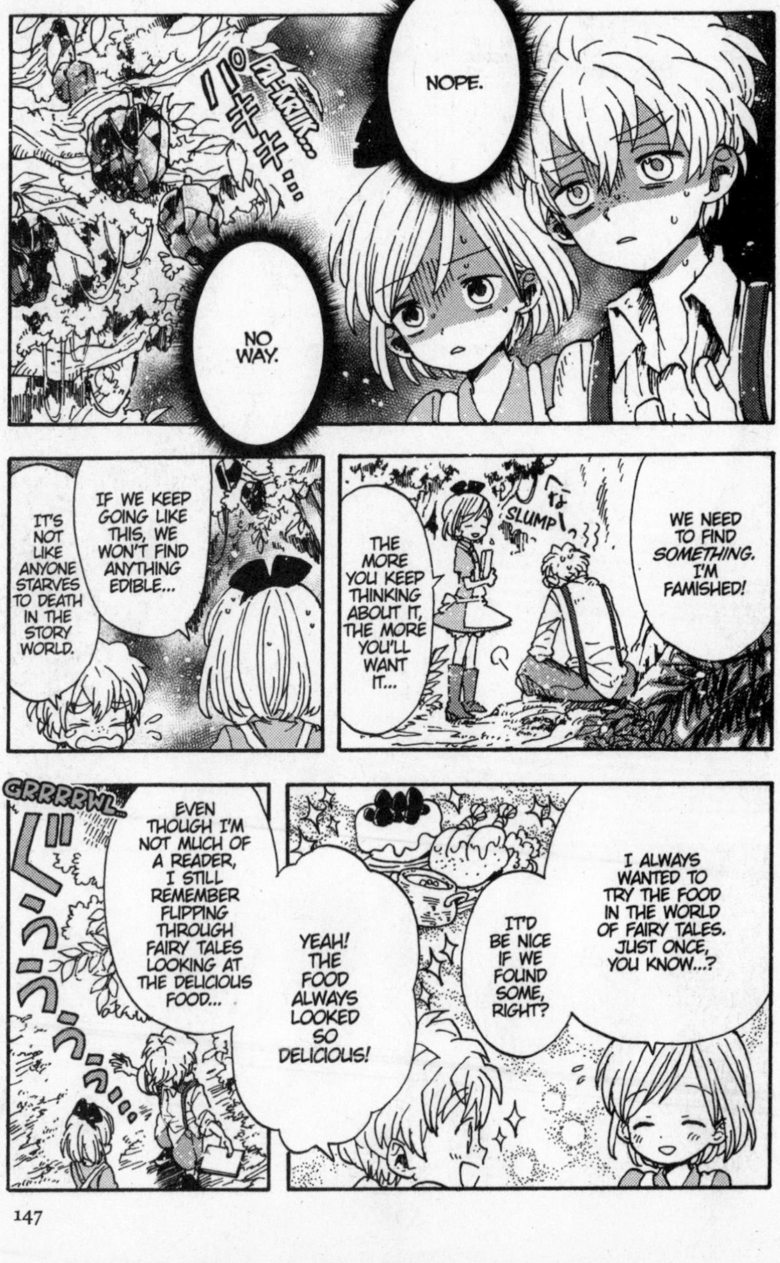
NOPE.
NO WAY.
PA-KRIIK...
パキキ...
SLUMP
WE NEED TO FIND *SOMETHING.* I'M FAMISHED!
THE MORE YOU KEEP THINKING ABOUT IT, THE MORE YOU'LL WANT IT...
IF WE KEEP GOING LIKE THIS, WE WON'T FIND ANYTHING EDIBLE...
IT'S NOT LIKE ANYONE STARVES TO DEATH IN THE STORY WORLD.
I ALWAYS WANTED TO TRY THE FOOD IN THE WORLD OF FAIRY TALES. JUST ONCE, YOU KNOW...?
IT'D BE NICE IF WE FOUND SOME, RIGHT?
YEAH! THE FOOD ALWAYS LOOKED SO DELICIOUS!
EVEN THOUGH I'M NOT MUCH OF A READER, I STILL REMEMBER FLIPPING THROUGH FAIRY TALES LOOKING AT THE DELICIOUS FOOD...
GRRRRWL...

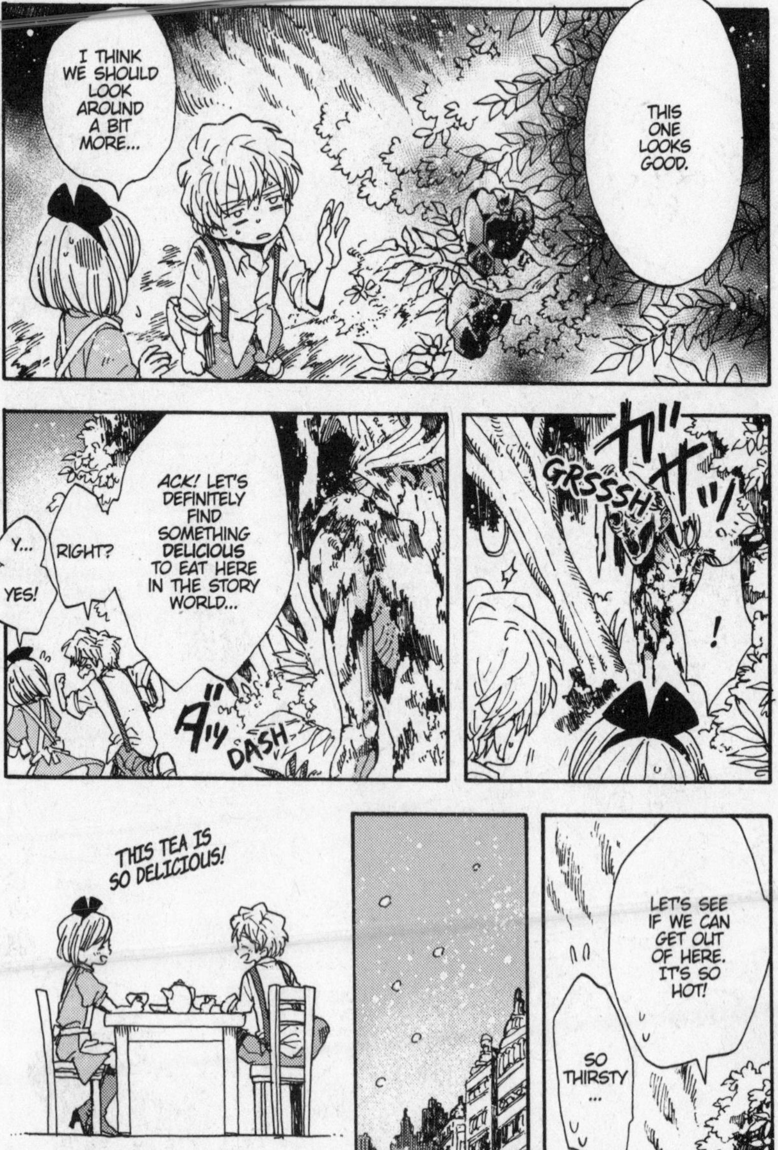
THIS ONE LOOKS GOOD.
I THINK WE SHOULD LOOK AROUND A BIT MORE...
GRSSSH
!
ACK! LET'S DEFINITELY FIND SOMETHING DELICIOUS TO EAT HERE IN THE STORY WORLD...
RIGHT?
Y... YES!
DASH
LET'S SEE IF WE CAN GET OUT OF HERE. IT'S SO HOT!
SO THIRSTY ...
THIS TEA IS SO DELICIOUS!

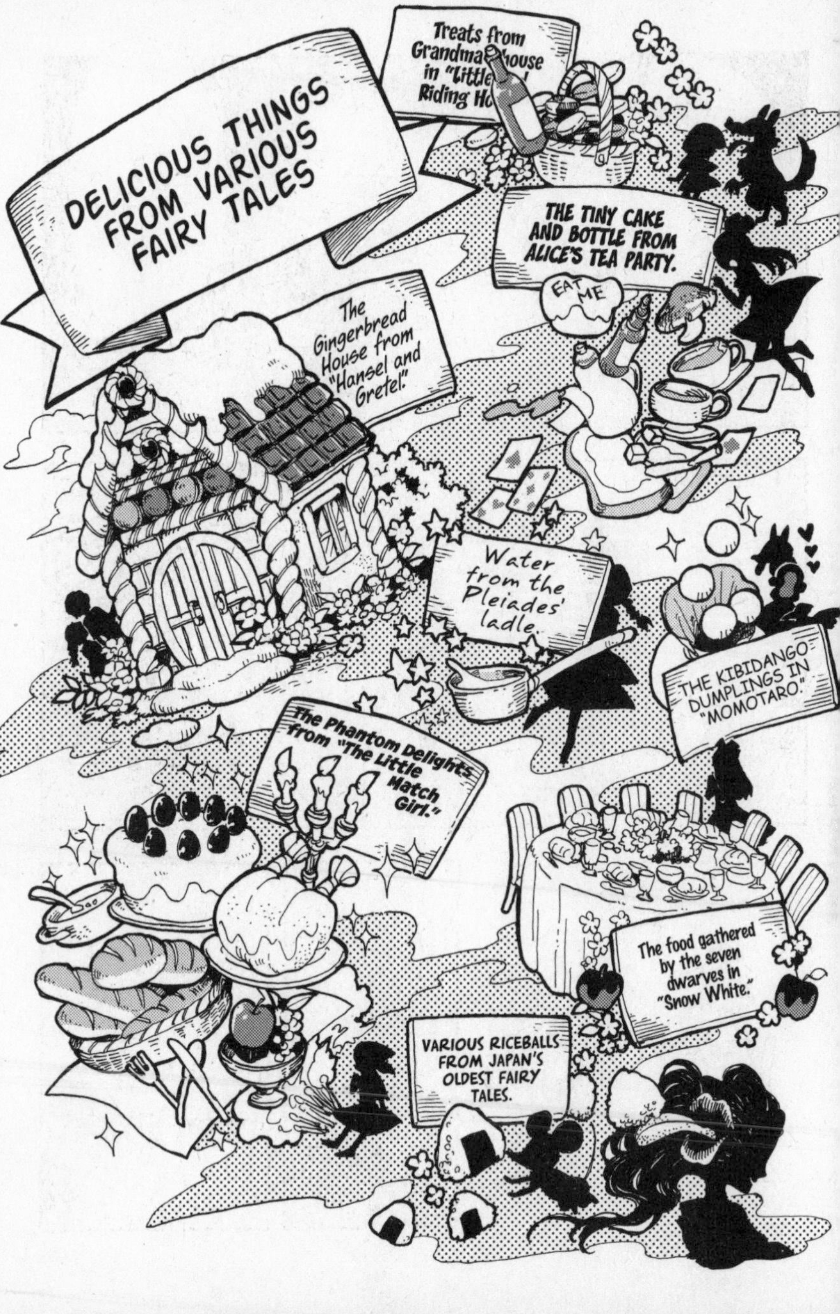
DELICIOUS THINGS FROM VARIOUS FAIRY TALES
Treats from Grandma's House in "Little Red Riding Hood."
THE TINY CAKE AND BOTTLE FROM ALICE'S TEA PARTY.
EAT ME
The Gingerbread House from "Hansel and Gretel."
Water from the Pleiades' ladle.
THE KIBIDANGO DUMPLINGS IN "MOMOTARO."
The Phantom Delights from "The Little Match Girl."
The food gathered by the seven dwarves in "Snow White."
VARIOUS RICEBALLS FROM JAPAN'S OLDEST FAIRY TALES.

FAIRY TALE BATTLE ROYALE

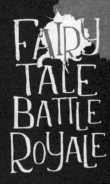

COMEDY SKETCH:

Hang in there, Kuninaka-san!

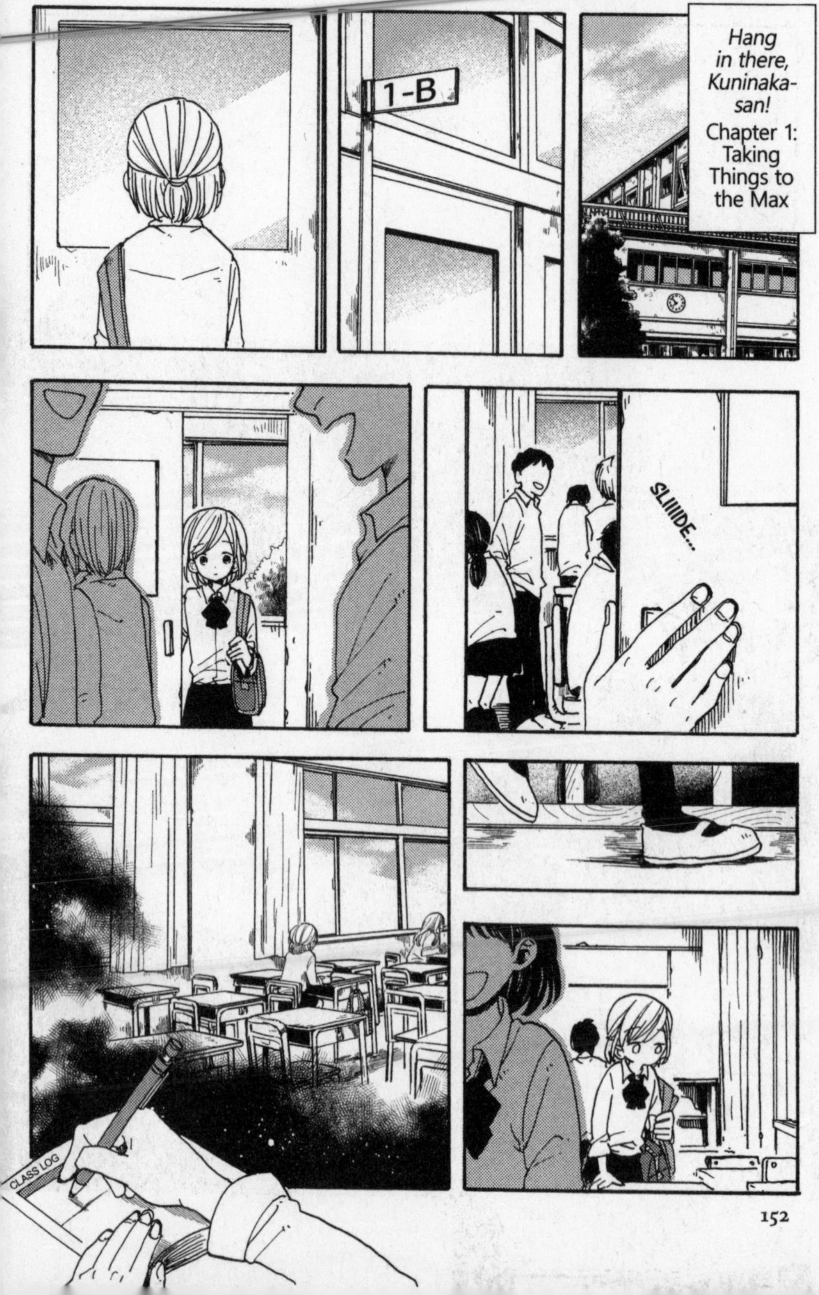
1-B
Hang in there, Kuninaka-san!
Chapter 1: Taking Things to the Max
SLIIIIDE...
CLASS LOG

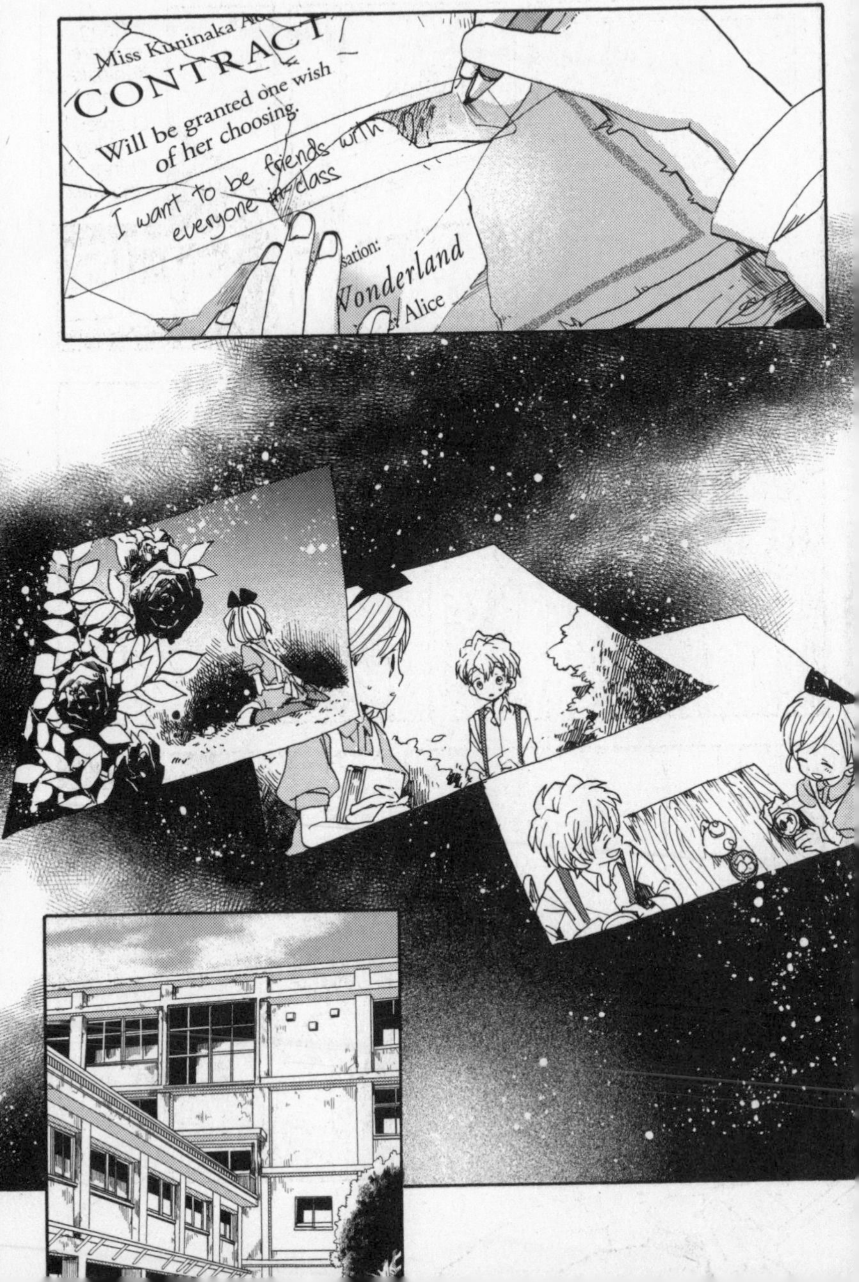
Miss Kuninaka
CONTRACT
Will be granted one wish
of her choosing.
I want to be friends with
everyone in class
Wonderland
Alice

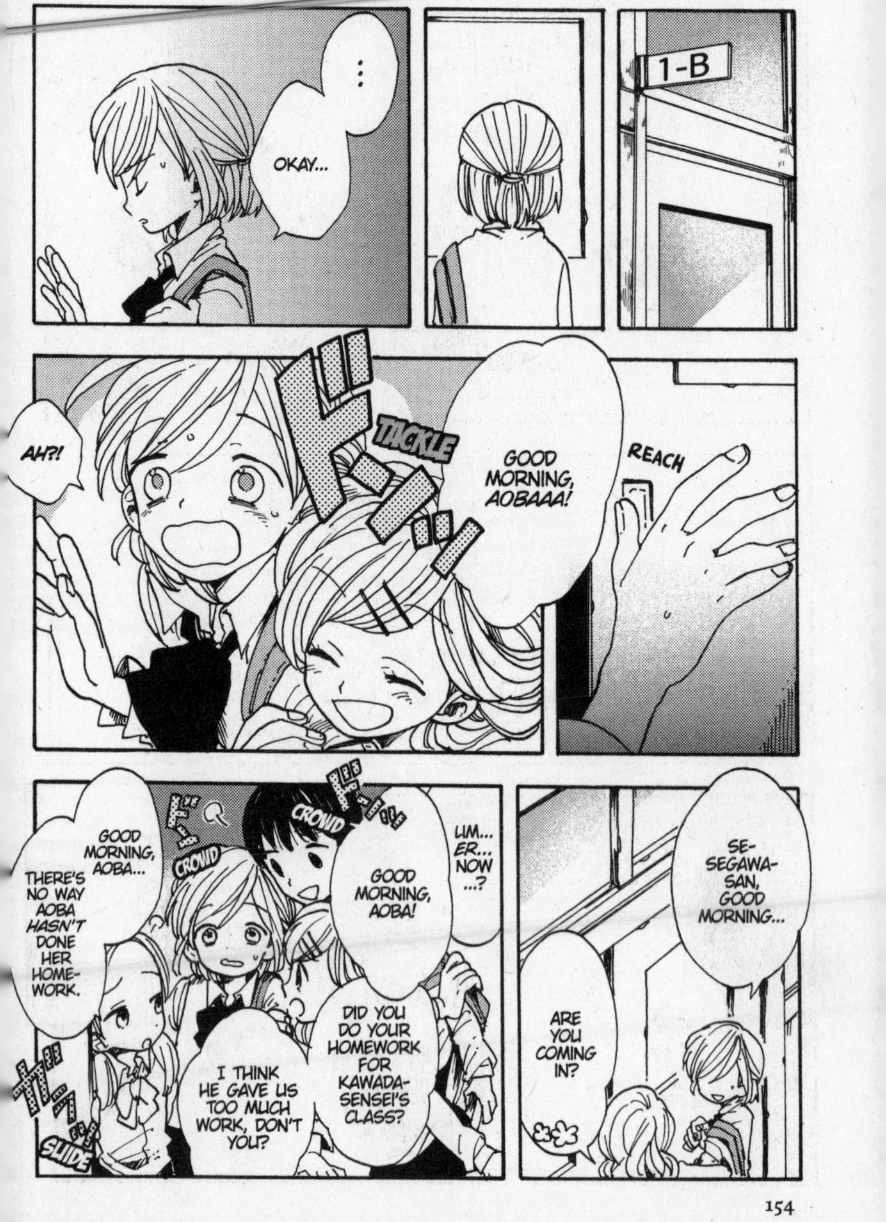
1-B
...
OKAY...
REACH
GOOD MORNING, AOBAAA!
TACKLE
AH?!
SE-SEGAWA-SAN, GOOD MORNING...
ARE YOU COMING IN?
UM... ER... NOW ...?
CROWD
GOOD MORNING, AOBA!
DID YOU DO YOUR HOMEWORK FOR KAWADA-SENSEI'S CLASS?
GOOD MORNING, AOBA...
CROWD
I THINK HE GAVE US TOO MUCH WORK, DON'T YOU?
THERE'S NO WAY AOBA HASN'T DONE HER HOMEWORK.
SLIDE

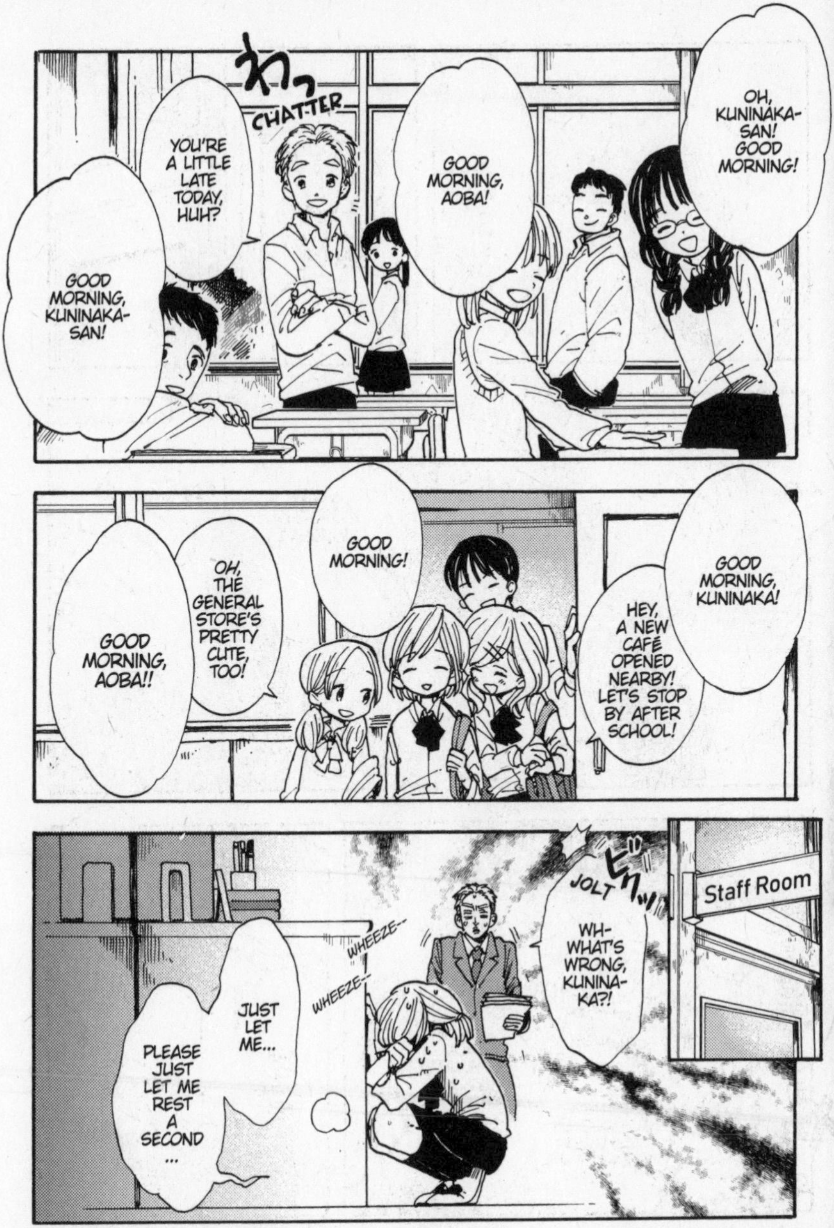
OH, KUNINAKA-SAN! GOOD MORNING!
GOOD MORNING, AOBA!
わっ
CHATTER
YOU'RE A LITTLE LATE TODAY, HUH?
GOOD MORNING, KUNINAKA-SAN!
GOOD MORNING, KUNINAKA!
HEY, A NEW CAFÉ OPENED NEARBY! LET'S STOP BY AFTER SCHOOL!
GOOD MORNING!
OH, THE GENERAL STORE'S PRETTY CUTE, TOO!
GOOD MORNING, AOBA!!
Staff Room
JOLT
WH-WHAT'S WRONG, KUNINAKA?!
WHEEZE
WHEEZE
JUST LET ME...
PLEASE JUST LET ME REST A SECOND ...

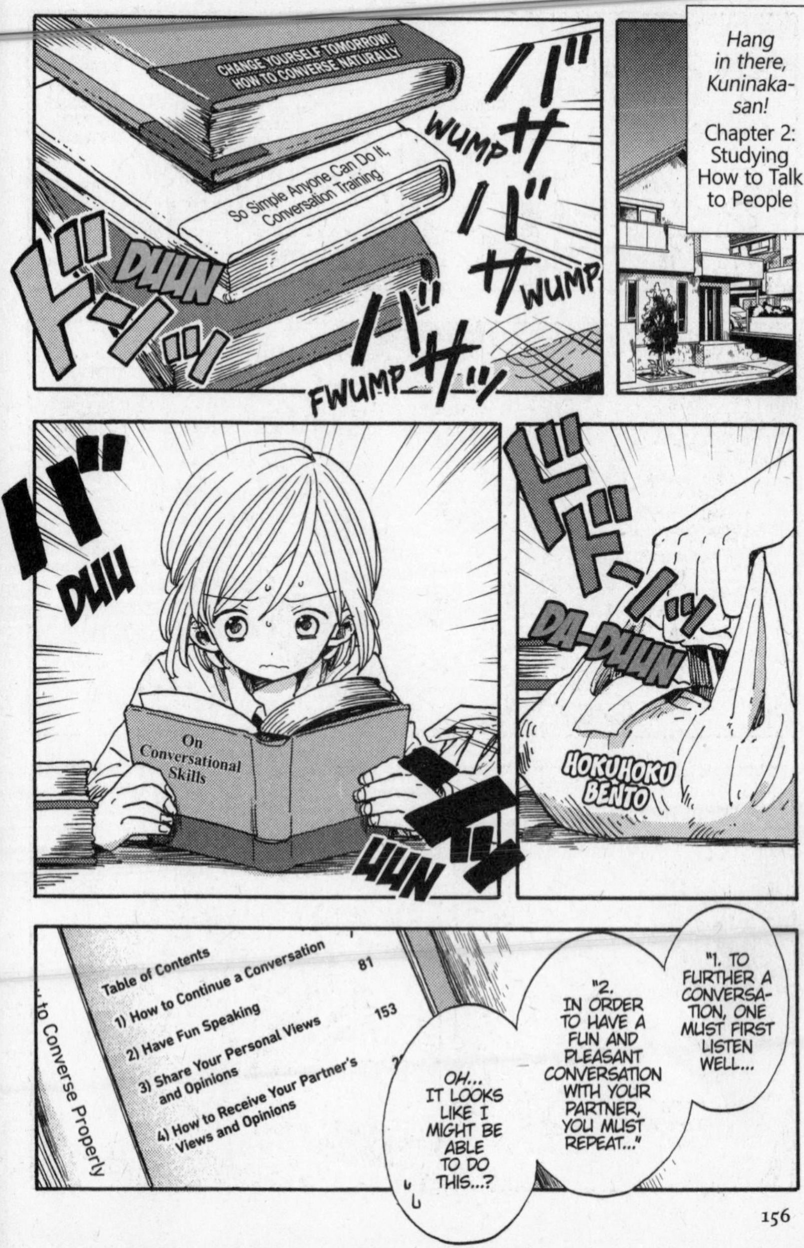

Hang in there, Kuninaka-san!
Chapter 2: Studying How to Talk to People
CHANGE YOURSELF TOMORROW! HOW TO CONVERSE NATURALLY
So Simple Anyone Can Do It, Conversation Training
WUMP
WUMP
FWUMP
DUUN
DA-DUUN
HOKUHOKU BENTO
DUU
On Conversational Skills
UUN
Table of Contents
1) How to Continue a Conversation 81
2) Have Fun Speaking 153
3) Share Your Personal Views and Opinions
4) How to Receive Your Partner's Views and Opinions
to Converse Properly
"1. TO FURTHER A CONVERSATION, ONE MUST FIRST LISTEN WELL...
"2. IN ORDER TO HAVE A FUN AND PLEASANT CONVERSATION WITH YOUR PARTNER, YOU MUST REPEAT..."
OH... IT LOOKS LIKE I MIGHT BE ABLE TO DO THIS...?

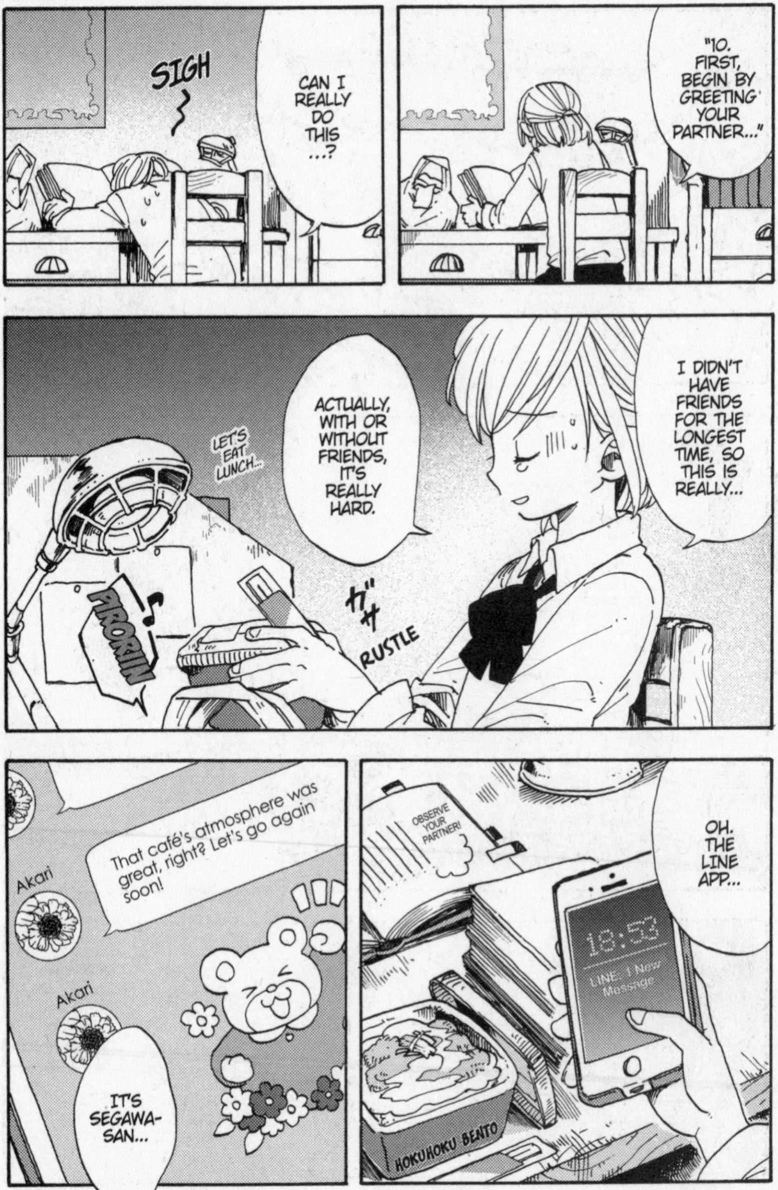
"10. FIRST, BEGIN BY GREETING YOUR PARTNER..."
CAN I REALLY DO THIS ...?
SIGH
I DIDN'T HAVE FRIENDS FOR THE LONGEST TIME, SO THIS IS REALLY...
ACTUALLY, WITH OR WITHOUT FRIENDS, IT'S REALLY HARD.
LET'S EAT LUNCH...
RUSTLE
PIRORIIN
OH. THE LINE APP...
OBSERVE YOUR PARTNER!
18:53
LINE: 1 New Message
HOKUHOKU BENTO
That café's atmosphere was great, right? Let's go again soon!
Akari
Akari
IT'S SEGAWA-SAN...

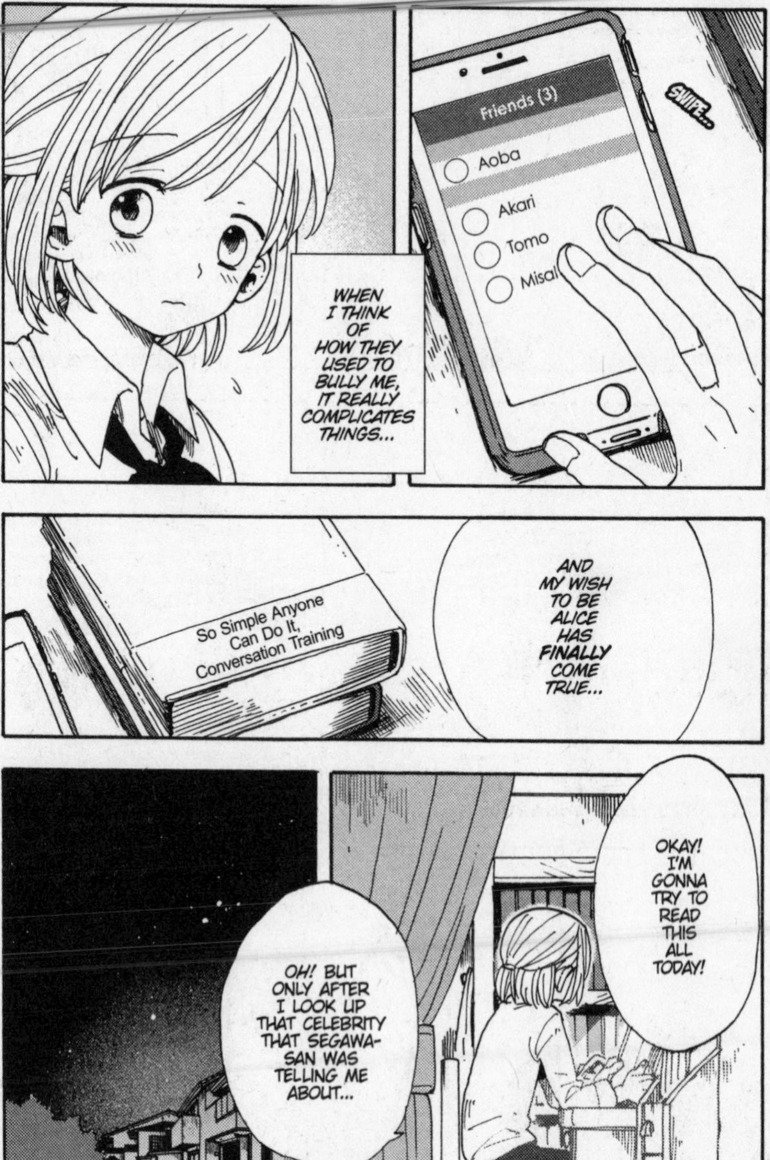
SWIPE...
Friends (3)
Aoba
Akari
Tomo
Misal
WHEN I THINK OF HOW THEY USED TO BULLY ME, IT REALLY COMPLICATES THINGS...
AND MY WISH TO BE ALICE HAS FINALLY COME TRUE...
So Simple Anyone Can Do It, Conversation Training
OKAY! I'M GONNA TRY TO READ THIS ALL TODAY!
OH! BUT ONLY AFTER I LOOK UP THAT CELEBRITY THAT SEGAWA-SAN WAS TELLING ME ABOUT...

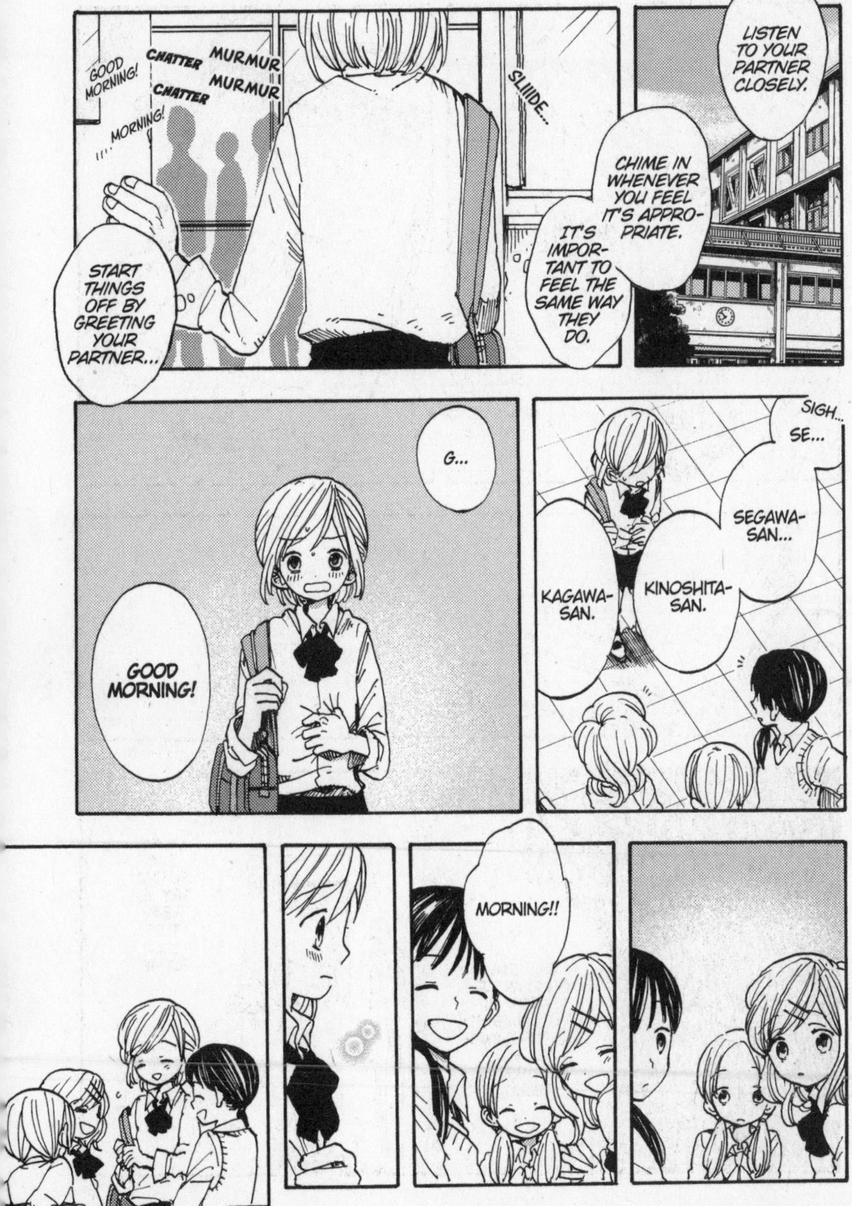

LISTEN TO YOUR PARTNER CLOSELY.
CHIME IN WHENEVER YOU FEEL IT'S APPROPRIATE.
IT'S IMPORTANT TO FEEL THE SAME WAY THEY DO.
SLIIIDE...
MURMUR MURMUR
CHATTER CHATTER
GOOD MORNING!
...MORNING!
START THINGS OFF BY GREETING YOUR PARTNER...
SIGH...
SE...
SEGAWA-SAN...
KINOSHITA-SAN.
KAGAWA-SAN.
G...
GOOD MORNING!
MORNING!!

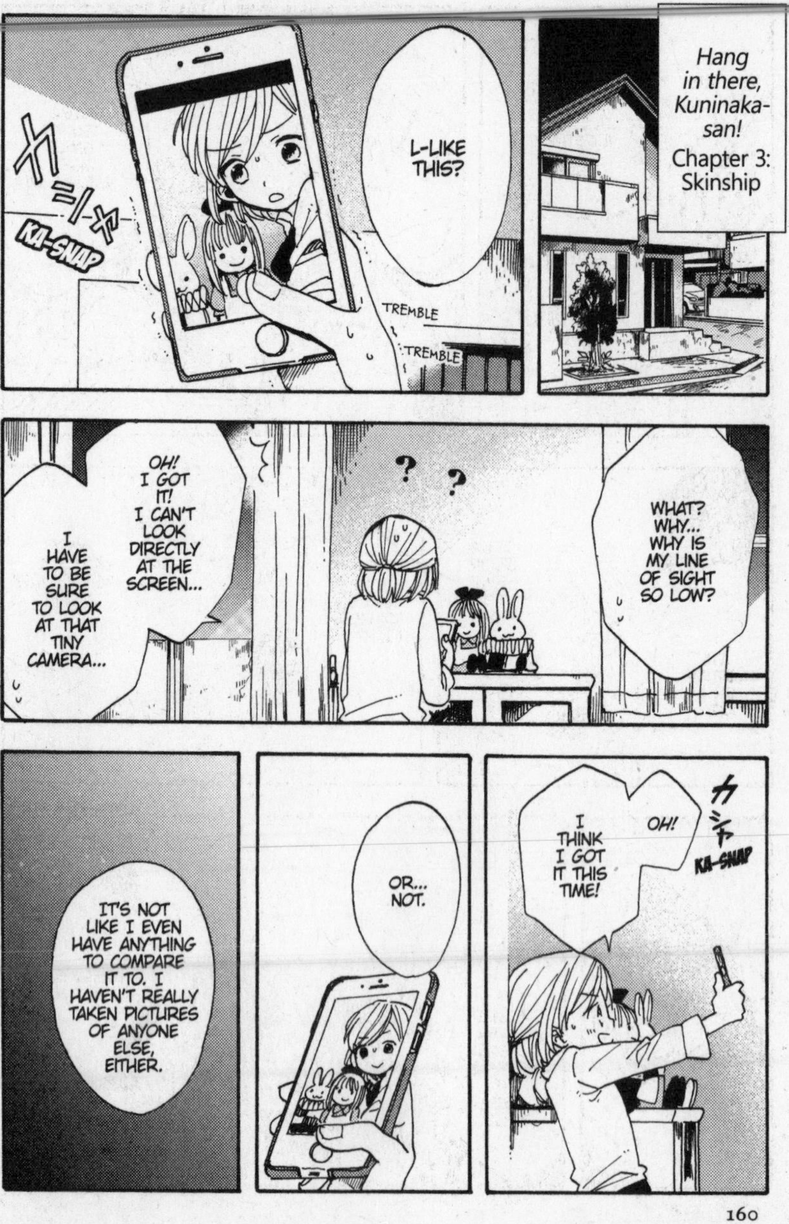
Hang in there, Kuninaka-san!
Chapter 3: Skinship
L-LIKE THIS?
KA-SNAP
TREMBLE
TREMBLE
WHAT? WHY... WHY IS MY LINE OF SIGHT SO LOW?
OH! I GOT IT! I CAN'T LOOK DIRECTLY AT THE SCREEN...
I HAVE TO BE SURE TO LOOK AT THAT TINY CAMERA...
OH!
I THINK I GOT IT THIS TIME!
カシャ
KA-SNAP
OR... NOT.
IT'S NOT LIKE I EVEN HAVE ANYTHING TO COMPARE IT TO. I HAVEN'T REALLY TAKEN PICTURES OF ANYONE ELSE, EITHER.

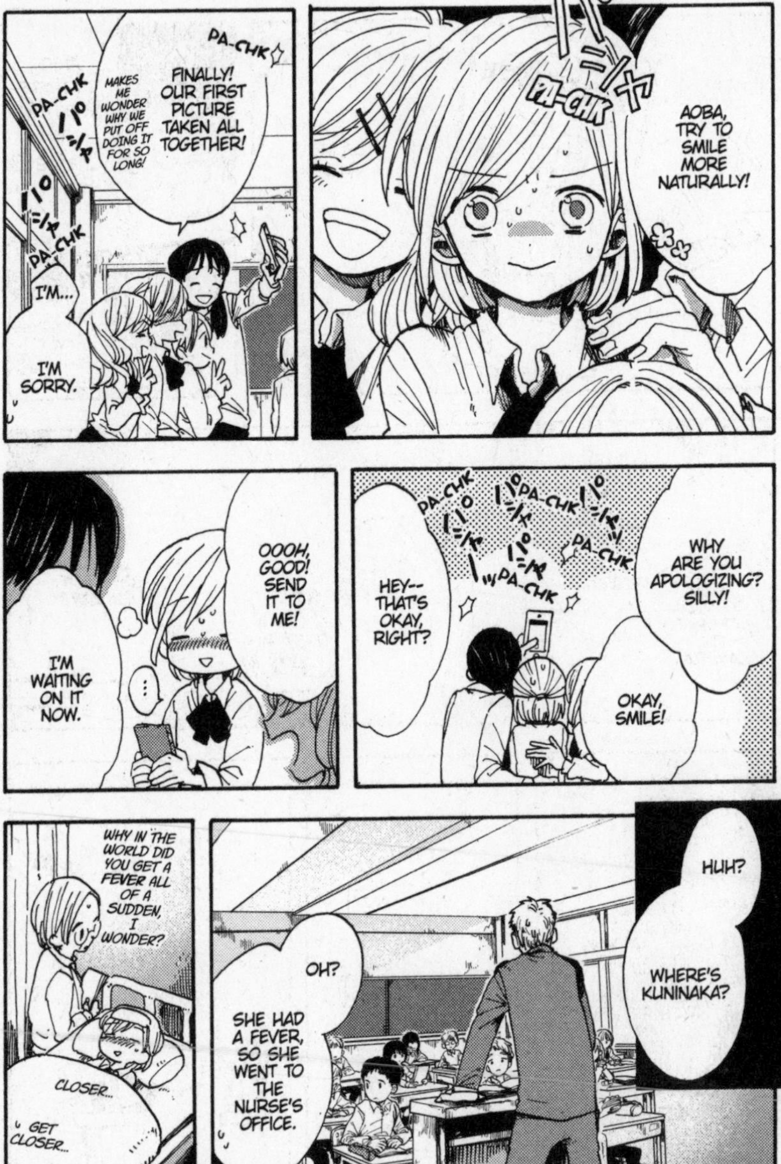
PA-CHK
AOBA, TRY TO SMILE MORE NATURALLY!
PA-CHK
FINALLY! OUR FIRST PICTURE TAKEN ALL TOGETHER!
MAKES ME WONDER WHY WE PUT OFF DOING IT FOR SO LONG!
PA-CHK
PA-CHK
I'M...
I'M SORRY.
WHY ARE YOU APOLOGIZING? SILLY!
PA-CHK PA-CHK PA-CHK PA-CHK PA-CHK
HEY--THAT'S OKAY, RIGHT?
OKAY, SMILE!
OOOH, GOOD! SEND IT TO ME!
I'M WAITING ON IT NOW.
...
HUH?
WHERE'S KUNINAKA?
OH?
SHE HAD A FEVER, SO SHE WENT TO THE NURSE'S OFFICE.
WHY IN THE WORLD DID YOU GET A FEVER ALL OF A SUDDEN, I WONDER?
CLOSER...
GET CLOSER...

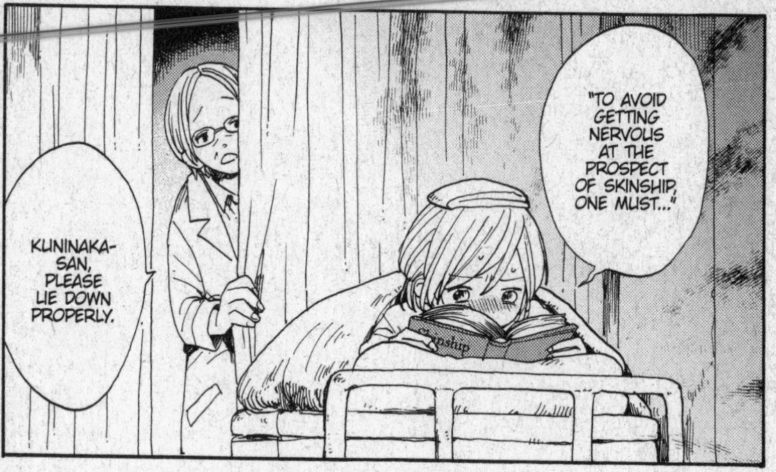
"TO AVOID GETTING NERVOUS AT THE PROSPECT OF SKINSHIP, ONE MUST..."
KUNINAKA-SAN, PLEASE LIE DOWN PROPERLY.

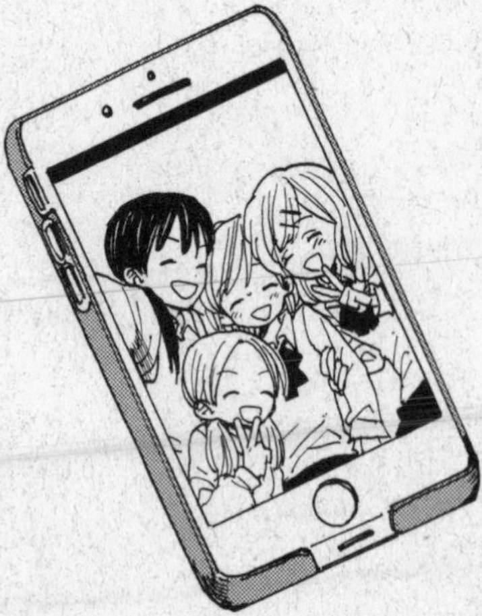

Volume ① : END

FAIRY TALE BATTLE ROYALE

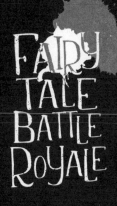

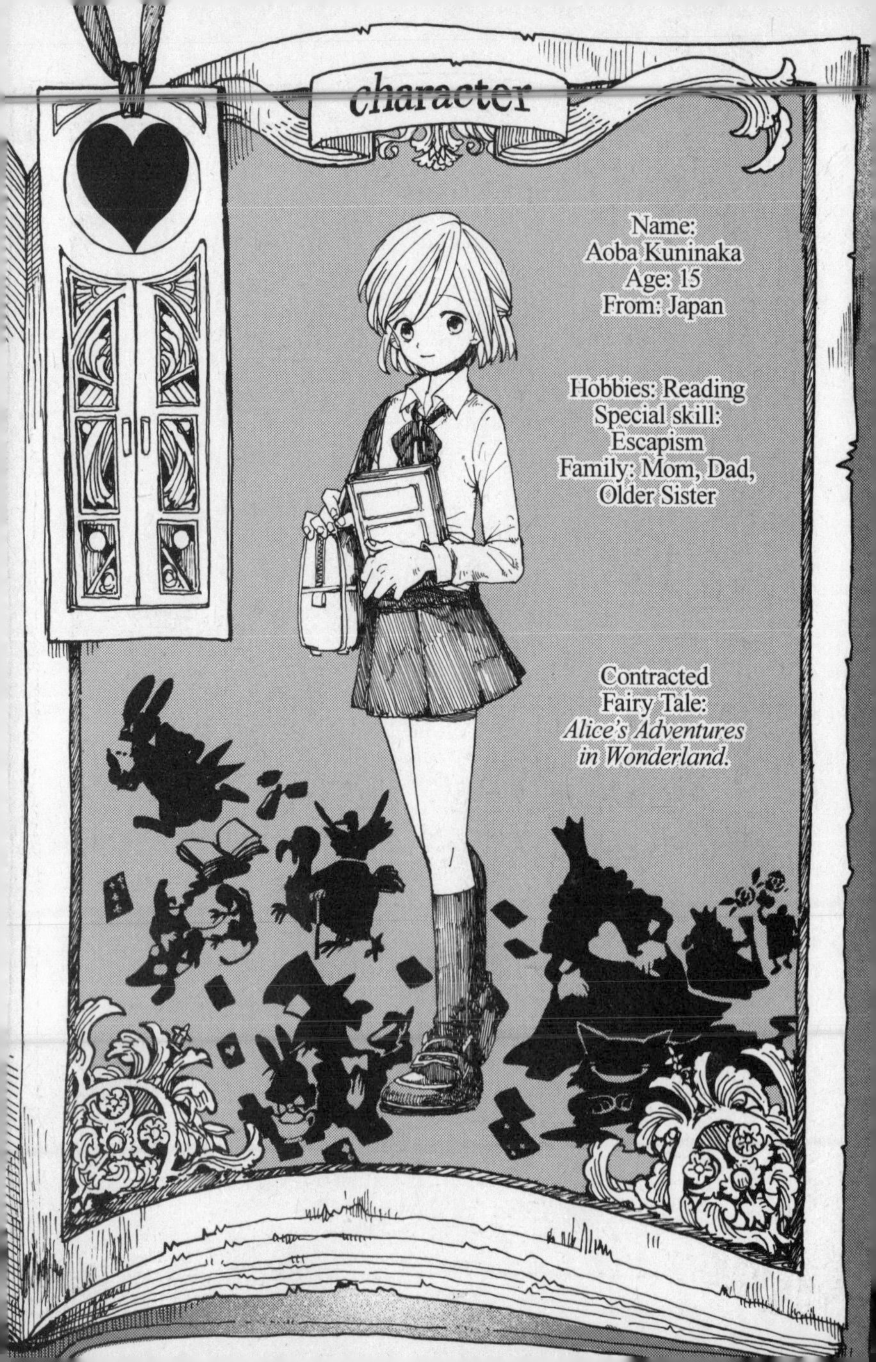
character
Name:
Aoba Kuninaka
Age: 15
From: Japan
Hobbies: Reading
Special skill:
Escapism
Family: Mom, Dad,
Older Sister
Contracted
Fairy Tale:
Alice's Adventures in Wonderland.

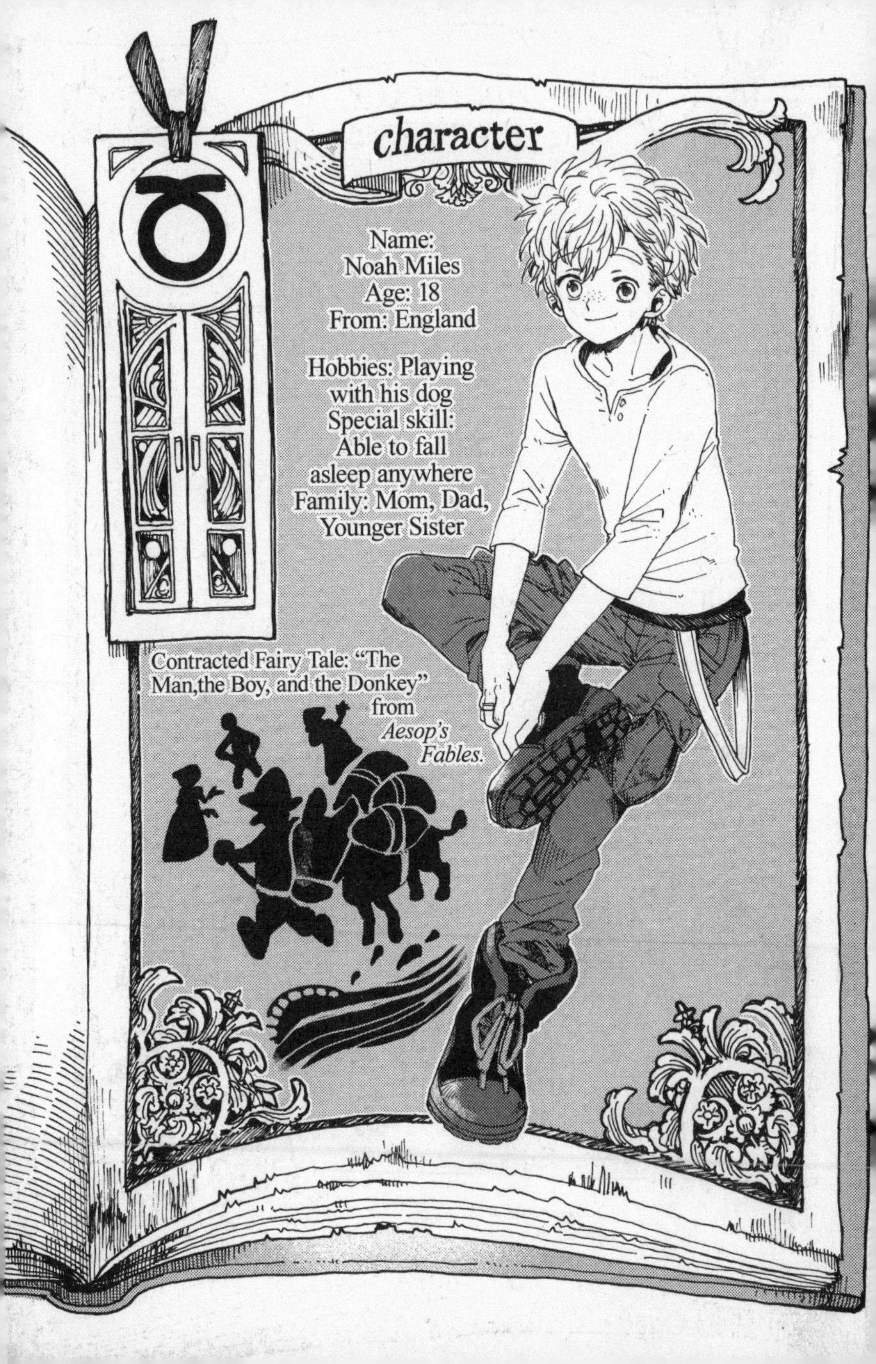
character
Name:
Noah Miles
Age: 18
From: England
Hobbies: Playing
with his dog
Special skill:
Able to fall
asleep anywhere
Family: Mom, Dad,
Younger Sister
Contracted Fairy Tale: "The
Man,the Boy, and the Donkey"
from
*Aesop's
Fables.*

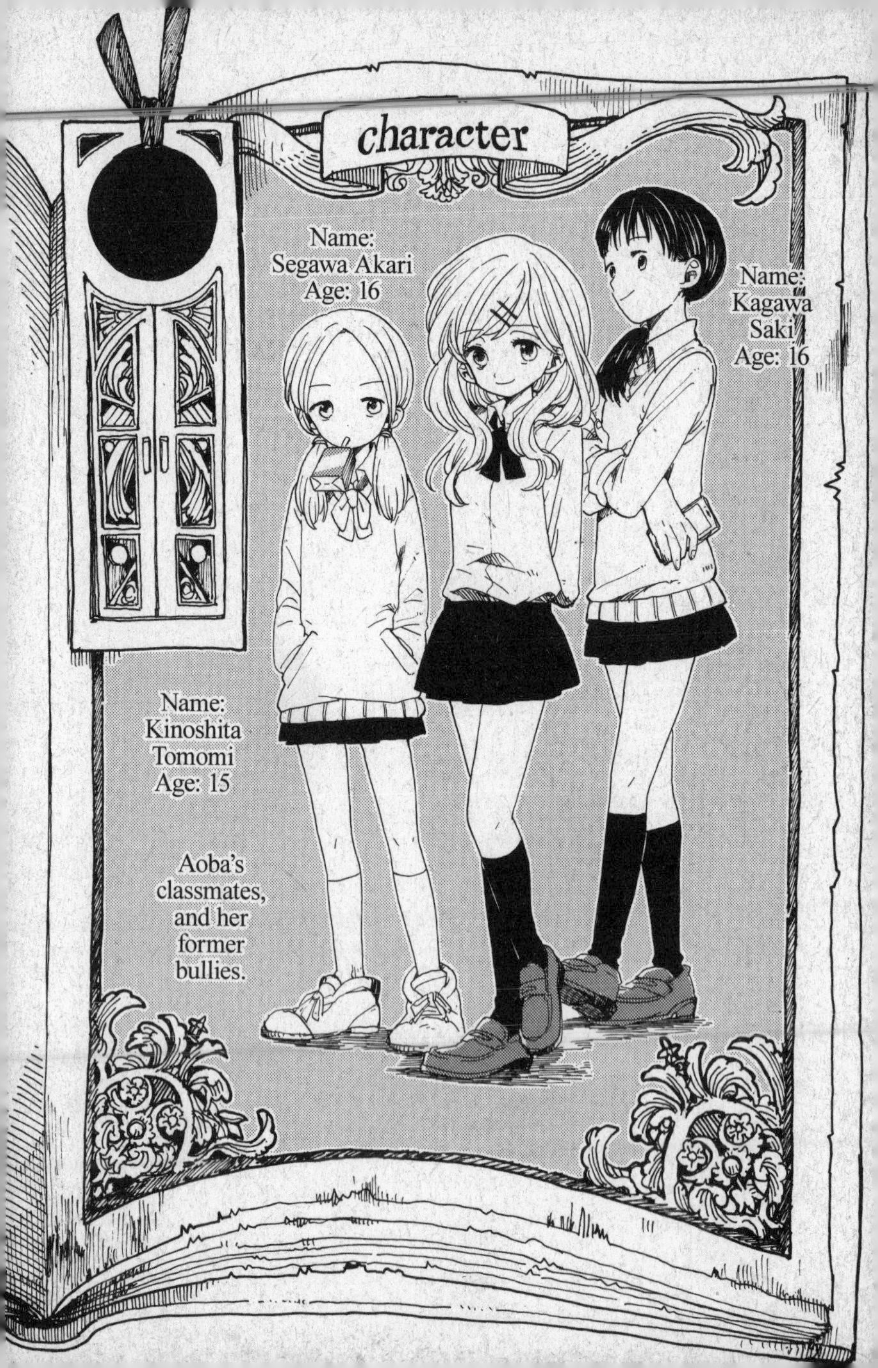

character
Name:
Segawa Akari
Age: 16
Name:
Kagawa
Saki
Age: 16
Name:
Kinoshita
Tomomi
Age: 15
Aoba's
classmates,
and her
former
bullies.

FAIRY
TALE
BATTLE
ROYALE

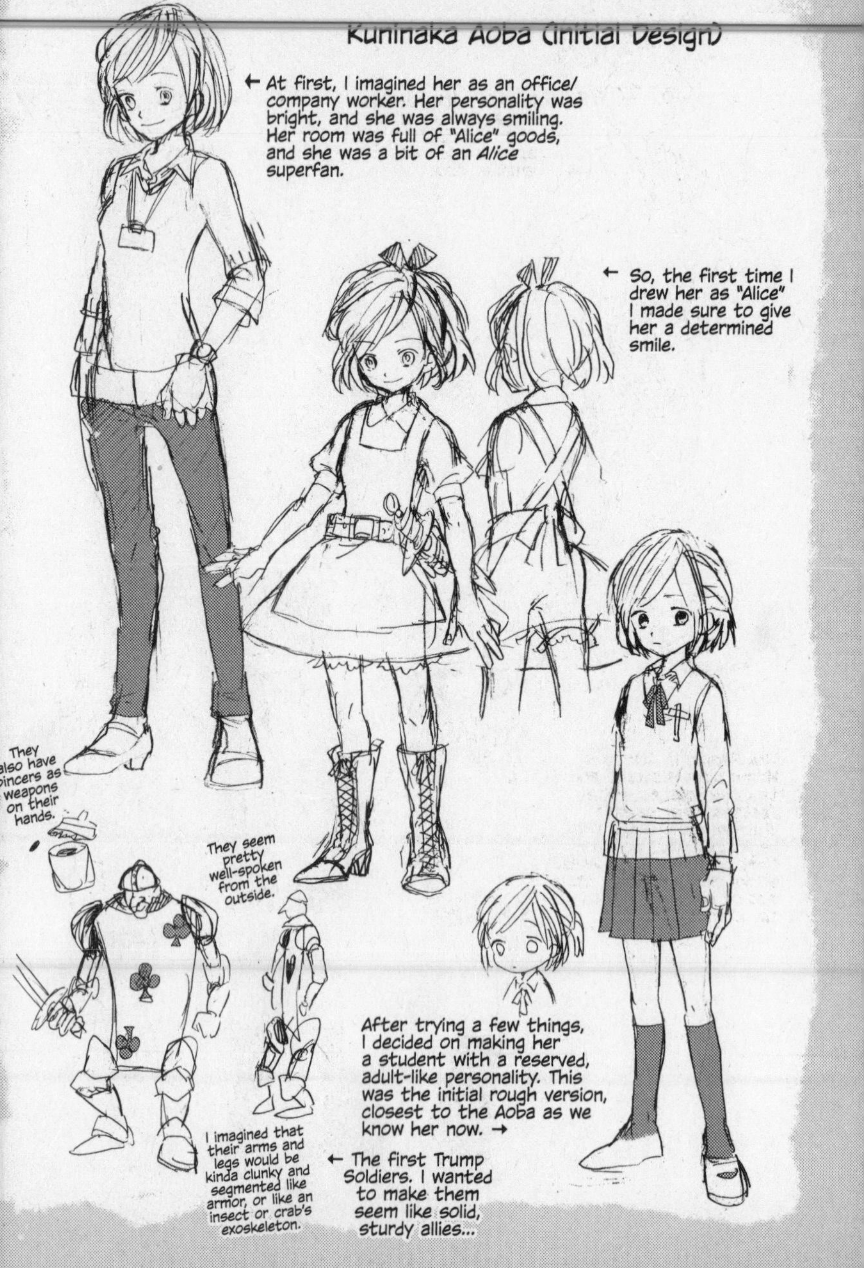
Kuninaka Aoba (Initial Design)
At first, I imagined her as an office/company worker. Her personality was bright, and she was always smiling. Her room was full of "Alice" goods, and she was a bit of an *Alice* superfan.
So, the first time I drew her as "Alice" I made sure to give her a determined smile.
They also have pincers as weapons on their hands.
They seem pretty well-spoken from the outside.
After trying a few things, I decided on making her a student with a reserved, adult-like personality. This was the initial rough version, closest to the Aoba as we know her now.
I imagined that their arms and legs would be kinda clunky and segmented like armor, or like an insect or crab's exoskeleton.
The first Trump Soldiers. I wanted to make them seem like solid, sturdy allies...

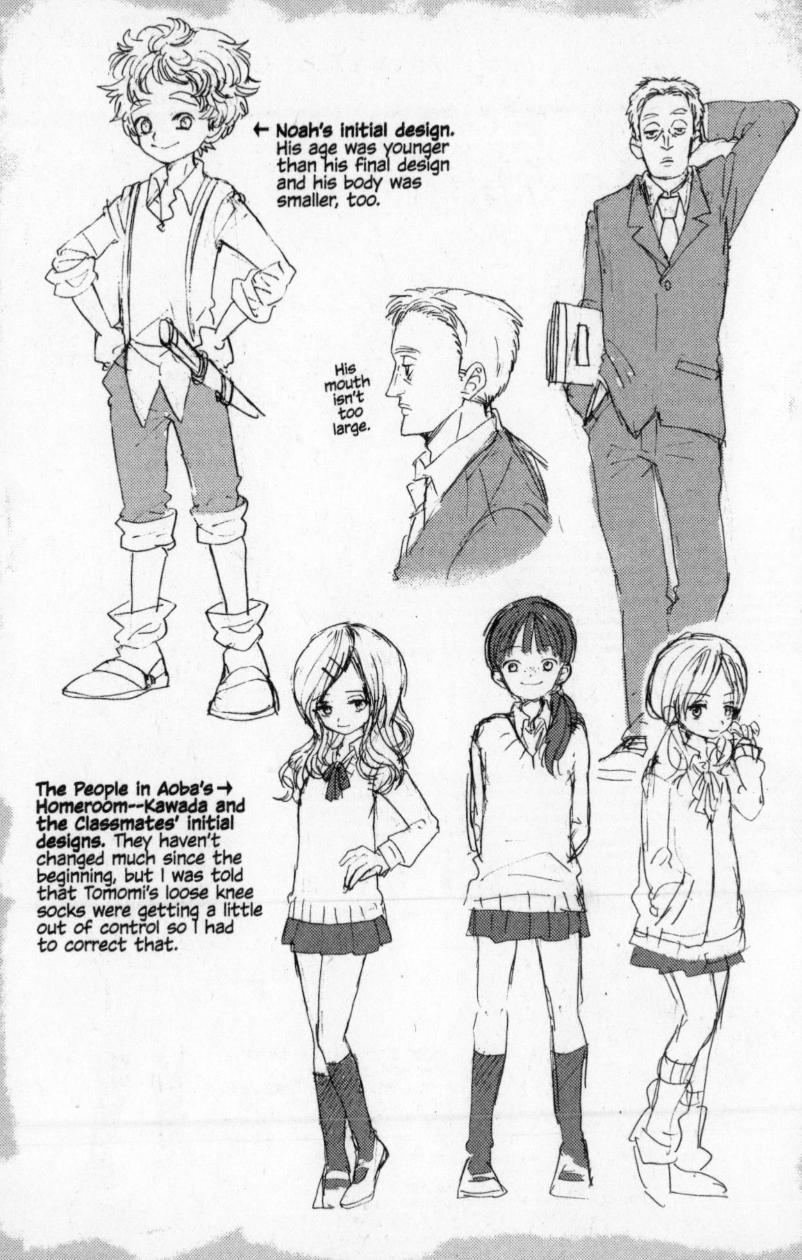
← Noah's initial design. His age was younger than his final design and his body was smaller, too.
His mouth isn't too large.
The People in Aoba's → Homeroom--Kawada and the Classmates' initial designs. They haven't changed much since the beginning, but I was told that Tomomi's loose knee socks were getting a little out of control so I had to correct that.

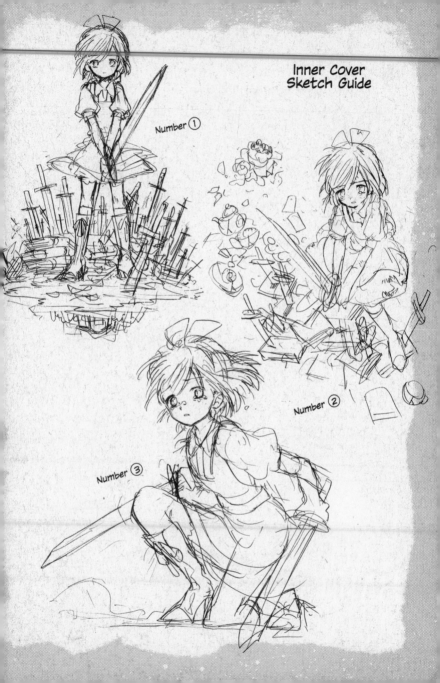

Inner Cover Sketch Guide

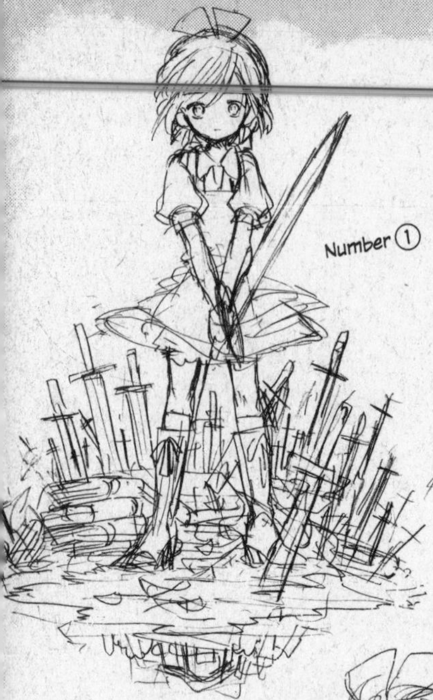

Number ①

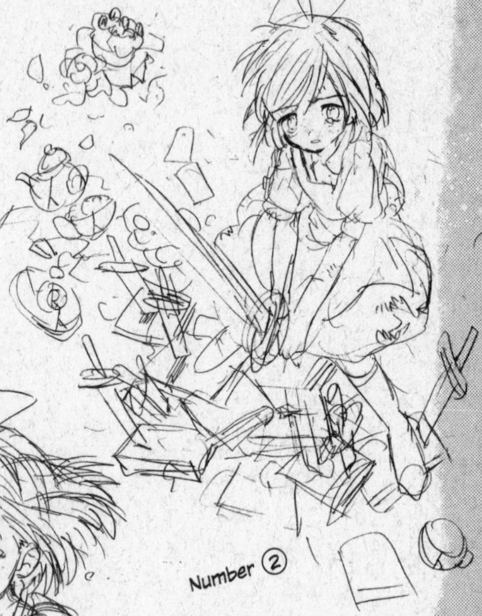

Number ②

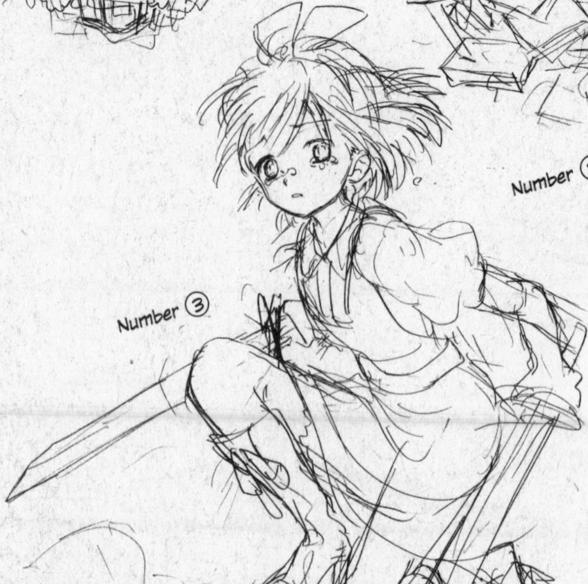

Number ③